Violence in France and Australia

Disorder in the postcolonial welfare state

Edited by Craig Browne and Justine McGill

SYDNEY UNIVERSITY PRESS

Published 2010 by Sydney University Press
SYDNEY UNIVERSITY PRESS
University of Sydney Library
sydney.edu.au/sup

Sydney University Press
Fisher Library F03
University of Sydney NSW 2006 AUSTRALIA
Email: sup.info@sydney.edu.au

National Library of Australia Cataloguing-in-Publication entry

Title: Violence in France and Australia : disorder in the postcolonial welfare state / edited by Craig Browne and Justine McGill.
ISBN: 9781920899479 (pbk.)
Notes: Includes bibliographical references.
Subjects: Social problems--Australia--History.
        Social problems--France--History.
        Welfare state--France--History.
        Welfare state--Australia--History.
        Minorities--Australia--History.
        Minorities--France--History.
Other Authors/Contributors:
        Browne, Craig.
        McGill, Justine.
Dewey Number: 361.65

Cover design by Miguel Yamin, University Publishing Service

Contents

1

Violence and the postcolonial welfare state in France and Australia

Craig Browne and Justine McGill

What can analyses of violence in marginalised communities in France and Australia teach us about the evolving structures of the postcolonial welfare state? This collection originates from a workshop that was held in October 2007 at the University of Sydney for the purpose of exploring this question. It represents a conversation between scholars working on violence in Australian Aboriginal communities and those studying violence in immigrant communities in France, particularly in relation to rioting. The rationale for bringing these two largely distinct bodies of research into communication is that in both countries violence in marginalised communities occurs in situations that can be interpreted in terms of two broad and superimposed frameworks that have not sufficiently been analysed in relation to one another: postcolonial society and the welfare state.

In analyses of the roots of violence in marginalised communities, there is a tendency, resisted in this collection, to draw exclusively on either one or the other of these frameworks—to suggest that the basis of the violence is broadly socio-economic, while neglecting its specific and long-term historical conditions, or conversely to see it as a feature of a culture that has been warped by the abuses of colonialism, without sufficiently acknowledging the more recent and generalised impact of welfare structures. The latter approach can be seen in 'culture'-based interpretations of Aboriginal violence, although interestingly, at the time of the workshop, a sharp focus on welfare structures as the primary underlying cause of Aboriginal violence was emerging in the context of the Intervention by the federal government into Aboriginal communities in the Northern Territory (NT) of Australia. This major political and social event had begun only weeks before the workshop. Of the chapters in this volume that focus on violence in Australia, two (by Watson and Howard-Wagner) deal explicitly with the Intervention, which is ongoing, and what it highlights about the governance of Aboriginal communities in Australia.

Despite their very different histories, Australia and France share the typical postcolonial experience of unresolved conflicts. In different ways, the legacies of colonial violence and appropriation are 'carried into the present as traumatic memory, inherited institutional structures, and often unexamined assumptions' (Good et al. 2008, 6). The persistent residues of colonial violence manifest in multifarious ways in contemporary outbreaks of violence both in Indigenous Australian communities and in communities in France with a large number of immigrants from former colonies and their descendants.

France and Australia are also highly modernised societies. Postcolonial violence in these societies can be clearly demarcated from those of decolonising nation-states undergoing modernisation, such as Zimbabwe and Pakistan. In France and Australia, the welfare state, in the broad sense of that social institution committed to the maintenance of a reasonably fair and dignified condition of living for the population of a nation-state, has modulated postcolonial conflicts. The structural limitations and policy failures of the welfare state have become sources of discontent and suffering in these two societies, leading to interactions between marginalised groups and the state that are punctuated by instances of violent contestation.

These broad commonalities and salient differences, which formed the starting point for the workshop's critical analyses of manifestations of violence in France and Australia, immediately raise the problem of how to understand the entanglement of the postcolonial and the welfare state. The precise relationships between the welfare state and the postcolonial have never been adequately characterised, being often regarded as distinct categorisations of institutional forms and states of historical transition. Yet, the recent comparative research on advanced marginality, which is itself motivated by a need to comprehend violent confrontations in contexts of persistent disadvantage, has drawn attention to a need to understand the intersections, as well as the variations, between the postcolonial and the welfare state (Wacquant 2008).

Particularly significant is the fact that the postcolonial background to contemporary violence throws into relief the racial and ethnic dimensions of forms of marginality. In order to account for this violence it is necessary to take into account the nexuses between the social and the racial within nation-states. Ethnically and racially marginalised groups tend to be comparatively limited in the scope and dimensions of their social agency, having limited access to mainstream politics and being subjected to normalising kinds of governmental regulation. These groups recurrently experience higher levels of policing and they regularly have higher imprisonment rates. It is clear in this context that the role of the state is not limited to that of mediating conflicts which arise independently in civil society. Rather, the exercise of state authority is itself a matter of conflict and disputed legitimacy. This disputation is disclosed by some of the ways in which marginalised groups instantiate violence, especially those modalities of violence that bear the marks of the frustrations of diminished citizenship and that are precipitated by perceptions of police abuse. The latter is exemplified, for example, by the riots that have sometimes followed the deaths in custody of Indigenous Australians and police shootings of youths of migrant descent in France.

Could there be a relationship between contemporary state sanctioned violence and the widely discussed ideas of the decline or crisis of the welfare state? One suggestion is that fiscal constraints and the broad trends of globalisation have resulted in the welfare state being reconfigured into an increasingly punitive regime (Bauman 1998; Wacquant 2008). It is claimed, in effect, that the state's resources are increasingly concentrated on the means of coercive regulation of populations, as demonstrated by certain nation-states increasing rates of imprisonment and the intensive policing of groups experiencing social dislocation and marginalisation. To the extent that they involve the selective application of state violence as a means of political governance, these developments have analogies with the dynamics of colonialism. The colonial analogy can be extended to the demands for these modes of state action emanating from broader public perceptions of the implications of social divisions, as in the need for force to manage unruly populations like the youth of housing estates and Indigenous communities. It is plausible to claim that these social processes amount to a type of internal colonisation, insofar as they legitimise unequal treatment and undermine the subordinated groups' capacities for self-determination. In this sense, these processes are seemingly paradoxical, being contrary to the explicit policy regimes of welfare state societies like France and Australia.

The postcolonial dimension of these welfare states is highlighted in their persistent forms of 'marginality' and impoverishment. A number of chapters in this collection concentrate on the recent violence in suburban France, which generally has involved a large number of youths of immigrant backgrounds, many of whom can trace their family history directly to former French colonies. In relation to Australian Aborigines, the postcolonial dimension of coercive regulation in the name of welfare is even more evident. At the time of the Australian Bicentennial in 1988, the anthropologist Jeremy Beckett made an initial contribution to understanding the interface between the welfare state and colonialism. With reference to the idea put forward by Robert Paine, Beckett drew attention to the contradictory and unstable juxtaposition contained in the term welfare colonialism; it simultaneously connoted 'citizenship (welfare) and its denial (colonialism)' (Beckett 1988, 14). In our view, the contemporary violence in advanced postcolonial societies exposes facets of this paradoxical combination that were not initially well understood and that require contemporary clarification.

Beckett rightly emphasised the logic of incorporation that shaped the development of welfare colonialism and how it represented a response by the postcolonial state, in countries like Australia and Canada, to the extreme poverty and marginality of indigenous communities, on the one hand, and to the increasing indigenous demands for self-determination and the full actualisation of the rights of citizenship, on the other. It is almost beyond dispute that the intervening period has revealed how the logic of incorporation can frustrate and negate the latter demands. As Beckett already appreciated, the contrast between the 'solicitous' treatment of citizens by the welfare state and the more straightforwardly exploitative quality of colonial domination did not signal any significant alteration in the asymmetrical distribution of power and decision-making. In his opinion, 'another contradictory feature of welfare colonialism is its need to secure the assent of its subjects as evidence of their political enfranchisement' (Beckett 1988, 14) However, later postcolonial welfare state policy developments, like the Intervention, challenge even this aspect of liberal-democratic citizenship and contribute to new forms of indigenous disenfranchisement. Recent manifestations of postcolonial violence highlight the limitations of the incorporative logic of 'welfare colonialism' and the dissatisfaction provoked by postcolonial states' modes of adapting to the advances made by movements for self-determination. This collection fulfils a need to re-examine these themes and to contextualise contemporary violence in relation to modifications in welfare states. It does this especially through the field research it draws upon, the innovations in social theory that it extends and the collection's comparative format, which provides novel insights into the particular configurations of the postcolonial and the welfare state.

The comparative aspect of this project is facilitated by the fact that a number of scholars working on violence in Australian Indigenous communities draw upon the rich conceptual resources of French theory in developing their interpretations of experiences in the field. This use of frameworks and ideas generated in a foreign context enables insights not available from within a purely local perspective, but it also involves a degree of adaptation, testing and extension of the theoretical material in response to problems and ethnographic material specific to Australian settings.

The opening chapter, by Gillian Cowlishaw, is a good example of this process. Cowlishaw takes up Axel Honneth's theory of recognition, also employed by Emmanuel Renault in his analysis of the perspective of young French rioters, included later in this volume. Cowlishaw uses Honneth's theory as a frame within which to interpret the everyday engagement in violence of the Murri people living in Bourke. The fact that conventional societal sources of recognition and respect are inaccessible for many of these people helps to explain the violence that forms part of everyday life, and occasionally flares into greater visibility in the form of riots. Violence is a way both to protest against the experience of invisibility and discrimination, and to force a highly ambiguous measure of recognition and respect.

Cowlishaw then extends this analysis in two directions. She introduces the dimension of gender, observing that like Murri men, Murri women also engage in violence and regard it as socially appropriate and enjoyable in situations where it would invoke censure from whitefellas. This ethnographic data contradicts the stereotype which depicts Aboriginal violence as essentially a matter of male aggression, typically directed toward submissive women. Secondly, she examines the courtroom process which is the usual sequel to Murri violence, especially riots, noting that while this process affords a certain form of recognition or at least visibility, it comes in a form that tends to confound any political impulses. It is not designed for the purpose of providing the kind of political recognition that could result from listening to and understanding Aborigines. Instead, in the courtroom as in the media, Aboriginal violence tends to provoke either moralistic judgment or pity in the form of compassionate discourses which Cowlishaw critiques as disrespectful. Both these approaches fail to recognise the immediate experiences of pleasure and power, as well as the underlying powerlessness or political ineffectiveness in the Aboriginal relationship with violence.

Aboriginal scholar Irene Watson provides another perspective on the relationship between violence and politics in Aboriginal experience. Like Cowlishaw, she also draws upon the resources of French theory, including concepts developed by Derrida, Rancière and Badiou. She deploys these in conjunction with insights drawn from personal experience as a legal activist to provide a challenging critical response to the Intervention as it had unfolded by the time of the workshop. In her chapter, this initiative is situated in relation to the violence that is historically and conceptually embedded in the Australian nation and the lives of its citizens, white and Aboriginal. Watson mounts a cutting critique of the paternalism which continues to allow the Australian government and other organisations to assume the mantle of 'saviour', 'crusader', or 'protector' in relation to Indigenous peoples. In exploring this problem, she picks up Wendy Brown's question regarding human rights as a framework for addressing violence: 'if [humanitarian interventions] reduce suffering, what kinds of subjects and political (or antipolitical) cultures do they bring into being as they do so, what kinds do they transform or erode, and what kinds do they aver?' (Brown 2004, 453). In applying this question to the raft of measures involved in the Intervention, Watson suggests that the consequences for Aboriginal political agency have been disastrous: the 'political subjects that are re-produced [by the coercive measures of the Intervention] are Aboriginal peoples who continue to be subjugated by the state/colonial body, having no possibility of shifting to or opening up a de-colonised space.'

Dierdre Howard-Wagner comes to similar conclusions in her chapter, which seeks to situate the Intervention in its more recent historical and political context. She examines the logic of governmentality that structured the Australian government's dealings with Aboriginal communities in the early years of the twenty-first century, culminating in the Intervention. She shows that under the Howard government the approach taken to Indigenous affairs was dominated by the interplay between neoliberal and neo-conservative modes of governance. On the one hand, in pursuit of neoliberal economic goals, the rhetoric of 'shared responsibility' was used, not to recognise and enhance Indigenous Australians' capacities to direct the process of recovery and revitalisation of their own communities, but rather to justify the introduction of neoliberal 'market values' and 'mainstream' Australian norms of private home-ownership and 'active entrepreneurship' as the solution to the dysfunction of Aboriginal communities. On the other hand, particularly once the Intervention was underway, neo-conservative politics simultaneously justified the withdrawal of certain liberal rights of Aboriginal citizens, and the abrogation of the limited rights to self-determination that had earlier been granted to some of their communities, in favour of paternalistic controls which claimed to address the moral deficiencies of Aboriginal parenting and guarantee social order.

The contradictions of this approach—demanding greater individual economic responsibility, while withdrawing basic individual liberties, and at the same time undermining communal structures of responsibility—were obscured in the atmosphere of crisis which was cultivated in the wake of a damning report on child abuse and neglect in Indigenous communities of the Northern Territory. Although this report provided the catalyst for the Intervention, its recommendation of genuine consultation with Aboriginal peoples to design initiatives to overcome the problems it identified was notably disregarded in favour of a style of governmental response more consonant with previous with the version of 'shared responsibility' already evident in the Howard government's approach to Indigenous affairs.

The shift to a neoliberal/neo-conservative mode of governance in relation to Indigenous communities has been justified by identifying welfare dependency as the key to understanding the problems of alcoholism, child abuse, pornography, entrenched unemployment and despair evident in many Indigenous communities, suggesting that if this is eliminated in favour of integration of Indigenous peoples into the liberal market then the primary cause of these problems will have been removed. As Howard-Wagner points out, what is overlooked in the simplicity, and short memory, of this analysis is the trauma of violence, including abuse and neglect: its long history reaching back to the beginnings of colonisation; its entrenchment in institutionalised racism; its burden as suffered in the form of economic and social exclusion; its transgenerational perpetration within Indigenous families; its destructive power (Dodson 2003).

Justine McGill also challenges the idea that violence in Indigenous and other marginalised communities can be attributed to a failure of or incapacity for responsibility on the part of their members, and proposes a mode of 'sharing responsibility' that is radically different to the thinking which gave rise to the 'Shared Responsibility Agreements' introduced in 2004 by the Australian government in an attempt to promote self-regulation in Indigenous communities. Her analysis indicates that the violence of the 'powerless' represents a vitality which demands and could support a radical shift in the relationship between marginalised citizens and the state, provided that the state relinquish the fantasy of total control and leave space for marginalised peoples to contribute actively to the future not only of their own communities, but also of the state itself.

McGill reaches this conclusion via an analysis of power and powerlessness in the context of rioting, arguing that it is not only the powerlessness of the marginalised that is exposed at these crisis points. The powerlessness of the state also comes into focus when governments, whether in Australia or in France, respond to explosive violence in marginalised communities with displays of repressive strength that mirror the impulsive and spectacular violence of the rioters. Underlying this typically disproportionate reaction of the state to a visibly weak and politically disorganised opponent lies a potent sense of the failure of the state to meet the needs of these disaffected citizens. In spite of decades of government programs designed to address the social problems in sectors of the population that carry the weight of postcolonial history, such problems appear to be increasing rather than diminishing. From this perspective, riots can be understood as a periodic form of 'counter-violence' pitted against the less visible, but far more destructive violence of institutionalised racism.

If the Intervention and the many issues it raised provided the framing example of violence in the postcolonial welfare state of Australia for the workshop, the French counterpart was the 2005 riots. There are several reasons for the detailed engagement with the late-2005 riots in France: first, the riots received widespread coverage in the international mass media and they generated innumerable commentaries. However, there undoubtedly was a substantial degree of false projection to these analyses. In the Australian context, for example, the 2005 French riots were subjected to the diametrically contrasting analyses of attributing them to either the surfeit of multiculturalism in France or the absence of French multiculturalism (see Browne & Mar 2006). It is likely that the 2005 French riots actually served as a pretext in these analyses for expressing positions on the unresolved meaning of multiculturalism in Australia. There is then a need for a better understanding of the context of the 2005 French riots and the claims that are being made in this enacting of discontent.

Second, the riots obtained a substantial signification and were sometimes seen as crystallising a basic social dilemma of the age. There are a number of variations on this interpretation and differences can be seen in the scale of analysis: the riots were viewed as emblematic of the problems and crises of globalisation, from another angle the riots were viewed as instancing the generic problems of European welfare states and the difficulties that these nation-states encounter in integrating migrant populations of different ethnic and religious orientations to that of the dominant culture (see Balibar 2007; Annales 4/2006; Lagrange & Oberti 2006), another framework of analysis emphasised the national particularity of the French state and economy, especially the alleged failures of the state and economy from the perspective of liberal market reforms, such as was espoused in the anniversary of the riots issue of the magazine *The Economist*. On this view, the riots revealed the substantial malaise and denial that had gripped France, thereby pointing to a society at an impasse owing to economic paralysis and a lack of social and cultural integration. In some respects, this perspective too seeks to fit the riots into a pre-existing agenda, while nonetheless drawing attention to some difficult and intractable social problems: urban decline, discrimination, resentment and social exclusion.

Third, the riots and their underlying social problem have been the topic of specific debates within France. These discussions are surveyed in several papers, giving an English-language readership an opportunity to assess the various positions that have developed. Even so, the debates concerning the riots in France have been marked by attempts to define an appropriate or adequate framework of analysis. In part, this reflects the riots' different registers of signification, but there are other complications, such as their relationship to the history of political contestation in France and the difficulties of an appropriate representation of the rioters' own perspective. The chapters by the two French contributors to the collection, Didier Fassin and Emmanuel Renault, each seek to clarify some dimensions of the riots that have been the subject of misunderstanding, or some measure of misrepresentation. In fact, the context of the riots, outer suburban *cités* (housing estates) and *banlieues*, appear to offer an already well-established framework of interpretation.

The *banlieues* have come to be equated with a decaying urban milieu, populated by immigrants and their children. More often implicit, but occasionally explicit, in this vision are the connotations of criminality, incivility and ethnically generated violence. However, as Emmanuel Renault explains in this collection, there are actually a considerable variety of *banlieues*. Not all of them fit the stigmatised stereotype of the outer suburban housing estates. Given the specificity of the term *banlieue* and its regular use in this collection, it is necessary to clarify the connotations of *banlieue* at the outset, particularly for English-speaking readers that are unfamiliar with its meaning. In his recent book *Urban outcasts*, Loïc Wacquant makes the following clarifying comments about the term *banlieue* that are worth quoting at length:

> Technically, the term *banlieue* designates a peripheral town or zone administratively attached to a larger urban centre. Originally, in the French medieval city, it referred to the ring on one league (*lieue*) falling under the ban or juridical authority of the city. A *banlieue* can thus be bourgeois or working class, affluent or impoverished. Since the mid-1980s, however, the word has been increasingly reserved to denote lower-class districts of the urban periphery harbouring high densities of deteriorating public housing (projects known as *cités*) considered prime breeding grounds for the 'urban ills' of the age, combining economic deprivation, ecological degradation, social dislocations, postcolonial immigration and youth delinquency (Boyer 2000). Such cités are typically composed of large estates of cheaply built high rises that generate an atmosphere of monotony and dread. (Wacquant 2008, 4, Note 5)

The meanings and resonances of the contemporary violence in France can only be properly understood in terms of the historical background that has shaped the patterns of immigration and the public imagination. In 'Colonial violence and post-colonial France', Robert Aldrich surveys the historical connections between French colonialism and violence, as well as the legacy of this violence and its persistence as a form of memory and a symbol for contemporary social struggles. Violence was an important part of the 'arsenal' of colonialism and it was a major factor in imperial expansion and resistance to it. Violence was present in the European metropole, but Aldrich emphasises the key difference of colonial violence was its links to the racial cleavage of the periphery. Frantz Fanon (1968) famously saw in this a justification for the necessity of decolonising violence in order to cleanse the colonised of the psychic taint of the coloniser. While acknowledging the importance of Fanon's views in underlining the presence of violence in colonialism and decolonisation, Aldrich seeks to correct the simple polarity of Fanon's account of coloniser and colonised. Aldrich finds that violence in the French colonial world was far more manifold, multidimensional and multifaceted, for example, he points to how violence reached a point in Algeria where it had 'erupted in all directions'. Indeed, this is one of a number of reasons why the heritage of violence has 'proved longer lasting' than Fanon 'foresaw'. In fact, the complications of colonial and decolonising violence, which Aldrich establishes through a detailed analysis of various episodes, have produced a history of veiling and obscuring. It is only recently that some major features of colonial violence, including the fighting for the French nation by troops sourced from colonised populations, have been revealed in France, especially in the popular media and public commemorations.

Like many of the contributors to the collection, Aldrich highlights how French colonialism and French republicanism involve a considerable tension of basic principles. The history of their co-existence raises then a number of questions. If republicanism and colonialism do not negate each other then is it possible that one can inhabit the other? If the latter is the case then is the colonial within the Republic or are the Republican values within the colonial? Interestingly, these respective alternatives are the points of reference for two contrasting women's political organisations that have recently emerged within French immigrant communities. Their disagreements over these questions are conveyed by their respective titles: '*Ni putes ni soumises*' [Neither whores nor submissives] and '*Les Indigènes de la République*' [The natives/Indigenous of the Republic]. Elizabeth Rechniewski examines these two protest movements in the chapter 'Violence, identity and the postcolonial French state', considering each of them to be variations on identity politics. Rechniewski contends that the situation of women in the *banlieues* and *cités* has been overlooked in the recent public discourses on violence. These women's struggles are, she argues, initially ones of self-definition. Violence towards women by men from the *banlieues* as well as the disputation by women of the ethnic and religious origins of male violence served as catalyst for these two movements. By contrasting the politics and identity claims of '*Ni putes ni soumises*' and '*Les Indigènes de la République*', Rechniewski shows that homogenising claims about the political position of women of migrant descent are misleading. Both of these women's movements, she argues, 'can be seen as positioning themselves to speak with an exclusive voice for the populations of the *banlieues*, in a field left largely vacant by mainstream and alternative political parties.'

In their respective political organisations, '*Ni putes ni soumises*' and '*Les Indigènes de la République*' each conforms to new social movements, especially in their emphases on struggles over social identity. Rechniewski draws on the theoretical perspectives of new social movement theory but qualifies their frameworks through the use of the notion of social fields, which is inspired by the work of Pierre Bourdieu (1990). The notion of field draws attention to the more structural and relational facets of contestations over identity. Rechniewski is then able to propose correlations between a typology of different orders of violence: physical, symbolic and distributive, and the origination or constitution of this violence in the state, civil society and community. On the basis of this typology, Rechniewski shows that the orientations of the different women's movements reveal differing focuses, either on physical, symbolic or distributive violence. Given that '*Ni putes ni sou-*

mises' and '*Les Indigènes de la République*' very much define themselves in relation to the state and Republic, at issue are the values of the Republic and whether they should be extended or limited. Although the movements may have an interest in presenting this as a stark choice between alternatives, this not the case in Rechniewski's opinion, neither the state nor the Republic are monolithic entities according to her.

Emmanuel Renault turns to the struggles of the youth in the *banlieues* and seeks to explicate the underlying demands of the 2005 French riots. In 'Violence and disrespect in the French revolt of November 2005', Renault contests the view that the riots were without political content. The riots or revolt, he argues, involved processes of politicisation. In other words, the riots concerned the construction of the definition of the political and therefore the definition of the threshold that separates the political from the prepolitical. The social denial of this feature of the riots has certain similarities with what Gayatri Spivak (2000) described as the denial of subaltern insurgencies in colonial India. That is, these denials show that the definition of the threshold between the prepolitical and the political is itself a matter of political conflicts. Renault finds a common thread to the youths' own justifications of the revolt and that which recurs in different guises in scholarly analyses. The violent reactions of November 2005 were to experiences of social disrespect and humiliation. Renault then draws on Axel Honneth's (1995) theory of the struggle for recognition to describe the moral content of these violent reactions to social disrespect. The resulting conceptualisation of how it is that collective experiences of injustice can lead to revolt enables Renault to evaluate and synthesise different perspectives on the riots. Significantly, what Honneth's framework provides is a way of comprehending the 'moral wound that justifies violent reactions' and Renault's own interviews with youth from the *banlieues* highlight these negative experiences of injustice. Renault's analysis demonstrates that the 2005 revolts had a rational component, even though it is not so much rationally articulated. In a recently published paper Renault and Jean-Philippe Deranty argue for a politicising of Honneth's theory of recognition (Deranty & Renault 2007). Renault makes use of the distinction developed at greater length in the earlier paper between a struggle *for* recognition and a struggle *of* recognition to show how in the 2005 riots a demand for respect took the more politically confrontational conflictual form of an accusation concerning denied respect.

In 'The violence of racialisation: the 2005 riots as event', Didier Fassin overviews the complexities and ambiguities of the notion of race in France, in both popular and academic discourses. Despite its history of postcolonial immigration, race had been denied as a feature of French society for a long period. Race was rather viewed as a category of relevance to nation-states that institutionalised racial boundaries or a colour line, like the USA and South Africa. In French sociological and political discourses, race was largely assimilated to the categories of social inequality and Fassin recounts the resistance that the invocation of race encountered. However, the 2005 riots suddenly generated, Fassin argues, the exactly contrary position, that is, not simply the discovery of the salience of the category of race but also the dominance of discourses in the public sphere that reduced the riots and their implications to race, thereby obscuring the riots' connection to the social. Nevertheless, despite the deficiencies of this sudden reversal in perspective and the less than sanguine political connotations of some of the associated discourses, Fassin considers that the 2005 riots constituted a significant 'event'. The 2005 riots made racialisation visible in France, establishing then a temporal demarcation of before and after the explicit problematisation of race. Fassin suggests that what was specific to the veiling of race in France was the importance that had been ascribed to three overarching signifiers of social unity and identification: 'class', 'nation' and 'republic'. The riots then challenge some dimensions of each of these signifiers and hence, in turn, problematised basic assumptions about French society.

Of course, the veiling of race in France involved a certain denial of the forms of engagement with race that were actually occurring. Fassin's analysis is based on the ethnographic research that he had undertaken into police patrols in the *banlieues* and *cités*. Fassin's 'fragments of an ethnography' reveal how, far from conforming to the prevailing expectations concerning delinquent populations, the *banlieue* youth, especially those of immigrant backgrounds like Blacks and Arabs, have developed relatively servile relations to the police, as a form of self-protection against police harassment and potential brutality. The police patrols, that Fassin observed, had an overtly racialised modus operandi. Like the riots of the past two decades that had preceded them, the 2005 riots were precipitated by the deaths of two youths of North African backgrounds and whose actions (which were to culminate in their electrocution) are comprehensible in terms of their prior experiences of police patrols. Drawing on EP Thompson's arguments on crowds, Fassin argues that the riots in the *cités* and *banlieues* have been triggered by the police crossing the threshold of the local moral order. He makes the important point that rioting is rare and never the immediate first option for these French citizens. Although the rioters were mainly male youth from these suburbs, there was nonetheless, Fassin notes, connections between them and the broader communities of the *banlieues*, which while they may not have condoned the riots, certainly understood the tensions that produced the discontent.

Craig Browne and Phillip Mar seek to explain the links between the lived experience of the collective violence and the broader structural sources of the discontent. Even though they find that these are irreducible to one another, Browne and Mar consider that the actions of the rioters gave certain expression to experiences of injustice and humiliation that can be traced to the major institutional structures of French society. In their chapter 'Enacting half-positions: creative disrespect in the 2005 French riots', Browne and Mar emphasise the non-discursive character of these actions and suggest that the novelty of the 2005 riots consisted especially in their unplanned coordination, turning a single incident into the massive riots which were national in scale and extended over several weeks. Despite the intensity of the riots and their spectacular character, they led only to the single death of a bystander from a heart attack. Given the riots then involved quite defined forms of interaction with the police and a rather limited range of physical targets, they argue that it is necessary to explicate the meanings inherent in these acts of violence and the ways in which the dynamics of a dialectic of control are mediated by those resources and normative rules that shape the rioters' actions. On the basis of their analysis of the riots' originating contexts, active participants, developmental extension and concomitant factors, Browne and Mar claim to discern a distinctive structure to the riots. In their opinion, the riots should be understood as a kind of non-discursive action that embodied the frustrations of those members of French society with the least access to a public voice. Drawing on the distinction between the processes of system integration and social integration, Browne and Mar perceive that these violent actions are intrinsically related to the youthful actors occupying 'half-positions' in French society. Particularly that half-position of possessing citizenship rights but lacking full-time paid employment, and the attendant experiences of humiliation owing to the youth of the *banlieues*' ethnic and racial backgrounds.

In light of their analysis of the contradictions of half-positions and the particular modalities of these violent actions, Browne and Mar develop two central theses. First, that the riots themselves were a form of retribution for the perceived and experienced damages of material and symbolic denigration. Retribution being a kind of moral claim that is moulded in this case by the expectation that full membership in French society, whether as a citizen or paid employee, cannot be taken for granted and that even the tacit rules regulating the subordinated groups relations to the institutional authority of the police has been transgressed and violated. Second, the riots involved actions of creative disrespect, that is, performative actions that give expression to a frustrated social agency in the absence of other means of effective access to the public sphere, on the one hand, and, on the other hand, these actions are creative in making explicit the contestation over values and legitimacy. Creative disrespect arises out of the attempt of a collective to reassert some form of self-control in relation to institutional subordination. While careful to distinguish their understanding of creative disrespect from that of Gillian Cowlishaw, Browne and Mar draw on her analysis of riots among Indigenous Australian communities and find some parallels in the manner in which the 2005 French riots enacted meanings. According to Cowlishaw

> Riotous, destructive or outrageous behaviour in Indigenous communities
> is usually explained reductively as the consequences of alienation,

> unemployment and poverty. I contend that the logic of such public events goes far beyond such sympathetic but superficial diagnosis of aberrant behaviour. Riots are not sophisticated or effective politics but nor are they simply reactive violence. They contain coherent, logical and positive meanings and messages about Indigenous experience. (Cowlishaw 2004, 315)

The French riots of 2005 brought persisting but veiled circumstances to public attention. Even if the French state could effectively address the most direct sources of the rioters' discontent, it would not amount to anything like the end of a problem. France's legacy of postcolonialism is both a product of past action and continuing circumstances owing to the situation of the substantial immigrant populations from former colonies, such as Algeria. The latter has given rise to continuing questions in France over difference and integration, though tending to focus on the latter in relation to immigrants and their children. The difficulty here is the ambivalence, and in some cases hostility, among the broad French public towards citizens that due to their ethnic and racial composition do not meet the self-representation of the nation. It is now a long time after the so-called glorious years of economic recovery that underpinned the growth of the welfare state and that provided employment for migrants from former colonies. It is a cliché to speak of an impasse in the present circumstances, yet the violence of recent riots points to conditions of sustained discontent and the reliance of the French state on the coercive actions of the police in the *banlieues* and *cités*. The use of emergency measures that utilised laws framed for colonial conflicts, reflected the fact that the postcolonial applies not just to citizens from former colonies but also to aspects of the French state itself.

The chapters that address the recent violence point to different thresholds of these conflicts: Fassin highlights the threshold that made the riots an event that disrupts the occlusion of race in France and the implications of racialisation; Renault shows how the violent revolt in seeking to make visible the moral wounds of disrespect disclose the politicised conflicts over the threshold between the prepolitical and the political; Browne and Mar delineate the threshold at which the violation of the informal norms that had regulated conflicts escalates certain aspects of their structuration and eventuates in actions that are circumscribed in a way that leads to creative disrespect and that are oriented toward retribution; Rechniewski draws attention to how the thresholds between the state, republic and collective identity are shaped in radically different ways by two women's political movements. Similarly, Aldrich points to how the threshold between past colonial violence and the postcolonial present is marked by persisting tensions that neither the colonisers, nor the colonised, as well as their descendants, have been able to come to terms with in its full complexity. The present circumstances that are shown to have shaped the violence in France make such a process even more necessary while contributing to the improbability of agreement over the past and the probability of the continuation of demands for justice and violent acts of discontent.

The chapters dealing with violence in Australian Indigenous communities can similarly be read as reflections on violence as a live marker of lines of power. Like Renault, Cowlishaw highlights the contested interpretative dimension of violence; in her case the focus is on who holds the power to define social interactions as unacceptable interpersonal violence. Watson emphasises the lines of colonial power that frame the constructions of Aboriginality which both organise practices of state violence and provoke and sustain resistance to it. Howard-Wagner's analysis of the Howard government's Intervention in the Northern Territory shows how it marks a significant shift to a new, coercive mode of governance; while McGill analyses riots in marginalised communities and state responses to them as moments when, against the flames of burning cars, the interdependence of the powerless and the powerful is sharply outlined. As a whole, the collection's diverse critical perspectives build a complex picture of the contemporary violent disordering of postcolonial welfare states.

*   *   *

We would like to thank the Faculty of Arts, the University of Sydney for the Strategic Development Funding that facilitated the workshop that was held in October 2007. We would also like to express our appreciation for the work that was undertaken by the school's administrative staff in the organising of the workshop and particularly to Michael Slezak for his assistance, including for his work on the workshop's website. In addition to the presenters to the workshop whose subsequently revised papers are represented in this collection, papers were delivered by two leading scholars in the field of Australian anthropology and Indigenous studies: Diane Austin-Broos and Judy Atkinson. We thank them both for their participation and later support with the preparation of this volume.

We believe that the extremely rich and varied body of theoretical knowledge and ethnographic experience of violence in different contexts that characterised the workshop's discussion are reflected in this collection's papers. All of the chapters have been subjected to peer-review by experts in the field and we would like to thank the reviewers for their time and expertise. There are many people who assisted in different ways with the preparation of this volume, particularly through making available their knowledge, experience and expertise. We would especially like to thank Judy Atkinson, Diane Austin-Broos, Katherine Auty, Étienne Balibar, Larissa Behrendt, Harry Blatterer, Geoffrey Boucher, Marguerite La Caze, Ian Coller, Frederick Cooper, Chris Cunneen, Natalie Doyle, Robert Fine, Ghassan Hage, Daniela Heil, Richie Howitt, Andrew Jakubowicz, Andrew Lattas, Tess Lea, Brett Neilson, Scott Poynting, Sandy Toussaint, and Nicole Watson. The production of an edited collection is a complex process and we very much appreciate the contributions of Sydney Press University. Susan Murray-Smith has been a delight to work with and source of wise advice.

References

Annales. Histoire, Sciences Sociales (4/2006) vol. 61.

Balibar E (2007). Uprisings in the banlieues. *Constellations*, 14(1): 47–71.

Bauman Z (1998). *Globalization: the human consequences*. Cambridge: Polity Press.

Beckett J (1988). Aboriginality, citizenship and the nation state. *Social Analysis*, 24: 3–18.

Bourdieu P (1990). *Logic of practice*. Stanford: Stanford University Press.

Boyer JC (2000). *Les banlieues en France: territoires et sociétés*. Paris: Armand Colin.

Brown W (2004). 'The most we can hope for … ': human rights and the politics of fatalism. *South Atlantic Quarterly*, 103(2/3): 451–63.

Browne C & Mar P (2006). The French riots: events and circumstances. *Australian Mosaic*, 13(1): 27–29.

Cowlishaw G (2004). Difficulties, desire and the death of ATSIC. *The Australian Journal of Anthropology*, 15(3): 312–16.

Deranty JP & Renault E (2007). Politicising Honneth's ethics of recognition. *Thesis Eleven*, 88(1): 92–111.

Dodson M (2003a). Violence dysfunction Aboriginality. Speech presented at National Press Club 11 June 2003 [Online]. Available: law.anu.edu.au/anuiia/dodson.pdf [Accessed 1 September 2007].

Economist (2006). The art of the impossible: a special report on France, 28 October–3 November.

Fanon F (1968). *The wretched of the earth*. New York: Grove.

Foucault M (1980). *Power/knowledge: selected interviews and other writings*. C Gordon (Ed). Brighton: Harvester Press.

Good MJDV, Hyde ST, Pinto S & Good BJ (Eds) (2008). *Postcolonial disorders*. Berkeley: University of California Press.

Honneth A (1995). *The struggle for recognition*. Cambridge: Polity Press.

Lagrange H & Oberti M (2006). *Émeutes urbaines et protestations*. Paris: Presses de Sciences Politiques.

Spivak G (2000). The new subaltern: a silent interview. In V Chaturvedi (Ed), *Mapping subaltern studies and the postcolonial*, (pp324–40). London: Verso.

Wacquant L (2008). *Urban outcasts: a comparative sociology of advanced marginality*. Cambridge: Polity Press.

Weber M (1972). Politics as a vocation. In HH Gerth & CW Mills (Eds), *From Max Weber* (pp77–128). New York: Oxford University Press.

2

Framing violence: an ethnographic perspective on rioting[1]

Gillian Cowlishaw

> The political efficacy of an act of violence is also an aesthetic efficacy that provides pleasures of consumption and reception that positions aggressor and victim respectively in an iconic and stylised relationship. (Feldman 1997)

The analysis of violence is usually conducted by journalists and academics that are positioned outside and above its practice, and from a position of unequivocal condemnation. Ethnographic work begins from a different position, in this case from inside a group that is outside the circuits where public imagery is constructed. The physical assertiveness here is different from that of the urban middle class, as is the relationship with police and with the concept of violence. It may be banal to assert that violence means different things in different places, yet the significance of this banality needs exploring. By examining *relationships* of violence, it is possible to understand 'riots' in a way that is, I believe, both more true to the events, more morally ambiguous and more politically effective.

Framing violence

There is danger in allowing public scandals to determine where we apply our analytic attention. The media discourse about public violence such

---

1 The material in this article is taken from my book, *Blackfellas, whitefellas and the hidden injuries of race* (2004), in which chapter six contains a broader discussion of violence in an Australian town.

as rioting threatens to overwhelm any cultural and historical analysis that could reveal the complex significance of such events, particularly to those involved. My study of contemporary social relations in Bourke, a country town in Australia, was framed by the narrative of a riot that occurred in December 1997 and its effects that unfolded over the following four years. Rather than deploring the riot, I aimed to explore its existential nature, the meanings it expressed and the conditions from which it arose. Bourke is notorious for, among other things, a history of racial violence.[2] I interpreted the riot as one expressive moment in a long-standing struggle to assert Murris' rights and difference, and to contest the hegemony that whitefellas exercise through their shops, their institutions and their moralising gaze, all prefaced on their assumption of ownership of the land in the 1860s. The Bourke riot itself may seem inconsequential, a symbolic crisis or the culmination of far more significant forces. There was some property and bodily damage, but the violence was short lived and was arguably a result of police interference. It aroused local passions but hardly registered in the national media.[3]

That is why my title refers to framing. We need to reframe our ideas about where and what violence is, as well as to recognise the ways that violence frames the relationship between subordinate peoples and those they live among. What is viewed as deplorable violence also needs relativising, as illustrated in this example of an ordinary Aboriginal response to the problem of racial affront. Joe explained that when he was a university student he sometimes came upon people 'talking about blackfellas'. While other Aboriginal students were not very confident, he said:

> Me, I'll go straight in ... Situations might arise where, say you might be getting in the car and they'll say, 'Oh don't let that blackfella in there.' I'll

---

2 Bourke has a certain iconic status in Australia with the phrase 'back o' Bourke' typifying the remote outback. It was one of a number of towns on the Darling river where a series of violent confrontations between police and Aborigines has occurred since the late 1970s (Cunneen & Robb 1987; Morris 2001).

3 Thus this riot provides a stark contrast with Didier Fassin's argument in this volume that the French riots marked a major change in the national imagination and discourses.

just retaliate and give them a clip around the ear-hole or tell them not to be opening their mouth without a real reason for it … You couldn't get much clearer than that, when you give them a good jab in the jaw.

A similarly decisive response was made to the expression of contempt from white fellow residents:

You see in the clubs and pubs around town here, you see whitefellas talking about blackfellas and as soon as a blackfella comes along, they're real quiet … At the Central one night a couple of whitefellas was teasing Cliffy and his son walked in, and went over and downed one of them. He was all blood. But that's life; they look for it, they got it. Local blokes, they still drink there, same pub. But they don't talk like they used to. They know not to.[4]

These glimpses of a world where physical punishment is accepted as part of social life stands in sharp contrast with the discourses favoured at those institutional sites which offer cultural awareness courses that aim to overcome racist attitudes through instruction in intellectual ways of understanding difference. An Aboriginal woman expressed frustration with these talking cures: 'We can't stop what they think, but we can stop them saying it'. Explanations of public violence in terms of national or international forces tend to leave out such specific characteristics of the cultural context, and my ethnographic purpose is to attend to such omissions. I do not want explanation to erase the contentious presence of the people I am quoting. Structural conditions may comprise some necessary conditions for a riot to occur, but I want to enrich, modify, complicate and extend their explanatory reach.

The topic here is not violence as a generic category, but a specific kind of public and politicised violence, an understanding of which must begin with recognising its cultural embeddedness in local regimes of violence and in the social relations between groups and classes of people. Norbert Elias traced the development of 'mental self-restraint'

---

4 Such attacks on whites by Aborigines are rare. There was little in the way of interracial violence in the 1980s and 1990s, although this has changed somewhat with the increase in illicit drug use.

that emerged among citizens as states achieved the 'monopolisation of physical force' (Elias 1982, 235). The kind of self-restraint that has become 'second nature' enables the erasure, the apparent absence, of violence from urban cosmopolitan spaces. We conveniently forget that this absence relies on the police force to keep order. Cosmopolitan citizens routinely eschew and denounce all violent practices. We have little experience even of robust physicality and *habitually* deplore its practice, unlike the Murris (local self-designation of Aboriginal people) quoted above. The disavowal of violence in the name of eradicating it seems to me a discursive ploy that at once removes legitimised police and military violence from consciousness and as well negates the political meaning that may be important in the violence of others. It also suppresses the analysis of violence.

Feldman (1994, 405) has observed what he calls 'cultural anaesthesia' among academics, a nervous distancing from any exploration of those social realms where violence is not only a part of mundane social existence, but where positive merit and legitimate pleasure is taken in forms of behaviour that are elsewhere condemned as violent. It is true that the pleasures associated with many forms of violence are on display and obvious to all in the media and entertainment industries. Pub brawls and bikies' fights comprise the frank style and enjoyment of those who participate, while being rendered as shocking public spectacle for the vociferous disapproval of the public. The surreptitious enjoyment of violence in sport has been exposed in the humour of Australian comedians and commentators, Roy and HG Nelson.[5] These muted pleasures are denied legitimacy as part of urban cosmopolitan life. Thus, because Aboriginal social life in Australia is suffused with a sense of the violence done to and by them, it carries a sense of abnormality and embarrassment in egalitarian Australia. I will show what this means below. For the moment, following Feldman, I emphasise that violence defines the other, the outsider, confirming 'the exceptionalism

---

5   Roy and HG, as they were known, began as maverick sports commentators, broadcasting 'This sporting life' on Sydney radio station 2JJJ in 1986. They gained a huge cult following for their irreverence as they revelled in naming and celebrating practices usually subject to extreme disapproval such as fighting and gouging, 'groping' and 'pig rooting'.

of the historical and geographical periphery' (Feldman 1994). Violence, especially the domestic violence that has been the subject of media attention in 2007, is an active element in the continuing positioning of Aborigines at the periphery of normal citizenship because 'violence and its consequences are automatically associated with aberrant cultural difference' (ibid, 405). It appears to explain their excluded position and justify their hugely disproportionate rate of incarceration.[6]

My study of conditions that underlay the 1997 riot in Bourke argued that commonly expressed rage and resentment among Murris carried important insights into prevailing social conditions. Characteristic subjective and emotional orientations were reflected in shared discourses, habitual attitudes and foundational concepts. The lack of positive public recognition and the experience of being disrespected were community wide chronic realities illuminated through concepts of stigma (Goffman 1963), transgression (Stallybrass & White 1986) and interpellation (Butler 1997). Thus I approached Axel Honneth's book *The struggle for recognition* (Honneth 1995) in a different way from others engaged in the comparison between riots in Australia and France. Rather than inviting abstract arguments about internationally comparable conditions, Honneth offered me a broader, more 'political' interpretation of the specific events in Bourke.

Honneth gives a technical precision to the terms honour, respect and recognition, and examines how these social processes and the emotions they generate can become the basis for social movements. He argues that human beings have a 'constitutional dependence ... on the experience of recognition' (Honneth 1995, 136), so that when social subjects lack this experience an emotional space is made for the negative reactions of shame and rage. Honneth's notion of 'evaluative disrespect' refers to assaults on 'honour', 'dignity', or 'status', or more generally to 'the degree of social esteem accorded to his or her manner

---

6 The outpourings of outraged journalists and commentators in mid-2001 and again in mid and late 2007 have made domestic violence and sexual abuse the most well-known characteristics of Indigenous communities. Indigenous writers that have provided analyses of violence and suffering within Aboriginal communities include Langton 1997, Lucashenko 1997, Pearson 2000, Atkinson 2002 and McDermott 2002.

of self-realisation within a society's inherited cultural horizon'. Where forms of life and manners of belief are deemed inferior or deficient, then the subjects in question are robbed 'of every opportunity to attribute social value to their own abilities' (Honneth 1995, 134). Such social conditions can result in 'collective resistance stemming from the socially critical interpretation of commonly shared feelings of being disrespected' (Honneth 1995, 164). Subordinated groups will then engage in a social struggle for recognition and against 'what is referred to colloquially as "disrespect" or "insult"' (Honneth 1995, 132). Honneth's theory of the moral grammar of social conflicts can be applied to the systematic misrecognition and disrespect that Aborigines experience.[7] Many examples of such 'collective resistance' could be instanced, and 'commonly shared feelings of being disrespected' were certainly present in the Bourke riot, and would not be difficult to find expressed in the riots in Redfern, Palm Island, Macquarie Fields and Cronulla, as well as among the rioters in France.

If it is true that 'the experience of being disrespected carries with it the danger of an injury that can bring the identity of the person as a whole to the point of collapse' (Honneth 1995, 131–32), then the entrenched and systematic disrespect directed towards Indigenous people must be a major constitutive force which threatens, not just individuals, but the coherence of contemporary Indigenous society. I need to add that disrespect can come in the guise of benevolent, patronising concern for the helpless and injured victim of colonial history. That is, pity for the subaltern can also be disrespectful. But now I want to present three observations, to be illustrated below, that stem from placing Honneth in Bourke.

First, we must recognise the double-edged *consequences* of 'collective resistance' that takes the form of public, communal violence. To argue that public violence partakes of political intent says nothing of its effectiveness either as a considered political strategy, or as an

---

7   While there is extensive documented evidence of this condition, often glossed as racism, it has become so widely referred to as to have become platitudinous and suspect as a personal source of suffering. Dennis McDermott (2002) considered the way neural pathways are worn out by general, clichéd claims of injury.

opportunistic tactic in local struggles. The communal violence that became characteristic of the towns on the Darling River in the 1980s (Cunneen & Robb 1987) appeared to reinforce and justify local fellow residents' refusal of recognition. On the national stage the disorder may have contributed to the increase in official concern for deprived conditions, but as I have argued elsewhere, compassionate discourses seldom entail respect for the subordinated peoples they profess to help (Cowlishaw 2003).

Second, local social groupings produce and identify with rival moral discourses about historical and present injury, both sides of which have empirical support and vigorous supporters. In Bourke there is competition between blackfellas and whitefellas for moral ascendency. As one side shouts in fury, the other is morally outraged; as the subordinate commits passionate crimes against injustice, authority's cool reason becomes punitive, and the national audience entertains itself by taking sides.[8]

Third, the difference between in-group and public experiences of disrespect must be recognised. Honneth says subjects can be robbed 'of every opportunity to attribute social value to their own attributes' (Honneth 1995, 134) but he does not discuss the ability of a stigmatised group to confer value within its boundaries. It is well recognised that minorities promote alternative sources of pride, celebrate different manners, and use the amplification of stigma as a defensive weapon.[9] Even family life (usually) provides a foundational measure of respect and esteem for its members. The extent to which these internal social processes can dilute or undermine the effects of disrespect, contempt or exclusion from a hegemonic society would merit systematic empirical

---

8 This national audience presents another complication because a town that displays racial conflict is seen as peopled by rednecks and prejudiced police. These in turn are disrespected for disrespecting Aborigines. But because these are urban discourses of distaste, articulated in the national media, they are not experienced directly and are easily rejected because conservative discourses are more apparent in rural areas (Cowlishaw 2006).

9 Bourgois 15 (1996) work among the crack dealers in Harlem illustrates specific ways of gaining respect within the group that are at odds with those that confer respect outside it.

research. The significance of strangers' regard for the personal sense of self is a complex question, one that overlaps with the effect of reputation or stereotyping on particular subordinate groups. For instance, the experience of Bourke Aborigines in the city includes relief from habitual disrespect, well as shock at strangers' hostile, curious or presumptuous stares. I am arguing that public contempt directed to a particular group is mediated in various ways. The circumstances for experiencing respect and disrespect vary greatly. While Murri interaction in Bourke is mainly with in-group familiars, the white community cannot be avoided as they own and run the shops and institutions. These are the people who can cause what Goffman called psychic injury or in Honneth's terms threaten one's social honour.

While rage, resistance and sometimes riots are an inevitable, and rational, kind of response to structurally inferior conditions, their political efficacy is another question entirely. The rationality behind violent public protest is seldom attended to because violence itself is refused any relationship with reason. However, I follow Honneth in seeing social and psychological benefit in the overt expression of common grievances. These are matters that deserve empirical investigation rather than abstract speculation.

Transformations

By following the series of transformations that occur during and after a riot, we can glimpse the performative subjectivities that are evoked by these events and also reveal something of the social relations in which they are embedded. Some of these elements are common to riots generally. With the excitement of participants, riots take on an expressive, carnivalesque mood. Crowd behaviour enhances and amplifies emotions and concentrates the meanings into a spectacle. A riot also elicits the thrill and fear of battle for police who are facing off against highly aroused opponents. This is public combat, a disorganised battleground among surging crowds, spectacle, party and ritual combined (Stallybras & White 1986). We need to recognise that both hatred and love, as well as loyalty and betrayal, courage and fear are expressed in these events.[10]

---

10   Perhaps accident is also present, as in the TropFest film *Between the flags,*

The riot is then transformed in two directions. There is the impassioned public debate and there is the legal system's transformation of one set of participants into the accused. The media takes up and amplifies the emotive responses to the riot and plays the story back with a kind of moralising intensity that both exaggerates and trivialises the events. Thus the Bourke riot was headlined 'Rioters tear up Bourke', hysterically inflating the damage to bodies and property which followed the arrival of the police. But public debate is fickle, and the media loses interest in a riot when the slow and solemn legal consequences begin to unfold.

The court deprives the events of emotion by taking time and paying attention, not to any local narratives, but to the very specific details of individuals' actions. The legal process intervenes in the life of the town by positioning the protesting rioters as the accused, vested with an aura of guilt, yet no definitive findings accord with the local narratives. The law itself, in terms of statutes, legal principles, or lawyers' and judges' activities, is not directly responsible for this circumstance. The criminal cases *cannot* attend to any overall meaning of the riot, or pay any attention to its genesis or its justification in either any individual history or social conditions—although these matters may be attended to during sentencing. The price the accused must pay for legal protection is to subject themselves to the court's rituals and rules, and allow their actions to be (mis)interpreted, judged and made into the object of pity, anger or concern.

The legal system considers the rioters as responsible, not for a political event or a communal protest, but for individual crimes.[11] This individualisation, necessary to any criminal prosecution, renders the

---

(2007, Jayce White, dir.) about one Anglo and one Lebanese man who went to Maroubra by mistake and missed the Cronulla riot.

11   A series of criminal charges led eventually to 12 juveniles being tried and given non-custodial sentences, except for one custodial sentence of 18 months which was quashed on appeal. Five adults faced serious charges that carried substantial jail sentences. They were heard two to three years later; some were appealed and quashed. The most serious jail sentence of six months was served out four years after the event.

riot meaningless.[12] The rioters become embroiled in long drawn out and irresistible roles as court clients, supplicants before the justice system, transformed from assertive, violent and participatory citizens into abject, passive recipients of the law, occupying their place waiting on the courthouse steps, in the dock or in custody. These legal events should be seen as essential parts of riotous events, rather than sequels that override and empty the local conditions of their meaning. The humiliation and derogation experienced within the court system are ordinary elements of Aboriginal experience, whether as the accused, a relative, or one whose social identity is embroiled with this highly criminalised segment of the population.

Riots are further transformed when they become the subject of analytic writings that compete for the most incisive and powerful interpretations. The rioters' own sense of things can here become irrelevant, and explanations may show little appreciation of how the riot event may have reinforced or altered local social dynamics. That is, overarching explanations, appealing to economic, political or ideological conditions, may be directed to different questions from those that motivate the rioters. Even the pens of radical intellectuals transform the passions, the visceral experiences, the embodied rivalries that generate these events, into objects of cool analysis.

While I argue that the political *meanings* of the events to the riotous participants is essential to any interpretation, the ambiguous *effects* of such violence cannot be contained in any explicit or even inchoate political intention or meaning. I follow Feldman's argument that violence can be used to 'create the political' (in this case by challenging both ownership and propriety), but the rioters' politics may be local, short term and counterproductive. Intentions and motivations may also be contradictory; an endemic sense of injustice and rage may

---

12 Charges, such as 'affray' entailing the common purpose of a group are seldom pursued by prosecutors because they are notoriously difficult to prove (cf. Cowlishaw 2004, 235). Also, because the law has to assume a homogeneous citizenry, to whom a set of criminal laws applies equally, the legal system can generate further conflict by misrepresenting subordinate peoples and because of limited understanding of social conflicts.

contend or overlap with a personal vendetta toward particular police or shopkeepers or immediate desire for the looted goods.[13]

There are also pleasures and protections afforded by the law. The accused become important actors in a major site of institutional power before lawyers and judges who occupy positions of high status (Hebdige 1988). A lawyer is provided to take the part of the accused against police officers. Police are called to account in a public forum, forced to answer questions and respond to accusations before a judicial officer. Some Murris are proud of their expertise in legal processes. There are occasional opportunities to disrupt or challenge the process, although such disruptions may attract further punishment or simply be ignored. When an Aboriginal youth shouted from the courtroom foyer 'Give us a fair go, you poofters', the officers of the court rendered themselves deaf, though the moment was marked by grins and nudges among the Murris (Cowlishaw 2004, 73).

One immediate cause of the rage that erupted in the main street on the night of the riot was the sense that police were interfering in Murris' homely space, interrupting the usual Friday night fisticuffs in the street. This view, driven by a sense of moral outrage, expresses a passionate, opportunistic attempt to invert the moral hierarchy of white virtue and black sin. Violent actions then briefly shattered the complacency and moral superiority that accompanies and naturalises state power. But the cultural logic of black community life was quickly smothered under the hysteria of anger and pity, and by the foreign rhythm of long drawn out courtroom dramas.

Habituated and pleasurable violence

In the following section I illustrate the candid violence, the robust physicality that is part of the Murri repertoire in Bourke. Some behaviour that is conventionally considered violent is explicitly celebrated in Murri talk. Fights on a Friday night were spoken of as a regular source of enjoyment. One man said:

---

13 I should add that there is a peaceful and sober, perhaps more integrated, segment of the Murri population that will, mostly in private, dissent from, or show ambivalence towards these actions.

> That was the go, you go down there and watch the fights. People were fighting with their fists … it was just like going into one of those Michael Tyson boxing rings … If [the riot] had been, say one block down, … I don't think the police would've even got involved in it.

Further: 'Police used to never venture down there … they used to get stoned, rocks and bottles', another indication that Murris see themselves as protecting their own space from unwarranted surveillance. Frequent and pleasurable memories of fist fights among women as well as men evoke a sense of sporting contests. Cecily boasted of her response when a woman began to strip on the bar in a pub: 'I said "You won't show your tits to *my* husband" and decked her.' Another woman took satisfaction from planning a 'knuckle up' with the woman who had stolen her boyfriend. Fights which challenge the mental and physical strength of others stem from real conflicts, disputes and jealousies, that is, from normal aspects of human relations in a densely interacting community. These ways of settling conflict are effective because they are accepted as decisively completing disputes, at least temporarily. The failure to condemn physical violence, indeed the affirmation of the satisfaction of 'knocking' someone, can deeply shock whitefellas, myself included. Yet there is an appealing directness and honesty in responding to an offensive comment with a jab in the jaw.

Andy King told me the story of how he punched a policeman during the Riot: 'The police were just parked straight across the road … So I'm telling them, "*Why didn't you stop it when it started down the street down here. Yous all scared or what? What are you doing in uniform? Gutless bastard.*" And something I said there, well he said to me, "*Go on hit me big man, hit me*", like that … I went whack and I hit him once under the chin and knocked him out.'

Andy was not merely expressing his resentment towards the police. He was also using a familiar and honourable method of drawing this particular police officer, with whom he had clashed before, into his social world where men *and* women rely on their own physical strength. The police reliance on state-sponsored powers is exposed as cowardly in Murri eyes. Andy evokes a picture of himself as at home, comfortable in his knowledge of what is going on, and ready to contest those police actions and decision he sees as illegitimate in some way.[14] He professes outrage that next morning several police vehicles surrounded his house, and he was taken to the station and charged on nine counts, the last of which was resolved four years later. Police, he says, do not play fair. Such disputation is played out repeatedly as police officers are accused of concealing what Murris believe to be agendas of personal vengeance and mastery behind uniforms, weaponry and the courts. Many Murris interpret police violence as a voluntary practice, not necessitated by their work, but used illegitimately in their campaign of vicious contempt towards particular people. Violence is thus an intimate part of relations between police and Aborigines.

Elsewhere I have offered details of the way Aboriginal people experience being humiliated and derogated in the streets and shops. Being interpellated as a chronic suspect accompanies everyday life of many Murris. Such experience generates and shapes both bitter shame, anger and self-destruction as well as humour, energy and a creative spirit which mounts a barrage of backtalk to the white world. These performers of Aboriginality see themselves positioned outside the circuits that establish national truths about Aboriginality.[15] But our understanding of this condition would be severely limited without taking into account the assertion that the children have certain relevant skills. As one man boasted:

> You got kid anywhere from 10 to 15 in Bourke would know more about crime and how to commit it and how to get away with it than any of the coppers ... Them kids are a long way ahead ... They've been doing it ever

---

14 Andy's sense of being at home is also vividly apparent in his account of what happened next: 'There was fighting going on ... I could feel the batons into me, see, so I crawled away from there, out of the crowd and sat on the gutter, me and me nephew. ... I had a few bruises and that on me ... just sat in the gutter talking. I said "Don't worry about it, Bugger it" and I walked home and as I was walking home I seen all the windows being smashed.'

15 There is a quite different kind of institutional environment where the articulation of 'the Aboriginal viewpoint' is demanded in pursuit of 'hearing the Indigenous voice'. Such representations occur in social realms that appear independent of the social world I have been describing. The barriers between these domains illustrate another aspect of the cultural conflict I have been describing.

since they were old enough to walk. They're in the shops, out of the shops, and these cops don't even know, or they've gone before they get them.

Of course such bravado is not reliable evidence of child criminality, but rather of a rebellious orientation towards property, police and propriety that used to be played out in the regular smashing of shop windows until retractable metal roller blinds were installed.

Domestic and intra community violence is also familiar among Murris. One woman laughed as she said she wouldn't marry one of *that* family and 'have to go around with a face looking like a busted up camp oven.' Another said, 'I didn't raise my daughter to be someone's punching bag.' These are candid references to conditions that many resist but cannot entirely avoid without jeopardising primary social relationships. The term domestic violence usually refers to interpersonal brutality and cruelty perpetrated within private space in the home, carefully secreted from neighbours and public view. But in Bourke there is little secrecy. Men who cruelly and regularly beat their women are well known and criticised, but not ostracised. There are women who are seen as the instigators of physical violence and who fight with at least equal ferocity. Because domestic violence takes place in a context where physical force is accepted as a natural element in the settling of disputes and as a normal feature of human conflict and contestation, it is less remarked and shameful than elsewhere, although commonly deplored.[16]

The Aboriginal people who take part in riots are regularly construed as irredeemably recalcitrant, but the police are also traduced. In standard 'left' interpretations, police and local whites are readily stereotyped as rednecks, racists, and other epithets that distance them from what Hage calls cosmo-multiculturalists (1997). Police are also criticised by local whites for their inability to stop public disorder and delinquency. Of course the forms and degrees of 'disrespect' towards rednecks and police differ markedly from those directed towards

---

16 These circumstances make domestic violence hard to combat. Given the recent publicising of high levels of sexual abuse of children in Aboriginal communities, I should add that I only ever heard one hint of a small child being sexually abused. The sexualisation of young girls was a common condition often deplored by older women in terms familiar in urban contexts.

Aborigines, as does the threat disrespect poses to the social honour of each and the moral grammar that can be called upon to bolster the two positions. For Aboriginal residents of Bourke it is the local whites who can endanger the honour of Murris at any moment in the streets or the shops in a multitude of minute gestures whereas rural police and local whites do not have to interact with their urban critics.[17] Further, the normative self-image of white police is 'continually backed up by [local and institutional] others' (Honneth 1995, 131–32), so that the criticisms mounted by local blackfellas are rarely experienced as destructive disrespect. However, some individuals, such as Andy, deliberately target the pride of police officers. After describing incidents of being harassed, Andy explained: 'It doesn't worry me. I just turn to the side and spit on the ground and *they hate that. That's what I do to them.* Or I go "Woof, woof" cause that's all they are, dogs' (my emphasis).

Bourke police are the object of attack as perpetrators of oppressive injustice, and also for not protecting (white) people and property. In the face of these contradictory criticisms, police develop a well-recognised institutionalised defensiveness, based on a sense that their work lacks recognition, respect or understanding of their role in enforcing public order, and this contributes significantly I believe, to the conditions in which public disorder occurs.[18] There is a degree of familiarity and even intimacy between police and those they habitually try to control and subdue. Cultural commonalities among Murri men and policemen— beer drinking, football and macho competitiveness—rather than establishing common interests, appears to increase hostility. The senior police I interviewed in Bourke expressed sorrow, distaste and pity, and a hint of bafflement in the face of people they are assiduously policing,

---

17 The paranoid attitude of police towards the urban media has been documented by Morris (2001) and in the report of the Royal Commission into Aboriginal Deaths in Custody (RCIADIC).

18 Tony Birch (2004) noted that the quick response of police to the death of the young Koori that sparked the riot in Redfern, demonstrated their understanding of the local community's point of view and their desire to obviate its effect.
While the police force is better governed than thirty years ago, and explicit racist practices are no longer endemic, a range of structural and institutional sources of conflict remain.

that is, those most likely to be involved in riots and also the most abject and 'dysfunctional' families.[19]

The daunting fury which police fear from Murris as well as the pleasure that can be extracted from the narration of a physically violent drama is illustrated in the following story:

> One time they took G. into the court. Beautiful court, the dock's quite high, a good chest height. He's in the dock and all the cops are there. One of the police acted as a prosecutor and he's gone off on this spiel, legalese you know, talking multi-syllable words and G's wondering what's going on. He said 'Do I get bail or what?' He [the prosecutor] said 'No'. G. yelled, 'You fucken cunt'. He's leapt from a standing position on to the top of the railing and he launched himself across the bar table. All the coppers crash-tackled him. They rolled off the bar table and onto the floor and they're all wrestling around with him. He's got that mad strength; they reckon there's about six cops laying on top of him. He's going 'errrrr' like that. Anyway they looked up and where the chamber magistrate had been they reckon there's a big high backed chair going rrk rrk rrk. He's gone!!

I also perceived an involuntary form of abjection in habits of self-denigration where public judgements leak into self-consciousness. A man I call Jake reflected on his own reflection in the eyes of whites, saying: 'I don't think the rest of the whites give a stuff about us or what happens to us. They haven't took the time to get to know Aboriginal people. They see one walking along charged up, "Here's another one of them drunken black thieving bastards"' Jake places himself in the same frame as the ugliness perceived by whites. Unable to escape by any action of his own, he is trapped by this image of himself as a repellent creature. But he also showed understanding of the policeman's perception:

> If a young cop is posted to Bourke ... he's in town a week and gets confronted by an Aboriginal who's drunk ... he could be swearing

---

19 Police and Aborigines share something of an outsider status, apt to be characterised as other by a majority of their fellow citizens. I did not gain the confidence of the Bourke police. However, there is evidence that some members of the police force carry a concealed contempt for the niceties of the law and that such views are associated with treating Aborigines as personal antagonists (Morris 2001).

> or yelling loud at his missus, but he might do that all the time ... For
> someone who doesn't know and they're confronted by that they think, 'Oh
> yeah I've heard about these drunken blackfellas. This is one of them here.
> Listen how he's swearing. Come on, get him. Lock him up.' And all he is,
> is just probably half in the horrors, a person permanently in the horrors
> from all the cheap wine he's gotta drink.

The 'gotta' refers both to the man's compulsion to drink and his penury which precludes better quality alcohol, neither of which he is seen as responsible for. Wounds are alluded to here, not as individual experience, but as communal features of Aboriginal existence in a language which explains both behavioural characteristics and the town's problems.

Recognising repugnance

These stories not only confound the notion that Aborigines are passive victims, but also could be seen to complicate Honneth's argument about recognition. The whitefellas at the coal face, the local residents, the 'blow-ins' such as school teachers, health workers and even police, do not see themselves as refusing recognition to Aboriginal people. Rather, they are recognising, and rejecting, what Povinelli has called 'repugnant practices' that are beyond the pale for liberal citizens (Povinelli 2002). The fact that Murri women appear not only in the familiar female role as victims, but also as active participants in public displays of violence, adds to the repugnance and stigma carried by the Murri domain. The bulk of Murris who do not participate in this kind of violence have to defend themselves from the implication that they are exceptions, atypical, not authentic Aborigines.

While it is not surprising to find more primal forms of power well represented among people who experience a chronic threat to their social honour, many Aboriginal people firmly reject the 'repugnant' social persona, or stereotype, that is attributed to them. One man, for instance, angrily refused to be defined as a 'police client'. When such people refuse the sociality of the pub and face suspicion of disloyalty from other Murris, they assert an intact Indigenous identity free of public violence and negative stereotypes. They reject the idea that Aborigines' troubles are all due to an unremittingly racist social environment. This is part of an 'anti-victimhood' discourse that is becoming more explicit and powerful, I believe, as it is recognised that a victim status has become a burden on Aboriginal social life (Povinelli 1999).[20]

Honneth suggests that emotional reactions to the refusal of recognition hold out 'the *possibility* that the injustice done to one will cognitively disclose itself and become the motive for political resistance' (1995, 138; my emphasis). It is important to acknowledge that political resistance may not be realised, or if realised may not be good or effective politics as mentioned above. The Bourke riot could be seen as simply entrenching the blackfellas' reputation for destructiveness. But there are other sources of, and responses to, political inspiration. A man I call Joe provides an affirmation of Honneth's argument that 'negative emotional reactions, such as being ashamed or enraged, feeling hurt or indignant' can provide a psychological link 'from mere suffering to action by cognitively informing the person in question of his or her social situation' (Honneth 1995, 135). For Joe,

> Aboriginal people know that something is wrong in society and they know the white man's to blame for it. Because of the awareness around black history they've come to realise that they have been put down by the whites and that white people are responsible for the situation. Especially housing and inequalities of ownership of land and ownership of everything.

Thus a new emphasis in Australian history, often known as Aboriginal history, has enabled a fresh interpretation of Aborigines' position, a sheeting home to others and the responsibility for their communal plight. It is popular versions of postcolonial discourses that have allowed Aboriginal people to name white violence, injustice and hypocrisy and to make them the subject of legitimate public complaint. The need to create a political space through the symbolic power of

---

20 Noel Pearson (2000) has been a major catalyst of change in the public discourses, but there are other sources of this shift in Indigenous community politics towards renewed assertions of genuine self-determination in the face of the failure of many Aboriginal organisations. I believe that an increasing number of educated and articulate Aboriginal people are the major source of this shift.

violence and of racialised bodies indicates the political ambiguity of this position.[21] The robust assertion of the primal physical force of the body is a powerful challenge to the order of things, yet it cannot succeed as is evident in the deployment of riot gear for police protection. The challenge is also evident in that other response that protects the status quo, the barrage of delegitimising discourses, expressing revulsion, rejection and condemnation of what is named as merely disordered destructiveness.

There is ambivalence at the heart of the resisting and active psyche which is made in subjection, and which is evident in the distress and self destructiveness that characterises many, but by no means all, Aboriginal communities. These are well-known sources of the public's bemused concern or outraged despair, and these responses in turn reverberate in Aboriginal communities. They become both unconscious and self-conscious aspects of identities constructed in the reflected glare of national discourses.

The ethics of responsibility

We were invited to speak about 'the role of the state, and the ethics of responsibility'. When these grand topics meet up with the ability to fight and to frighten—that is, with elemental forms of power practised candidly by those we want to rescue from state power—they tend to sputter into silence and temporary insignificance. At a more mundane level, the contrast between the rioters' lives and sociological generalisations was evident in the magistrate's diagnosis of the causes of the riot. In sentencing some of the younger Bourke rioters, he proffered a familiar rhetoric of victimhood; the summer heat; boredom; unemployment; old tribal rivalries; old tensions with police. These are standard themes in a kind of reasoning that appears to exonerate the perpetrators of the Bourke riot, emphasising their social distress while erasing the intent and

---

21 I have described elsewhere how this power is activated in discursive constructions and in the performances of racialised identities in the streets, as well as within Aboriginal community life where dramatic fabulations are evoked in conversation and are part of the politics and poetics of everyday life. But there is collateral damage also, as older forms of adjustment and accommodation are displaced (Cowlishaw 2004).

intensity, the satire, humour and mischievousness. They become simply victims of a social pathology they are helpless to combat and a resentment they are bound to express. This seems a weak and unsatisfactory way to address what are frequent, passionate, and sometimes bloody conflicts, engaging the attention of many people and many resources over considerable periods of time and occasionally involving substantial prison sentences. Unlike populist and punitive responses, liberal thinkers do not attribute agency or serious purpose to the perpetrators of such acts. Thus any explicit or implicit *positive* meanings associated with the riot are forced to give way before the pity and concern of their supporters. We need relief from texts that similarly take up the white man's burden in their aim to shed light on others' suffering but which further ensnare these others in a language they do not make and cannot contest (e.g. Sutton 2001; Neil 2002).

It seems to me that, for the social analyst, 'the ethics of responsibility' begins with the obligation to recognise the meaning and the context of social events to those who instigated them, as well as to others directly involved. We need to listen to what the rioters are saying but also, ideally, to experience the condition of which the rioters are a constitutive part. But it is not enough to echo, or simply explore the legitimacy of, the rioters' explicit complaints. Populist debates are caught in a binary of either defending the indefensible (violence), or criticising the rioters (blaming the victim). Ashis Nandy developed a cultural analysis that probed the limits of both sides of these conventional arguments in relation to the hijackers of an Indian airline. Asserting that 'interpretation is a matter of choice, and the choice is both political and moral' (Nandy 1995, 18), he showed that another, non-violent moral order operated within the hijackers' violent actions. The hijackers showed respect to the elderly, responded to a child who called one of them 'uncle', and whispered to the man they had threatened to shoot that he was really quite safe. Nandy says that he would be derided by orthodox scholars who say we should not be trying to understand such people. Because it is so difficult to give any account of legitimate violence outside the structures of state authority, it becomes political work to offer a cultural analysis of rioters as well as hijackers and suicide bombers. This is not an offer to simply legitimise such violence, but to explain why these 'repugnant' behaviours *seem* legitimate and liberating to the actors involved, and to enable the question about a more general legitimacy to be raised. Paying attention to the participants' sense of these events entails examining the cultural and historical conditions that have established what appears as a population binary marking dramatically different moral conditions among contiguous peoples.

Where to from here?

I will conclude with some comments that both wrap up the above arguments and suggest some further considerations. Through an ethnographic approach I have tried to introduce empirical material to destabilise popular interpretation of riots, and to add depth, specificity and challenge to common sociological and philosophical approaches to public violence. By considering the actual experience of a riot, the feelings of fear, anger and excitement, I suggest we can get a vicarious feel for what physical violence is about and better comprehend public disorder.[22] Attention to the relationships being expressed, the visceral sense of resentment or anger towards local police, local shopkeepers or the wider society can only be properly understood by being 'with' the rioters—as well as 'with' the police and local residents. These social relations existed before and remain after the riot. For me, another aspect of 'being there' as ethnographer was following the long drawn out consequences through the courts. These legal processes are familiar to the rioters and have an organic relationship with a riot and related events. They are quotidian elements of the social conditions in Bourke, as is the fact that they do not vindicate the political convictions of either accused or accusers.

An emphasis on local meanings also highlights the significance of the distinct Indigenous struggles being enacted at the 2004 riots in Redfern (Birch 2004) and Palm Island (Glowczewski 2006) and the quite

---

22   I am not suggesting that we all need to be rioters to understand a riot, but we do need to allow our imaginations to explore what it would mean to be there (Canetti 1973). In this case I found my imaginative abilities greatly enhanced by living among those involved.

different trajectory of the immigrants in France. Still other intentions and experiences were present when Lebanese and Anglo-Australians clashed at Cronulla in December 2005.[23] As noted above, identifying common features of public violence in these events may obscure their cultural and historical specificity. There is a sense of disquiet about publicised violence that tends to disable political engagement with what is being expressed. Because the focus is on solving what is named as the problem of violence, attention is distracted from specific complaints which have emerged from long-standing, organic conditions that precede and energise riotous events.[24] Emphasis on the scandalous, the shocking and the violent keeps the quotidian nature of social control and conflict hidden. International comparisons usefully explore some of the broad conditions that give rise to these events, but they can also threaten to dissolve local significance and may derail or trivialise important local political meanings that need to be made visible.

I risk being accused of regressive politics in recognising the specificities, the salience and a degree of legitimacy in the violence of the Aboriginal community in Bourke. My insistence on the political meaning of behaviour that is widely condemned as social pathology has been dismissed out of hand by some critics. I am said to 'want to treat signs of Aboriginal personal dysfunction as expressions of ebullient rebelliousness' (Burchell 2007).[25] Like the popular press, such academic critics are refusing to take Aboriginal social life seriously and are eager to distance themselves from any engagement with a realm they prejudge to be repugnant. Even if there are real causes of repugnance— rather than it being a circulating self-fulfilling fantasy—why does this preclude social analysis? If Bourgois (2003) can analyse the social lives of crack dealers in Harlem and identify their 'search for respect', muting

---

23   Papers by A. Lattas, J. Lattas and A. Redmond on the Cronulla riot were published in The Australian Journal of Anthropology, December 2007.

24   See Lea, 2006.

25   Burchell's is the most recent and crude of a series of such dismissals, which have in common a lack of any engagement with either the theoretical alternatives or with the ethnographic material. For details of this dispute see *Oceania* 71(3), 2002, special issue 'Old contempt and new solicitude': race relations and Australian Aboriginal ethnography.

his moral impulses long enough to reveal a rich, real and fraught social arena where money and work, violence and status are played out in particular ways, then surely Australian social science can suspend its anxious moralism long enough to try to understand the less dangerous and destructive realm of Aboriginal life in Australia.

The violence that resulted when a street fight among Aboriginal people in Bourke was interrupted by police is part of a familiar exchange, one generated in specific historical conditions. Yet when the actors appear in the criminal courts they have no opportunity to speak their own lines. This is not a space where otherness as culture or as history can be recognised. The actors can only perform as pitiable and reprehensible evidence of marginality. In the public arena, and in academic analysis (Bolger 1991; Sutton 2001; Tatz 2001) with a few exceptions (Robinson 1995), Indigenous violence is examined only as a pathology, either a repugnant indigenous tradition or a symptom of colonial injury. If one does not join the universal opprobrium, the hounds of moral policing start to bay. Such moral hegemony obstructs the exploration both of local meanings attached to particular violent events and of the historical generation of such cultural expression.[26]

Considering how politicised ethnic or racial groupings are involved in rioting leads to a consideration of the ubiquity and inescapability of the social categories of race. The anxieties that characterise contemporary Indigenous studies are to do with fear and embarrassment—fear of feeding negative racist stereotypes—fear of rousing suffering and angry victims hidden in history's cupboards—embarrassment about intruding on private Aboriginal business. This latter seems to me a gesture of repentance and irresponsibility; the nation confesses to a damaging history and takes no responsibility for its effects except for cumbersome legal remedies which can exacerbate rather than heal historical wounds. The native title process, unsuccessful claims for compensation, applications for stolen wages, all make demands on Aboriginal people to prove who they are and what they have suffered. These are the only things the nation seems able or willing to recognise as Aboriginal.

---

26 The prevalence of police violence in the past, such as bashings in the police lock-up, should also be taken into account.

I have elsewhere discussed why, in the face of the goodwill that marked the moral ascendancy of self-determination and land rights in the last thirty years, Aboriginal people have not snuggled comfortably into the warm and welcoming embrace of the nation. This is the kind of question implied in much recent public debate, and reminds us that we cannot dismiss the state's official recognition of culture and heritage—in legal provisions for claims to land and heritage—as merely a shallow cloaking of a deeper rejection of alterity as Povinelli implies (2002). Recognition is not merely ideological; it is law and practice bolstered by a supporting body of impulses and sentiments, which comprise a complex and contradictory condition of existence for Indigenous people. As academics we participate in this sympathetic desire to recognise. But these benign intentions can also be a stifling fog, concealing painful experiences of interracial interaction and drowning emotional impulses in conventional compassion. Engagement with Indigenous people requires a tougher approach. It is useful, I suggest, to imagine public violence as a way of breaking through the suffocating, complacent façade of national solicitude. Rioting can be seen as expressing rage consequent on the recognition that true recognition has never occurred.

References

Atkinson J (2002). *Trauma trails: recreating song lines*. Melbourne: Spinifex.

Birch T (2004). 'Who gives a fuck about white society anymore?': a response to the Redfern riot. *Overland, 175*.

Bolger A (1991). *Aboriginal women and violence*. Darwin: NARU.

Bourgois P (2003). *In search of respect*. Cambridge: Cambridge University Press.

Burchell D (2007). Tears in, and over, the social fabric. *The Australian*.

Butler J (1997). *Excitable speech: a politics of the performative*. New York & London: Routledge.

Canetti E (1973). *Crowds and power*. London: Penguin Books.

Cowlishaw G (2003). Disappointing Indigenous people: violence and the refusal of help. *Public Culture, 15*(1): 103–25.

Cowlishaw G (2004). *Blackfellas, whitefellas and the hidden injuries of race*. Oxford: Blackwell Publishing.

Cowlishaw G (2006). Cultures of complaint: an ethnography of rural racial rivalry. *Journal of Sociology,* 42(4): 431–45.

Cunneen C & Robb T (1987). *Criminal justice in north-west New South Wales.* Sydney, Bureau of Crime Statistics and Research.

Elias N (1982). *The civilising process: state formation and civilisation.* Oxford: Basil Blackwell.

Feldman A (1994). On cultural anesthesia: from Desert Storm to Rodney King. *American Ethnologist,* 21(2): 404–18.

Feldman A (1997). Violence and vision: the prosthetics and aesthetics of violence. *Public Culture,* 10(1): 24–60.

Glowczewski B (2008). *Guerriers pour la paix: la condition politique des Aborigènes vue de Palm island.* Avec une contribution de Lex Wotton. Montpellier: Indigène Editions.

Goffman E (1963). *Stigma: notes on the management of spoiled identity.* New York: Simon & Schuster Inc.

Hage G (1997). At home in the entrails of the west: multiculturalism, ethnic food and migrant home building. In H Grace, G Hage, L Johnson, J Langsworth & M Symonds, *Home/world: space community and marginality in Sydney's west* (pp118–46). Sydney: Pluto Press.

Hebdige D (1988). *Hiding in the light: on images and things.* London: Routledge.

Honneth A (1995). *The struggle for recognition.* Cambridge: Polity Press.

Lattas A (2007). 'They always seem to be angry': the Cronulla riot and the civilising pleasures of the sun. *The Australian Journal of Anthropology* 18(3): 300–20.

Lattas J (2007). Cruising: 'moral panic' and the Cronulla riots. *The Australian Journal of Anthropology* 18(3): 320–35.

Langton M (1997). Rum seduction and death: 'Aboriginality' and alcohol. In G Cowlishaw and B Morris, *Race matters* (pp77–94). Canberra: Aboriginal Studies Press.

Lea T (2006). 'Violence as crisis: the vampiric qualities of policy making in the north.' Paper delivered at Cairns AAS conference, September.

Lucashenko M (1997). Violence against Aboriginal women: public and private dimensions. In S Cook and J Besant, *Women's encounters with violence: Australian experiences.* Thousand Oaks: Sage Publications.

McDermott D (2002). Bare feet, broken glass: Aboriginal poetry and the leaving of trauma. In X Pons, *Departures: how Australia reinvents itself* (pp271–81). Melbourne: Melbourne University Press.

Morris B (2001). Policing racial fantasy in the far west of New South Wales. *Oceania*, 71(3): 242–62.

Nandy A (1995). The discrete charms of Indian terrorism. In A Nandy, *The savage Freud* (pp1–31). Oxford: Oxford University Press.

Neil R (2002). *White out: how politics is killing Black Australia.* Sydney: Allen and Unwin.

Pearson N (2000). *Our right to take responsibility.* Cairns: Noel Pearson & Associates.

Povinelli E (2002). *The cunning of recognition: Indigenous alterities and the making of Australian multiculturalism.* Durham: Duke University Press.

Povinelli EA (1999). Settler modernity and the quest for an Indigenous tradition. *Public Culture*, 11(1): 19–48.

Redmond A (2007). Surfies versus westies: kinship, mateship and sexuality in the Cronulla riot. *The Australian Journal of Anthropology* 18(3): 336–49.

Robinson G (1995). Violence, social differentiation and the self. *Oceania* 65(4): 323–46.

Royal Commission of Aboriginal Deaths in Custody (1991). *National Report* Vol I [Online]. Available: www.austlii.edu.au/au/other/IndigLRes/rciadic/ national/vol1/ [Accessed 21 August 2007].

Stallybrass P & White A (1986). *The politics and poetics of transgression.* London: Methuen.

Sutton P (2001). The politics of suffering: Indigenous policy in Australia since the 1970s. *Anthropological Forum*, 11(2): 125–73.

Tatz C (2001). *Aboriginal suicide is different: a portrait of life and self-destruction.* Canberra: Aboriginal Studies Press.

3

In the Northern Territory Intervention: what is saved or rescued and at what cost?[1]

Irene Watson

The foundation of the Australian colonial project lies within an 'originary violence', in which the state retains a vested interest in maintaining the founding order of things. Inequalities and iniquities are maintained for the purpose of sustaining the life and continuity of the state (Derrida 1990, 927, 931, 943, 971–77). The Australian state, founder of a violent (dis)order is called upon by the international community to conform and uphold 'human rights', but what does this call to conformity require, particularly when the call comes from states which are also founded upon colonial violence? It is my argument that very little is required beyond the masquerade that 'equality' for Aboriginal peoples is an ongoing project of the state. So for what purpose does the masquerade continue? The masquerade of equality is essential to the notion of foundation and state legitimacy even though inside the colonial state 'equality' is never a possibility. The bare minimum notion of 'rights' is allowed, in what Rancière suggests is a space that is diminishing daily, until 'rights' appear empty and devoid of use (Rancière 2004, 307). Rancière compares the idea of rights of the oppressed to the charitable giving of second-hand clothes to the poor, or the sending of aid abroad to 'deprived peoples'.

Australia does not have to look overseas to extend the 'charity' of human rights; the colonisation of Aboriginal people's lives and territories

---

1 This chapter was first published in *Cultural Studies Review* 15(2): 45–60, September 2009. Reprinted with permission.

has been an ongoing project in the maintenance of inequality—inequality between Aboriginal life and a privileged colonial settler society. The standing inequality between the Aboriginal and settler societies provides fertile ground for human rights interventions. In June 2007 the Howard Coalition government announced it would lead an Intervention into Aboriginal communities in the Northern Territory (NT) as a response to the findings of the *Little children are sacred* report, which revealed high levels of community violence against Aboriginal children and women (Wild & Anderson 2007). Without negotiating with Aboriginal communities the Australian federal government announced its own strategy to intervene in the 'crisis' within Northern Territory Aboriginal communities, and enacted the Northern Territory National Emergency Response Bill (Cth) 2007.[2]

Soon after the announcement the Intervention commenced and was led, like those in Iraq and Afghanistan, by the military. According to the Australian government the Intervention will save and transform the lives of Aboriginal peoples living on Aboriginal lands that have been recognised since 1975 as such under the *NT Aboriginal Land Rights Act (Cth)*. The Howard federal government argued that its emergency Intervention was a 'just' and 'humanitarian' act, while the incoming and now current federal Labor government fully supports its opponent's Intervention laws. But are they just? Derrida argues that the mere application of a rule 'without a spirit of justice' might be protected to stand as 'law' but it would not be 'just' (Derrida 1990, 949). In this instance the Australian government stands protected by law, a law that continues to play out and re-enact its own unjust foundational position, one which took root in innumerable acts of colonial violence and continues today as violent re-enactments. But these violent re-enactments are not seen as violence. This is because the violence is normalised.

The Intervention was read by some as a contemporary invasion of Aboriginal lands but the Australian public and its political system read

---

2 The Howard government on 21 June 2007 announced its intention to use Commonwealth powers to impose a number of emergency measures following the *Ampe Akelyernemane Meke Mekarle 'Little children are sacred'* report.

it as a humanitarian intervention, as a lawful process of the Australian state (Derrida 1990, 983–85).

I understand the contemporary colonial project as one which has continued unabated from the time of the landing and invasion by the British in 1788, and which created a state founded on colonial or 'originary' violence.[3] It is from this foundation that the Australian state retains a vested interest in keeping the violence going, and the inequalities and iniquities that are maintained against Aboriginal peoples for the purpose of maintaining the life and continuity of the state. A question the Australian state is yet to resolve is its own illegitimate foundation and transformation into an edifice deemed lawful. Within this unanswered questionable structure the Australian state parades as one which has obliterated the 'founding violence' of its 'illegitimate' origins, and 'repressed them into a timeless past' (Zizek 2008, 99), while the survivors of this founding violence ask the state: by what lawful process do you come to occupy our lands?

The Commonwealth emergency response to Aboriginal violence is focused only on the Northern Territory—it is only the NT that has a federal Aboriginal land rights regime—but the NT is also earmarked for the opening of a number of new uranium mines. Coincidentally, a new railway line built by a consortium which included a subsidiary of Halliburton is routed from Adelaide to Darwin and crosses Aboriginal lands in the NT to provide easy access to shipping routes.[4] Clearly none of these facts have been cited as being relevant or having any connection to the new emergency laws—the media and public focus is solely upon child sexual abuse and the possibility of its prevention and protection—but they are certainly coincidental. Wendy Brown writing on humanitarian intervention suggests the state's Intervention in crisis events is probably more about a 'particular form of political power carrying a particular image of justice' (Brown 2004). In the

---

3 Derrida discusses the 'originary violence' that inheres in the foundation of states (Derrida 1990).

4 The 2008 economic crisis has impacted upon proposed uranium and other mining developments in the region and at the time of writing there is an indication of a slowing down of mining developments.

Australian context that image of justice is one which enables the violent foundations of colonialism to continue to hold territory and transform the life of Aboriginal peoples. It is a violent act which masquerades as being beneficial to impoverished Aboriginal communities across the NT, but one that once again boils down to the legitimising of the right to invasion of Aboriginal lands and lives (Rancière 2004).

Across colonial history, Australian law and society held and continues to hold the power to construct and identify that which is Aboriginal law and culture, a position which has resulted in translations and constructions of Aboriginal law and culture as being inherently violent against women and children. This position has allowed an opening for crusaders or 'white men to come to the rescue of brown women from brown men', as Gayatri Spivak suggested when commenting on the dynamics of a colonial India and the 'rescue' by white men of Indian women from the 'barbaric practice' of widow sacrifice (Spivak 1999, 284; see also Watson 2007; Watson 2005). The position of crusader is held up as the 'proper' solution to violence.[5] But in this universalised order whose concept of human rights and equality applies? And will the 'originary violence' be transformed into a lawful act of humanitarian intervention which obliterates its own past?

The federal government's concept of human rights was applied to provide 'protection' from violence in Aboriginal communities across the NT, but it remains important to examine what is being protected and the position and power held by 'contemporary Aboriginal Protectors'. It is my argument that the current emergency response laws are the contemporary representation of earlier colonial laws and protectionist policies of the Aborigines Acts, and that these (now repealed) laws were in their time of operation also characterised as being of benefit to Aboriginal peoples.[6]

---

5 For a critical discussion of the history of developments in the area of human rights see Douzinas 2000.

6 For examples of early colonial legislation see as follows: the *Aboriginals Protection and Restriction of the Sale of Opium Act (Qld) 1897*, s 9, 11, 13; *Aborigines Protection Act (Vic) 1886*; *Aborigines Act (Vic) 1890*; *Aborigines Protection Act (WA) 1890*; *Aborigines Protection Act (NSW) 1909*; *Northern Territory Aboriginals Act (SA) 1910*; *Aborigines Act (SA) 1911*.

Across time, from the moment of the original violence of foundation to this time now, the same question can be asked: what was it/is it that Aboriginal people are being protected from? In the past the black frontier experience was one of physical violence: white settlers effected massacres, murders and kidnappings, and as a result of their pressure, starvation and disease were also rife. Often official protection was ineffective. On the white side of the frontier however, it was and still is strongly contested that any frontier violence had occurred at all.[7] It is now claimed that under the recently imposed Commonwealth Intervention laws Aboriginal individuals, particularly women and children, would be protected from the violence of Aboriginal male members of their communities. Women and children would be protected from a 'failed Indigenous experiment' in respect of which the Howard government:

> would no longer stomach a policy regime whose many failings resulted in endemic poverty, alienation and disadvantage, and sickening levels of abuse of Aboriginal women and children.
>
> They rolled out a policy revolution. With the dis-establishment of ATSIC [Aboriginal and Torres Strait Islander Commission] and the removal of elected commissioners whose public reputations were in tatters following allegations of rape, corruption and incompetence, a new order swept in (Langton 2007, 147).

Langton's support for the new order fails to acknowledge the Howard government's complicity and power to determine otherwise; that is, during the previous decade the Howard government held power to intervene in Aboriginal community endemic poverty, alienation, disadvantage and community violence, but chose instead to do nothing, chose to sit back and observe like the vulture state it was and to swoop in upon communities at the point of implosion. So why did the state fail to intervene or act earlier? The implosion of communities was well represented by the Australian media but in their representation they failed

---

7   See in general the 'history wars' and revisionist writings on the truth of Australian history, most prominent being the works of Keith Windschuttle, e.g:Windschuttle 2002.

to provide a critical commentary of the Howard government's failure to engage with Aboriginal community development.[8]

The white settler frontiersman of the past has been transformed by the NT Intervention into the crusader of the present, rescuing Aboriginal women from Aboriginal men. The question to be asked is: what has happened in the intervening 200 years and why does the violence continue to occur intergenerationally in this changed and inverted context?

In coming to these questions it is important to distinguish the nature and character of violence in Aboriginal communities. Early colonial frontier violence was pitched against first peoples' laws and cultures, a foundational violence which established a colonial sovereignty. However, contemporary violence is more complex; it is characterised by violence of Aborigine against Aborigine, but the violence of the state also retains its original character against Aboriginal peoples' laws and cultures. It is a colonial violence which re-enacts itself to support its claim to legitimate foundation, and the Howard government emergency measures are such a re-enactment.

I don't think we can fully comprehend these recent developments without reflecting on history. In the past the colonial state cast the net of what I have called in previous works an illusion of protection or the masquerade of recognition of the humanness of Aboriginal peoples.[9] But under the protectionist policies of the Aborigines Acts our lives were totally controlled. Our old people were forced to live on reserve lands and were only allowed to leave the reserve once they obtained the permission of the Aboriginal Protector, or held an exemption certificate

---

8 The following media report profiles Aboriginal communities as failed states, 'A failed Indigenous experiment ends', *The Weekend Australian*, 23 June 2007, p. 16. While the intervention was implemented by the Howard government and is now supported by the current Rudd Labor government and it was met with resistance and a rally was organised in Canberra the day before the Rudd government apologised to the Stolen Generations (McClintock 2008).

9 The recognition of Aboriginality is seen as an illusion in Watson 1998. For further discussion on how this illusion is manifested in Australian native title laws see Watson 2009.

exempting them from being identified as an Aborigine under the Aborigines Acts.[10]

So who am I/are we today in this new so-called postcolonial landscape?[11] This question is particularly relevant to situations of native title claims where Aboriginal culture and identity is interrogated for authenticity, but apart from this it is also interrogated in another context. In the past our ability to truly live as Aboriginal peoples was subjugated entirely by colonial policies, but during the 1970s there was a symbolic shift to 'recognition' of Aboriginal lands, laws and cultures. However, recently we have been made aware most explicitly by the Howard government and also the Rudd government that these shifts in the 1970s were never based on firm ground but were vulnerable 'rights recognition' secured only by the 'human rights movement' of the times. So what are these times and how far if at all have we shifted from the original founding colonial intentions?

Prior to the commencement of the NT Intervention Aboriginal culture and collective forms of land ownership were deemed subversive to 'proper' forms of property ownership. In a speech to the Commonwealth Parliament Senator Mal Brough spoke in support of amendments to the *Northern Territory Land Rights Act (Cth) 1975*, arguing that private property rights would provide safer and more progressive developments for Aboriginal communities (Brough 2006). At the same time, negating the possibility for judicial consideration of Aboriginal cultural background was also considered by the Commonwealth as an advancement of universal human rights standards.[12] The build-up

---

10 *Aborigines Act (SA) 1934–39*, section 11a, provided Aboriginal individuals with an exemption from being identified as an Aborigine under the provisions of the *Aborigines Act*. For a further discussion on the history of the exemption system in South Australia, see Mattingley & Hampton 1998, 49.

11 I say so-called postcolonial because from my lived experience, there is very little which is postcolonial to the Aboriginal experience in Australia.

12 At the same time as the intervention was being talked up the Commonwealth sentencing laws were amended to remove the discretionary power of judges to consider the cultural background of the defendant, Commonwealth Parliamentary Debates, House of Representatives, 28 November 2006, see the amendment to the *Crimes Act (Cth)1914*, s16A, prior to the amendment the court could consider the

to the NT Intervention secured the passage of Commonwealth laws, marking a retreat from the 'recognition' of Aboriginal land rights, laws and culture.

The original colonial intentions were to establish colonies that were to become transformed into the Australian state. At the time of its foundation we were the non-native colonisers' natives, but we were ourselves Tanganekald[13] or other peoples, by our own names. Our identity and voices were unknown to the colonisers and unheard, but they have survived the attempted genocide. Today our voices are still talking while the colonial project remains entrenched and questions concerning identity politics, and the 'authentic native', are constructed and answered by those who have power to determine the legal and political categories of Aborigine and non-Aborigine. The categories of Aborigine and non-Aborigine were imposed by the colonial project and in this process of constructing Aboriginal and non-Aboriginal identities, the colonisers excluded themselves from having an Indigenous past.[14] I see this process of negating an Aboriginal identity as being tied to the idea of progress or the movement towards a 'vanishing future', away from an Aboriginal being, and relationships or connections to country.

While the colonial project from the outset denied and extinguished Aboriginality it seems contradictory that the commodification of Aboriginal culture brings an increased demand for authenticity— of Aboriginal art, and other tangible and intangible 'products'. Commodification occurs even while the survival of the 'authentic native' was and is threatened by colonialism, and while at the same time the state enables the space of annihilation, a space that at the same time demands the 'authentic native'. Who we are is often navigated from a violent space within which Aboriginality is measured for its degree

---

cultural background of the defendant, in the amended *Crimes Act (Cth) 1914*, new section 15AB.

13 Tanganekald is my mother's people of the Coorong of South Australia; our lands bordered with kin including the Meintangk, as our traditional identities mapped the land.

14 For further discussion on the construction of a non-Aboriginal identity as a result of colonialism. See Churchill 1994, 232–34.

of authenticity, and where those who do the measuring are ignorant or deniers of the history of colonialism. So when the struggle and desire for an Aboriginal life is depicted by the state as being no more than an invention or fabrication of culture and law, as was found in the Hindmarsh Island Bridge Royal Commission (South Australia) (Stevens 1995), we are deprived of our Aboriginality. The Hindmarsh Island Bridge Royal Commission inquired into the authenticity of Aboriginal women's law business and concluded that Aboriginal women had invented law business, and found that the practice had never been a part of Aboriginal cultures in the southern and south-eastern regions of South Australia. The commission was established to determine the truth or otherwise behind the claim that the building of a highway bridge from mainland Goolwa to Hindmarsh Island would destroy a significant Aboriginal women's site. Royal Commissioner Iris Stevens concluded that Aboriginal women's law was a fabrication or reinvention of traditional Aboriginal culture and law, for the purpose of preventing the building of the bridge. Since then the bridge has been built and a number of Aboriginal women continue to contest and resist the legitimacy of the decision which enabled the damage of an important Aboriginal site.

Aboriginal culture and identity is more likely to be supported when it is not challenging development projects and when culture performs as a commodity. However, when Aboriginality challenges the political agendas of the state, it is more likely to be attacked or demeaned as it was by Iris Stevens when she determined women's business was a fabrication and a reinvention of the past. Here the state determined the process of cultural translation, and the evidence relied upon was taken from white male experts, while the evidence of women's business was not presented to the commission because the proponents of Aboriginal women's business did not acknowledge the jurisdiction of the Royal Commission. How can anyone consider the possibility of cultural translation when the source of the translation has no status or even presence? When the information relied upon is that of the 'white expert' what is being translated? It is a compilation of their record of events; the Aboriginal record has no speaking voice. The outcome of the commission was to conclude an invention of tradition, a conclusion that resulted in the damage of a site of significance to Aboriginal women's law and cultural business. The discourse of progress framed and determined the processes of translation and the conclusions reached by the commission.

Zizek, in consideration of Scottish kilts, their origins and history writes, 'in the very act of returning to tradition, they are inventing it' (Zizek 2006, 29). He was referring to a specific history of place and people, a subject which cannot be conveyed to every known territory. However, the concept of invention of tradition is imposed broadly and occurred during the Hindmarsh Island Bridge Royal Commission. It was applied to a place where Aboriginal peoples are in struggle for the land and a space to re-establish a life beyond that of subjugated natives. The possibility for decolonisation or engagement with Aboriginal world-views on law and culture was rendered a fabrication by Iris Stevens, of the same species as Zizek's act of invention. Does a space in which there might be Aboriginality beyond a fabricated invention or a commodified Aborigine being exist? The cynic in me would say no; the resisting survivor would say it is the challenge.

In a critique of the 'tolerance' of liberal multiculturalism, Zizek reasons most unreasonably: 'an experience of Other deprived of its Otherness (the idealized Other who dances fascinating dances and has an ecologically sound holistic approach to reality, while features like wife-beating remain out of sight)?' (Zizek 2006, 38). Here Zizek renders the 'other' as 'real' without being so, for the real 'reality show' is not Aboriginal relationships to country but the out-of-sight wife-beating. This is real. But what of the reality of relationships to country; here they are demeaned as invention of tradition while the real is wife-beating. What is real and where is the reality space of colonialism as a determined player in the construction of the other's identity and responses to violence and the intergenerational traumas of colonialism? What has been stripped here is an Aboriginal context of life or an Aboriginal reality and not one as suggested by Zizek that is divested of substance resisting that which is real.

Colonial policies of protection were initially applied with the expectation that there would be a decline and eventual extinguishment of the 'native'. They would all die. When native populations, however, successfully resisted extinguishment, protectionist policies were replaced by policies of assimilation which assumed not that the natives would all die, but that cultural annihilation would occur. These policies more or less continue in various guises, but the recent Australian government Intervention into the NT works differently to colonial policies of the past. Aboriginal reserve lands which were set aside under the Aborigines Acts of the past for the purpose of sustaining protectionist policies of exclusion later formed the land base for the *Northern Territory Land Rights Act (Cth) 1975*. These lands have now been targeted for large-scale development and the bringing of both country and peoples into modernity. The 'emergency Intervention' is supported by a package of Commonwealth laws[15] which have been referred to by both major political parties as a necessary human rights intervention to relieve the crisis in Northern Territory Aboriginal communities.[16]

We might ask: was the sole purpose of the Commonwealth Intervention to save and transform lives and in particular the lives of Aboriginal children? The Intervention is being led by the Australian military and this raises the question whether this hard-line offensive precludes or negates other ways of dealing with violence in Aboriginal communities. For example, from early colonial times Aboriginal peoples have attempted to negotiate with the colonial powers on Aboriginal strategies that could work towards alleviating suffering in communities

---

15 The National Emergency Response comprises the following legislation; Northern Territory National Emergency Response Bill 2007 (Cth), Families, Community Services and Indigenous Affairs Amendment Northern Territory National Emergency Response Bill 2007 (Cth), and the Social Security and Other Legislation Amendment (Welfare Reform) Bill 2007 (Cth). This legislation will have an impact upon the following law, the *Aboriginal Land Rights Act 1975 (Cth)*, *The Racial Discrimination Act 1975 (Cth)*, and also the *Native Title Act 1993 (Cth)*, and the *Northern Territory Self-Government Act*.

16 The following provides a critical Aboriginal response to the intervention: Combined Aboriginal Organisations of the Northern Territory 2007; among media reports: Karvelas 2007, McKenna 2007.

across Australia. For more than 30 years Aboriginal strategies such as alternative justice models, and rehabilitation and healing centres modelled on Aboriginal cultural knowledge have largely been ignored or if they have been supported it has been in a tokenistic manner.

In considering the military Intervention into Aboriginal communities, I am interested in the question that Wendy Brown raises regarding humanitarian intervention: 'what kinds of subjects and political (or antipolitical) cultures do they bring into being as they do so, what kinds do they transform or erode, and what kinds do they aver?' (Brown 2004). It is a question which could also be applied to the early colonisation of Australia, and to this scenario we have an answer: what was brought into being was a large-scale dispossession of peoples from land, culture and law, peoples left without space to survive inside a colonial body that continually works to subjugate the 'native' to the trajectories of progress. Will Aboriginal communities be able to hold onto their land, or will they be removed? We have seen this history performed in the past. So what kinds of Aboriginal identities will form out of this most recent 'humanitarian intervention'? (Brown 2004, 454).

As the Intervention laws begin to peel back the provisions of the *Northern Territory Land Rights Act (Cth) 1975* we are yet to see the extent to which the Rudd Labor government will follow in line with that of its predecessor, the Howard government, and its original intention.

At the time of writing there is little to distinguish Rudd's policy from Howard's. It is, however, difficult to extrapolate all the intentions behind humanitarian intervention, because interventions by their nature are masked by the illusion of missionary goodwill, masking which is all the more powerful because of the real hardship and poverty of the peoples who are subjects of the intervention. What is to be saved or transformed by the NT Intervention, or what is likely to be achieved? Is the Intervention really about fixing the Aboriginal position of endemic poverty and violence or is it a land grab? Any answers to the above must critically consider that if intentions were sincere, why has the state taken so long to act, and why now? We know that the Australian government has spent the past decade de-funding and closing down Aboriginal initiatives and programs that were improving living conditions in

Aboriginal communities across Australia, and might have gone further if they had been allowed to continue.

The Board of Inquiry into the protection of Aboriginal children from sexual abuse report recommended collaboration of state and federal governments in consultation with Aboriginal communities to address the issue of child abuse as a matter of national emergency. But collaboration and consultation with Aboriginal communities and the Northern Territory was not considered by the Howard federal government. It has been suggested (and I am in agreement) that the Howard government's Intervention had less to do with addressing the question of child abuse and more to do with the government gaining greater access to Aboriginal lands, as well as weakening the position of Aboriginal law and culture.[17] The Intervention was planned and effected but to date it has not been proven that there is any link between the Intervention measures and child abuse.

As stated above, the Rudd government's response supports the Intervention and appears to share the same goal as the previous government: to gain greater access to and control over Aboriginal lands. The emergency Intervention laws, while covering a broad area, include three measures that have been identified as having the most potential to negatively impact upon the continuity of Aboriginal relationships to land. The first involves relaxing the Aboriginal permit system which allowed Aboriginal people to exclude or remove persons from 'common areas' and access roads into their communities and lands.[18] While the Coalition government and the supporters of this provision argued that greater access for the media and other members of the public would reduce the remoteness and increase public scrutiny of these communities, on the other side many Aboriginal peoples have argued that easier public access would open the lands to an increase in drug and grog runners into communities where the drinking of alcohol is restricted

---

17   For further discussion see Combined Aboriginal Organisations of the Northern Territory 2007; Balgo Women's Law Camp 2007; Altman 2007.

18   Families, Community Services and Indigenous Affairs Amendment Bill (Cth) 2007, Schedule 4, will amend the permit provisions under the *NT Aboriginal Land Rights Act (Cth) 1975*. The federal Labor government has indicated that it would not support this amendment and would retain the current permit system.

or prohibited. Secondly, the compulsory acquisition of Aboriginal townships for five years will provide for the compulsory transfer to government control of approximately 70 Aboriginal townships and settlements in the Northern Territory. Over these lands five-year leases will be compulsorily taken up by the Commonwealth using powers under Section 51 (xxxi) of the Constitution. The Howard government stated that compulsory acquisition of townships was necessary to allow unfettered access to Aboriginal townships; however, both state and federal bureaucrats already had access to meet and negotiate with communities on a range of issues. Compulsory acquisition would not provide any greater benefit to the Aboriginal communities in the critical areas of health, housing and education (National Emergency Response Bill, Pt 4). Thirdly, the Intervention laws disallow the consideration of customary law or the cultural background of an offender in sentencing or bail proceedings.[19] Critics of the Intervention laws have argued that these amendments are most likely to result in higher incarceration rates and also undermine the work of Aboriginal courts and their efforts at community involvement in a dialogue on culture and the increased involvement with community people and elders. In my current research, which maps the sentencing remarks of justices in the

---

19   National Emergency Response Bill, Pt 6, s91. These provisions are further explained in the 'Explanatory Memorandum' Pt 6. On 14 July 2006, the Council of Australian Governments (COAG) agreed that no customary law or cultural practice excuses, justifies, authorises, requires, or lessens the seriousness of violence or sexual abuse. All jurisdictions agreed that their laws would reflect this, if necessary by future amendment. COAG also agreed to improve the effectiveness of bail provisions in providing support and protection for victims and witnesses of violence and sexual abuse. The Commonwealth implemented the COAG decision through the *Crimes Amendment (Bail and Sentencing) Act 2006*, which applies to bail and sentencing discretion in relation to Commonwealth offences. The *Bail and Sentencing Act* amended the *Crimes Act 1914 (Cth)* to preclude consideration of customary law or cultural practice from sentencing discretion and bail hearings. The Bail and Sentencing Act also inserted provisions into the *Crimes Act* requiring the relevant authority to consider the potential impact on victims and witnesses, and specifically the potential impact on victims and witnesses in remote communities, when granting and imposing bail conditions for Commonwealth offences.

Northern Territory, I have found no evidence of a more lenient sentence of an Aboriginal offender where the courts have considered the 'cultural background' of the defendant but the government played upon populist sentiments that this in fact was happening.[20] The emergency response laws are now being challenged for contravening Australia's obligations under international law and the *Convention on the Elimination of All Forms of Racial Discrimination.*[21]

Initially, the National Emergency Response laws found their legitimacy in the findings of the *Little children are sacred* report. The report was the result of an eight-month inquiry which held consultations with 45 communities: 260 meetings, 60 written submissions, and 97 recommendations, most of which were ignored by the federal government. Instead, the government headlined the report's finding that child sexual abuse was endemic in Aboriginal communities, and decided upon fast-tracking and implementing the emergency response with all its powers to compulsorily acquire land. The *Little children are sacred* report's recommendation that it was necessary to address social, economic, violence and substance-abuse issues in close consultation with communities was ignored. Instead, the Australian military entered and targeted Aboriginal communities without prior consultation or their consent.

20 Watson, Aboriginal Women Law and Colonialism: Safe Places for Women; at the time of writing this research project is ongoing and has been supported by an Australian Research Council Discovery Indigenous Researchers Development Grant (2007–2008).

21 The challenge is taken pursuant to the *Racial Discrimination Act 1975 (Cth)* section 132, arguing that the National Emergency Response Bill by invoking the special measures provision in the *Racial Discrimination Act 1975 (Cth) (RDA),* enables the exclusion of the operation of Part II of the RDA, so as to avoid a challenge under the RDA. Similarly the *Native Title Act (Cth) 1993* invoked the special measures provisions to avoid a challenge under the RDA, however unlike the current challenge the *Native Title Act* went unchallenged, because at the time it had received popular support for being an 'act of reconciliation' this was even though the *Native Title Act* validated non-Aboriginal land titles that would have been otherwise claimable lands under the principles in Mabo, for further discussion on Mabo and native title see, Watson 2002, 253.

There have been a number of Aboriginal responses to the Intervention—mine, like many, is an outsider's view. I am not an Aboriginal person living in any of the communities which were the subjects of the *Little children are sacred* report and now targeted by the emergency response. From experience and long-term connections and relationships with friends living in some of the targeted communities, however, I know that the physical and economic violence suffered by some members of those communities is critical and it has been for a long time. I was the director of the Aboriginal Legal Rights Movement in Adelaide in 1988, and I was contacted by members of a remote South Australian community and asked to assist in their negotiations for a greater police presence within their community. For me, it was a difficult position to be placed in. In my life, led in more 'settled' areas of South Australia, police practices had deliberately targeted Aboriginal men, women and children as part of a strategy of maintaining an Aboriginal-free space for white people. We were the enemy for no reason other than our Aboriginality. So to consider the need to call upon the police to aid and protect members of Aboriginal communities was a very different proposition to the one I had lived with and known. The 1988 call for a greater police presence was to assist with the alarmingly high levels of substance-abuse related violence. That call has been consistent for some 20 or more years, not only from communities within the NT but from across Australia. But the call for increased services was not only for improved policing, it was also for services that would improve the overall wellbeing of communities in health, education and housing.

But while there is widespread criticism of the emergency response, a number of communities have expressed support. I would argue this support is an indication of how critical the situation has become in those communities rather than being an expression of support for the manner in which the federal government has acted. It's hard to see enthusiasm for sending in the military and amending the *Northern Territory Land Rights Act (Cth) 1975* so as to transfer control of Aboriginal townships to the Commonwealth government.

I have recently written about the long Australian media campaign waged against Aboriginal culture and law prior to the announcement of the emergency response, and I have argued the many acts of demonisation by the media have enabled the space for the current emergency response to enter and occupy with very little opposition (Watson 2007). In post-Intervention media debate the focus shifted to ideological differences within Aboriginal communities concerning the emergency response. The media facilitated a public slanging match between two Aboriginal women, both members of the NT Labor government, who held opposing views on the response. Alison Anderson, in line with Kevin Rudd's national Labor policy, publicly supported the emergency response and condemned Marion Scrymgour's rigorous opposition to it for being out of touch with 'grass roots' community concerns (Scrymgour 2007). Scrymgour had argued that there appeared to be no rational linkage between the need to rescue women and children from sexual abuse and the compulsory acquisition of their land. The emergency response has taken on the mantle of being the bringer of 'human rights' and to speak against it for whatever reason is to be against the advancement of the human rights of Aboriginal communities and an advocate for violent black men (see Watson 2005). At least this is how both major Australian political parties and their investors, both Aboriginal and non-Aboriginal, in the lead-up to the federal election allowed the event to be characterised by the Australian media. I, among others, would characterise the emergency response differently.[22]

As I have flagged earlier in this article the emergency response is a continuing play for legitimacy, and the act of legitimacy is the rescue of Aboriginal women and children from the violence of Aboriginal men. In the protection racket of shielding and protecting subjects from certain abuses they also become subjects in the tactics of their disempowerment. In the story of the NT Intervention that disempowerment comes in the form of weakened land tenure and the loss of opportunity to build communities from an Aboriginal centre and knowledge base (Brown 2004, 459). In the rescue mission Aboriginal townships will be taken over by the federal government for the purpose of providing access to health, housing and education, but the provision of essential services

---

22 For a further discussion on the construction of Aboriginal culture and the role of the media see Sheehan 2001.

will be at the cost of Aboriginal autonomy over township areas (National Emergency Response Bill, Pt 4). Instead of shifting the colonial imbalance towards a decolonised space the state further entrenches the colonial project by reviving protectionist policies, this time under the rubric of human rights. We are returned to the stereotype of the barbaric violent bashing native, one that is in need of protection from one's 'own kind'. Here it is not my intention to deny the experiences of chronic poverty, violence, poor health, housing shortages and poor education outcomes existing in the life of many Aboriginal peoples, or the need for action to remedy this critical condition, but to critically evaluate the Intervention processes. Wendy Brown makes the point that 'there is no such thing as *mere* reduction of suffering or protection from abuse— the nature of the reduction or protection is itself productive of political subjects and political possibilities' (Brown 2004, 459–60). The political subjects which are reproduced are Aboriginal peoples who continue to be subjugated by the colonial body state, having no possibility of shifting to or opening up a decolonised space. The Intervention has had the effect of foreclosing any possibility of that because the construction of the 'violent native' provides the legitimacy to that foreclosure.

What are the possibilities of having healthy safe, Aboriginal futures and should indeed our efforts be focused on decolonising the space as a strategy to this end? The continuing colonial cycle revisits the site of originary violence and has a vested interest in retaining its own violent foundation. So as a strategy towards having a life and better still an Aboriginal one I am in agreement with Wendy Brown's suggestion that there should be a more direct challenge of imperialism and support for 'indigenous efforts to transform authoritarian, despotic, and corrupt postcolonial regimes' (Brown 2004, 460).

The emergency response to the 'Aboriginal crisis' has misrepresented the causes of violence against Aboriginal women and children and reinforced the colonial myth that violence against women is inherent in Aboriginal culture,[23] rather than considering that the source of violence lies in the invasion and colonisation of Australia and the imprisonment of its Indigenous population. Alternative views on the source of violence

---

23   See Watson 2007, and for a different position Zizek 2006, 38.

in Aboriginal communities have not been given much of an airing in the debate around the Aboriginal 'emergency'. In general, the public knows very little about the complexities of Aboriginal law (beyond the perception of it being acquiescent in violence against women and children).[24] Aboriginal women are portrayed as victims in need of rescue from violent black males but this view is rarely inverted to reflect on the Australian legal system's failure to protect white women from white male violence.[25] While the concept of an 'inherent violence' in Aboriginal culture is deployed to explain the rape of small Aboriginal children and the focus is shifted from the social, economic and political environment of those being raped, culture is not deployed to explain the same in the white community. That is a policing matter. The emergency response instead engages the military to resolve sexual assault in Aboriginal communities living on Aboriginal lands in the Northern Territory. On Aboriginal ground, at home, reality is more complex. The violence in Aboriginal communities in my view is more a comment upon the Australian government's management of the colonial project than it is about the culture of the perpetrators of violence. Aboriginal communities across Australia continue to resist the pressure of assimilation, while the public gaze turns away (as it has done before) from the colonial violence of poverty and dispossession of Aboriginal Australia to cultural profiling of the other as barbarian (cf. Zizek 2007).

The violence of the colonial foundation was a means to an end: the creation of the Australian state. But this endpoint requires constant maintenance and, as I have argued, this maintenance occurs through continuous re-enactments of state violence. Derrida writes that European law prohibits individual violence of the military and its

---

24 Wohlan discusses the complex interaction between Aboriginal and Anglo-Australian laws and the failure of law to comprehend the high levels of violence in Aboriginal communities (Wohlan 2005, 1–10). Wohlan contextualises the problem as not being sourced in Aboriginal law, instead suggesting that Aboriginal law 'has the potential to be a useful tool in addressing community justice' (Wohlan 2005, 1).

25 In a recent South Australian court decision His Honour Judge Gordon Barrett, referred to 'culture sickness' when referring to the impact of Aboriginal people disconnected from country as an explanation for the rape of a woman. See 'Rapist's "Cultural Sickness"', *Advertiser*, South Australia, 10 June 2006, 21.

police not simply because the state's laws would be thereby threatened but because individual violence 'threatens the juridical order itself'.[26] In Australia it is the state which is threatened by its own founding violence (Derrida 1990, 989).

It was just prior to his 2007 election defeat that then Prime Minister, John Howard, announced at the Sydney Institute his new interest in reconciliation between Aboriginal and non-Aboriginal Australia,[27] as he declared: 'We are not a federation of tribes. We are one great tribe, one Australia' and in line with his government's proposed amendments to the *Aboriginal Land Rights Act (Cth) 1975* he also announced that 'group rights are, and ought to be, subordinate to both the citizenship rights of the individual and the sovereignty of the nation' (Shanahan 2007).

In the space of a united Australia where the many become the one-Australia tribe, what is it that we the Aborigines become? Is this the restaging of Badiou's 'new man', where the creation of a 'new humanity' requires the destruction of the 'old one'? (Badiou 2007, 8) In the destruction of the old one Badiou cautions us on the capacity of science to make the new man along with the power of profit to determine its making or unmaking (Badiou 2007, 9). The century Badiou reviews, the 20th, was one in which it is impossible not to see the 'unceasing burden of questions of race' (Badiou 2007, 14–15). Along with race there were the questions of contested sovereignties, and lawful and unlawful foundation. The impact of these unresolved 'burdens' provides for the continuation of a violent colonial foundation and one that leads to

------

26 Derrida writes 'militarism is a modern concept that supposes the exploitation of compulsory military service, is the forced use of force, the compelling to use force or violence in the service of the state and its legal ends' (Derrida 1990, 1001–7). See also Hunter 2006, 30 in reference to Derrida's argument on how Western law prohibits individual violence not because it poses a threat to this or that law (or person), but because it threatens the juridical order. In other words, law seeks to monopolise violence not in order to protect legal subjects, but to protect itself from challenge—in particular, from new acts of revolutionary violence, which might found a new legal order.

27 The Howard position had previously been against reconciliation in terms of a 'rights' discourse, preferring the pragmatic approach of 'practical reconciliation'.

skewed and colonised readings on violence and its origins. This is as well as the negation of the many hundreds of Aboriginal 'tribes' that co-existed in this land we now call Australia at the time of the coming of an 'originary colonial violence'.

References

Altman JC (2007). The 'National Emergency' and land rights reform: separating fact from fiction [Online]. Available: www.anu.edu.au/caepr/ Publications/topical/Altman_Oxfam.pdf [Accessed 30 March 2010].

Badiou A (2007). *The century.* Cambridge: Polity Press.

Balgo Women's Law Camp (2007). Aboriginal women have answers themselves [Online]. Available: www.womenforwik.org/pdfs/ BalgoWomensLawCamp100907.pdf [Accessed 30 March 2010].

Brough M (2006). Aboriginal Land Rights (Northern Territory) Amendment Bill 2006 Second Reading, Canberra: Commonwealth Parliament of Australia, Canberra, 31 May [Online]. Available: parlinfo.aph.gov.au/ parlInfo/genpdf/chamber/hansardr/2006-05-31/0012/hansard_frag. pdf;fileType=application%2Fpdf [Accessed 30 March 2010].

Brown W (2004). The most we can hope for … human rights and the politics of fatalism. *The South Atlantic Quarterly,* 103(2/3): 451–63.

Churchill W (1994). *Indians are us? Culture and genocide in Native North America.* Ontario: Between the Lines.

Combined Aboriginal Organisations of the Northern Territory (2007). A proposed emergency response and development plan to protect Aboriginal children in the Northern Territory: a preliminary response to the Australian government's proposals [Online]. Available: nla.gov.au/nla. arc-105901 [Accessed 30 March 2010].

Derrida J (1990). Force of law: the mystical foundation of authority. *Cardoza Law Review,* 11(5–6): 920-1045.

Douzinas C (2000). *The end of human rights: critical legal thought at the turn of the century.* Oxford: Portland.

Hunter R (2006). Law's (masculine) violence: reshaping jurisprudence. *Law and Critique,* 17(1): 27–46.

Karvelas P (2007). Crusade to save Aboriginal kids, Howard declares 'National Emergency' to end abuse. *Australian*, 22 June: 1.

Langton M (2007). Trapped in the Aboriginal reality show. *Griffith Review*, 19: 143–62.

Mattingley C & Hampton K (Eds) (1998). *Survival in our own land*. Adelaide: Wakefield Press.

McClintock P (2008). Thousands to march against NT intervention. ABC News, 11 February [Online]. Available: www.abc.net.au/news/ stories/2008/02/11/2159837.htm [Accessed 30 March 2010].

McKenna M (2007). Damaged generation. *Australian,* 22 June: 13.

Rancière J (2004). Who is the subject of the rights of man? *The South Atlantic Quarterly,* 103(2/3): 297–310.

Scrymgour M (2007). Whose national emergency? Caboolture and Kiribilli? or Milikapti and Mutitjulu? *Charles Perkins Oration*, 26 October, The University of Sydney [Online]. Available: www.usyd.edu.au/alumni/ images/content/activities/uni_events/perkins-scrymgour-speech.pdf [Accessed 30 March 2010].

Shanahan D (2007). Howard's new reconciliation. *Australian,* 12 October: 1&4.

Sheehan N (2001). 'Some call it culture': Aboriginal identity and the imaginary moral centre. *Social Alternatives,* 20(2): 29–33.

Spivak GC (1999). *A critique of postcolonial reason: toward a history of the vanishing present*. Cambridge Mass.: Harvard University Press.

Stevens I (1995). *Report of the Hindmarsh Island Bridge Royal Commission,* Adelaide: State Government Printer.

Watson I (1998). The power of Muldarbi and the road to its demise. *Australian Feminist Law Journal,* 11: 28–45.

Watson I (2002). Buried alive. *Law and Critique,* 13(3): 253–69.

Watson I (2005). Illusionists and hunters: being Aboriginal in this occupied space. *Australian Feminist Law Journal,* 22: 15–28.

Watson I (2007). Aboriginal women's laws and lives: how might we keep growing the law? *Australian Feminist Law Journal,* 26: 95–107.

Wild R & Anderson P (2007). *Ampe Akelyernemane Meke Mekarle 'Little children are sacred'*: report of the Northern Territory Board of Inquiry into the protection of Aboriginal children from sexual abuse, 30 June [Online]. Available: www.inquirysaac.nt.gov.au/pdf/bipacsa_final_report. pdf [Accessed 30 March 2010].

Windschuttle K (2002). *The fabrication of Aboriginal history.* Vol 1: *Van Diemen's Land 1803–1847.* Adelaide: Wakefield Press.

Wohlan C (2005). *Aboriginal women's interests in customary law recognition.* Background Paper 11, Law Reform Commission of Western Australia.

Zizek S (2006). *How to read Lacan.* London: Granta Books.

Zizek S (2007). How China got religion. *New York Times*, 11 October.

Zizek S (2008). *Violence.* London: Profile Books.

4

The state's Intervention in Indigenous affairs in the Northern Territory: governing the Indigenous population through violence, abuse and neglect[1]

Deirdre Howard-Wagner

> Tonight, in our rich and beautiful country, there are children living out a Hobbesian nightmare of violence, abuse and neglect.
>
> Many are in remote Indigenous communities in the Northern Territory. To recognise this is not racist. It's simply an empirical fact.
>
> If anything, our duty of care is greater because of who and where they are (Howard 2007a, 1).

The purpose of this chapter is to consider the strategies and technologies deployed by the state to govern violence, abuse and neglect in the 73 Indigenous communities identified in the Northern Territory national emergency response laws. It situates this response within the context of the broader federal policy governing Indigenous affairs during this period.

In adopting a governmentality approach, the chapter undertakes an analysis of the specificities of governance—the specific ways of thinking about violence, abuse and neglect (rationalities) and the specific ways

---

1 The author wishes to thank Professor Duncan Chappel, Dr Murray Lee, Professor Pat O'Malley, Dr Rebecca Scott Bray, Professor Julie Stubbs and Associate Professor Robert van Krieken for their comments on the first draft of a longer version of this paper.

of acting (technologies) used to govern the problems of violence, abuse and neglect in Indigenous communities (Garland 1997, 174). Following a governmentality approach, the chapter analyses how as objects of knowledge, violence, abuse and neglect in Indigenous communities are rendered in a particular conceptual form and made amenable to *intervention* and *regulation* (Rankin 2001, 22; Howard-Wagner 2006). Importantly though, in accordance with the governmentality approach, it investigates the exercise of political rule in a way that allows the state to be conceptualised as more than simply a ramifying apparatus of social control (Miller & Rose 1990, 3). In its conception of the state, the chapter is then referring to the governmentalised state or the governmentalisation of the state. This differs from a Weberian-inspired way of thinking, in which states are solely defined in terms of their outcomes (Rodgers 2006, 324). The state is given no universal or general essence. Rather state governmentality is viewed here in terms of: the tactics of governmentality; the governing of populations and citizenry; and, as an instrument and effect of political strategies (Butler 2004, 96; Jessop 2007, 36–37; Lemke 2007, 2). Thus, an underlying theme of the chapter is how state governmentality in relation to the Indigenous population underwent at a particular historical moment a significant transformation. Accordingly, its focus is on the Northern Territory national emergency response and its intent in relation to the governance of violence, abuse and neglect in Indigenous communities of the Northern Territory. In doing so, the chapter demonstrates that the interplay between neo-conservatism and neoliberalism is a striking feature of the Northern Territory national emergency response.

A 'radical, comprehensive and highly interventionist' Intervention

In early June 2007, the Report of an Inquiry into Child Protection in Indigenous communities titled *Ampe Akelyernemane Meke Mekarle 'Little children are sacred'* was publicly released. The report had been commissioned by the Northern Territory government 'to break through the veil of silence and inaction on this issue' (Martin 2006). The report indicated that child abuse and neglect in Indigenous communities of the

Northern Territory was 'serious, widespread and often unreported'.[2] It also acknowledged that there was 'nothing new or extraordinary about the allegation of sexual abuse of Aboriginal children of the Northern Territory' (Wild & Anderson 2007, 5).[3] The report declared that the situation had long warranted Aboriginal sexual abuse being designated a matter of urgent national significance, and recommended that the Northern Territory government and the federal government commit to genuine consultation with Aboriginal peoples in designing initiatives for Aboriginal communities in the Northern Territory to overcome violence, abuse and neglect (Wild & Anderson 2007, 7).

Despite this recommendation, within two weeks of the report's release, the state, using its constitutional and political powers combined with its *parens patria* power, asserted its 'duty of care' and intervened in Indigenous affairs in the Northern Territory (Howard 2007a, 1). The state's emergency response to violence, abuse and neglect was 'radical, comprehensive and highly interventionist' and involved seizing control of 73 Indigenous communities in the Northern Territory and initiating a major rebuilding of social order in these Indigenous communities (Howard 2007a, 1). It denied both the Northern Territory government and Indigenous peoples the right to engage in the designing of initiatives and strategies to overcome violence, abuse and neglect in Indigenous communities in the Northern Territory.

The Intervention, as it became commonly known, involved sending in the army to the identified Indigenous communities to re-establish law and order. It also involved putting in place legal mechanisms to regulate access to alcohol, pornography and gambling, such as harsh penalties for the purchase, supply or consumption of alcohol and pornography in Indigenous communities. Violence, abuse and neglect

---

2 *Ampe Akelyernemane Meke Mekarle 'Little children are sacred'* made 97 recommendations to directly address child sexual abuse in Indigenous communities. The findings and the recommendations were not new. Quantitative facts and figures and qualitative accounts detailing the extent and effects of violence and child sexual abuse in Indigenous communities had been presented to federal, state and territory governments since the late 1980s.

3 The sudden and urgent shift from a state of denial to a state of emergency is given consideration in Howard-Wagner 2010.

in Indigenous communities of the Northern Territory were governed and regulated through the conducting of health checks of Aboriginal children. Town camps in the Northern Territory were compulsorily acquired and the permit system was scrapped.[4] Welfare payments were managed too to limit the amount of cash available for alcohol, gambling and pornography.

The Intervention, and the five interrelated Northern Territory Emergency Response laws that gave effect to the Intervention, went beyond addressing violence, abuse and neglect and restoring law and order in the 73 Indigenous communities of the Northern Territory.[5] The Intervention turned to the governance of welfare dysfunction and alcohol dependency, as well as the apathetical unemployed and economically disengaged welfare subject (Scullion 2007). The Second Reading Speeches that accompanied the introduction of the Social Security and Other Legislation Amendment (Welfare Payment Reform) Bill 2007 and the Northern Territory National Emergency Response Bill 2007 into federal parliament indicated that one of the main intents of the new laws was to reduce community reliance on 'passive welfare' (Scullion 2007, 15–16). The Northern Territory National Emergency Response Bill 2007 Second Reading Speech declared that welfare had given no point to education, no point to work and no point to life beyond abuse and despair (Scullion 2007, 16). As stated in the Northern Territo-

---

4 The federal government faced a High Court challenge by Maningrida residents, one of the 73 Indigenous communities identified within the legislation, over the invalidity of certain aspects of the Northern Territory National emergency response laws in relation to the scrapping of permits and compulsory acquisition of land and assets and the provision of 'just compensation'. On 19 March 2008, the Commonwealth demurred to the plaintiff's statement of claim on the ground that no property had been acquired. While the High Court held that proper provisions needed to be made for the compensation of Aboriginal peoples and communities affected by the NT Intervention, a 6:1 majority allowed the demurrer.

5 See the Northern Territory National Emergency Response Bill 2007, the Families, Community Services and Indigenous Affairs and Other Legislation Amendment (Northern Territory National Emergency Measures) Bill 2007, the Social Security and Other Legislation Amendment Bill 2007, Appropriation (Northern Territory National Emergency Response) Bill (No.1) and Appropriation (Northern Territory National Emergency Response) Bill (No. 2).

ry National Emergency Response Bill 2007 Second Reading Speech, the new laws were aimed at 'establishing a life beyond welfare' and creating 'viable economies' through encouraging Indigenous communities to be more economically productive (Scullion 2007, 16). Another intent of the new laws, as set out in the Northern Territory National Emergency Response Bill 2007 Second Reading Speech, was to restructure land usage and tenure with the aim of facilitating entrepreneurial initiatives through the move away from a community-based approach to land management and ownership to a model of individual housing/leasehold tenure (Scullion 2007, 16–18). Other mechanisms within the new laws encouraged the promotion of business and enterprising initiatives (Scullion 2007).

This was consistent with a more general shift in the governance of Indigenous affairs. Three years earlier, the then Federal Minister for Aboriginal and Torres Strait Islander Affairs, Senator Amanda Vanstone, had announced that the main federal policy objectives for Indigenous affairs were 'reducing dependency on passive welfare and boosting employment and economic development in Indigenous communities' (Vanstone 2004a). These earlier objectives continued to be pursued through changes to the welfare system and land tenure under the Northern Territory National Emergency Response legislation.[6] The failed apparatuses of welfarism were to be dismantled along with the vestiges of self-determination and autonomy in the initiating of new mechanisms of *intervention* and *regulation*. Indigenous peoples were to be assimilated into the neoliberal body politic.

What was lost through such interpretations of the breakdown of Indigenous society as symptomatic of welfare dysfunction, alcohol dependency and lack of economic viability was the trauma of violence, including abuse and neglect: its history, its entrenchment, its burden, its

---

6 See Part 4—Northern Territory National Emergency Response Bill 2007—Acquisition of rights, titles and interests in land—Div 1—grants the Commonwealth five year leases. Part 4—Acquisition of rights, titles and interests in land—Div 2—deals with the acquisition of rights, titles and interests relating to town camps. See also Outline Families, Community Services and Indigenous Affairs and Other Legislation Amendment (Northern Territory National Emergency Response and Other Measures) Bill 2007—Access to Aboriginal Land.

dysfunction, its exclusion, its perpetration and its destruction (Dodson 2003). For Indigenous peoples, violent colonisation, the often-violent enforcement or imposition of discriminatory laws and social policy, and individual experiences of violation and violence, had produced perpetual trans-generational violence (Dodson 2003). Violence, abuse and neglect, as Wild and Anderson (2007) had found, dominated what Dodson (2003) had referred to three years earlier as 'the rhythm of life'.

The state's response also ignored three decades of significant Indigenous scholarship concerning family violence in Indigenous communities, including child abuse and neglect (Stanley et al. 2002; Howard-Wagner 2007a).[7] Within such scholarship, family violence had been described as multi-dimensional and related to historical, structural and situational factors, such as the sly grog trade, the lack of autonomy and self-determination, historical violence, government failure to address the inadequacy of government strategies, the inability to use cultural lore, the failure of the criminal justice system, and lack of community infrastructure (Robertson 2000; Howard-Wagner 2008). Self-determination was identified as critical to overcoming family violence, including child abuse and neglect (Atkinson 1990a, 1990b, 1990c, 1991, 1995, 1996; Martin 1992; Hunter 1993; Robertson 2000; Stanley et al. 2002; Dodson 2003; Behrendt 2006). Within such political rationalities, the empowerment of Indigenous communities was consistently linked to culturally appropriate alternative dispute resolution mechanisms. For example, the constructive features of Indigenous strategies and dispute resolution approaches, such as night patrols, were increasingly put forward as an alternative to law and order

---

7 Violence in Indigenous communities has been constructed as a community-based social problem, rather than an individual-based psychological problem commonly associated with the abuse of power in intimate non-Indigenous relationships. Indigenous scholars in particular directed attention away from references to the dominant paradigm of Western conceptualisations of domestic violence, preferring instead to use the concept of family violence. This notion of family violence too was deeply rooted in a social context of colonisation, loss of culture and poverty and in terms of the community and inter-generational effects (Atkinson 1990a, 1990b, 1990c, 1991, 1995, 1996, 2001 and 2006; Robertson 2000; Keel 2004).

and Western models of policing (Wright 1997; Blagg 2000; Stanley et al. 2002; Dodson 2003). Indigenous scholars argued that the state had inhibited Indigenous autonomy and self-determination, rather than facilitated it, which had only exacerbated the problems of family violence in Indigenous communities (Robertson 2000). *Ampe Akelyernemane Meke Mekarle 'Little children are sacred'* had presented similar findings.

Neoliberal rationalities and technologies of governing

At the beginning of the 21st century, the Indigenous population was declared to be in *crisis* as a result of poor management of Indigenous autonomy instigated through welfare dependency. It was claimed that this *crisis* was at the heart of all problems experienced by Indigenous individuals, families and communities (MacDonald & Muldoon 2006, 219). Federal government discourses had set about quantifying 'passive welfare', making regular reference to Indigenous disadvantage (such as high rates of unemployment, low levels of education and poor health statistics), and socio-cultural dysfunction (such as petrol sniffing and family violence), attributing these to welfare dependency (MacDonald & Muldoon 2006, 219). Initially, in discussing how to overcome Indigenous disadvantage, constant reference was made to the 'practical ways' that this disadvantage could be addressed through programs aimed at health, housing, education and employment. The nation-state's role was redefined as one that removed the barriers that prevented Aborigines from fully participating as Australian citizens in Australian society, premised on the rights 'to work, to good health, to a sound education, and to a decent home' (Commonwealth of Australia 2002, 1). The effects of 'passive welfare' or 'sit-down money' were condemned, signalling the intent to change the policy direction of federal Indigenous affairs through the application of neoliberal principles for the governance of Indigenous affairs in the forms of 'reciprocity', 'mutual obligation' and 'active welfare' (Vanstone 2003; Vanstone 2004a,b; Howard 2005). The objective was to attempt to incorporate Indigenous peoples into the mainstream economy through initiatives that were entrepreneurial in nature. Yet, such rationalities also codified moral injunctions indicating the possibility of making parenting payments conditional on school attendance and regular health checks (Vanstone 2004a), evidencing the influence of neo-conservative logic for the governing of Indigenous affairs.

This combining of an advanced or neoliberal logic with a neo-conservative logic manifested in state discourses, which operated to constitute a 'disadvantaged' Indigenous subject, one who was produced through references to economic conditions and social dysfunction. Such discourses normatively interpolated Indigeneity through focusing simply on 'economic and social disadvantage' and 'individual and social dysfunction', denying the right to self-determination or what were referred to as the symbolic gestures of Indigenous rights (Howard-Wagner 2007a). State Intervention was continuously premised on the basis of economic and social failure of Indigenous communities; a moral logic used to justify a restructuring of the delivery of services to the Indigenous communities more generally. State discourses attributed violence, abuse and neglect to the breakdown and social dysfunction within Indigenous communities resulting from 'passive welfare'. For example, the then Secretary of the Department of the Prime Minister and Cabinet, Peter Shergold described Indigenous communities as:

> imploding, their social structures are in collapse, respect for law and order has plummeted, and key social norms (such as responsibility and authority) are in tragic disrepair ... too many Aboriginal and Torres Strait Islander people have become trapped in a cycle of dependency, relying on welfare for their income and government payments for their livelihoods, unmotivated to take advantage of even the limited opportunities that are available. Passivity has been born of government handout and sit-down money ... Idle time, free money and a right to drink have concocted a dangerous cocktail ... [and] too many Indigenous communities are, in effect, being preserved as museum pieces, kept locked in poverty in socially dysfunctional communities, out of sight of mainstream Australia.

This contrasted with an Indigenous subjectivity produced through references to dispossession, self-determination and Indigenous rights and a political rationality that extended to the wider ethical and moral debates about Indigenous empowerment. Many Indigenous people argued, for example, that violence, abuse and neglect in Indigenous communities was the result of the interplay between historical, structural and situational factors, such as dispossession, lack of adequate government funding for programs and infrastructure, cyclical poverty and alcohol dependency (Robertson 2000; Stanley et al. 2002; Dodson 2003; Behrendt 2006). In this context, empowerment referred to both the need for Indigenous people to be 'the architects of their own solutions' and the need for governments to provide adequate funding and resources to implement culturally appropriate, self-identified strategies and programs for overcoming social dysfunction within Indigenous communities, including violence, abuse and neglect (Robertson 2000, 195; Dodson 2003; Behrendt 2006).

Instead though, the mainstream way of delivering services was discursively constructed as 'promising a *quiet revolution* in Indigenous affairs' in terms of a more effective way of not only delivering services to the Indigenous communities, but also incorporating Indigenous citizens into the mainstream (Shergold 2004; Vanstone 2005). It was through indirect attacks upon Indigenous rights, self-determination and substantive liberalism that Vanstone justified the abolition of ATSIC and the federal government's reforms to the delivery of services to Indigenous Australians (Vanstone 2005). In an attempt to move away from the logic of empowerment through self-determination, economic independence and entrepreneurship became the new mechanism for empowering Indigenous peoples and communities. Federal policy aimed to empower Indigenous people, overcoming the *crisis* resulting from welfare dependency, through economic independence and entrepreneurship. It was announced that 'building wealth, employment and entrepreneurial culture' was the new blueprint for 'building an economically sustainable future for Indigenous Australians' (Brough 2006a). The fostering of economic development was considered integral to the development of Indigenous communities and could be achieved through the 'removal of barriers to economic opportunity' and 'through reforms aimed at Indigenous Australians leading independent lives and benefiting from the economy in the same way as other Australians' (Brough 2006a,b). It is a powerful form of Intervention in which the federal government arbitrates in Indigenous politics and, in fact, reconfigures Indigenous politics. The federal government's Intervention in Indigenous affairs more generally works to limit the possibility of Indigenous Intervention.

This neoliberal vision aimed to lift the status of Australia's Indigenous population through empowering the entrepreneurial Indigenous citizen and community to govern the self in accordance with market rationalities. Indigenous entrepreneurship was identified as a mechanism for creating economic independence, for example, through the forging of links with the business sector, such as the model put forth in the Cape York Agenda and related strategies. An accompanying array of federal laws, programs and initiatives, were set up with the aim of fostering Indigenous entrepreneurship, including the Business Leadership initiative, the Work Initiatives General Business Support program, the Asset and Wealth Management initiatives (such as private sector involvement in home ownership and business development initiative and the coordinated economic development and land initiative, investment initiative and initiatives that increased skills in economic and business development). The objective of these initiatives was to foster entrepreneurial governance within Indigenous communities.

Neoliberal governance involved welfare responsibilities being transformed into commodity forms that were regulated according to market principles, economic entrepreneurship replacing regulation, active individual entrepreneurship replacing passivity and dependency on welfare (Rose & Miller 1992, 198).[8] The market provided the

---

8 Neoliberalism has its own epistemological character in terms of the strategies
for exercising power over the conduct of individuals and the collective and
securing the good of each and all (Rose 1999, 23). The language and programs
of neoliberalism extend beyond the realm of the economic to the social, ensuing
a restructuring of society and the welfare state that has resulted in a 'profound
transformation in the mechanisms for governing social life' (Rose & Miller 1992,
200). With a governmentality approach, neoliberalism, therefore, is conceptualised
as a constructivist project As Brown states: 'it does not presume the ontological
genesis of a thoroughgoing economic rationality for all domains of society, but

incentive for social order and social life in Indigenous communities. Alongside this, neo-conservative modes of governance tightened the grip on social regulation and constraint, targeting the Indigenous citizen and community, who are seen as needing to be morally disciplined (Garland 2001, 99).[9]

An exemplary example of how the interplay between neoliberal and neo-conservative modes of governance played out was in relation to the new Shared Responsibility Agreements introduced in 2004 in the wake of the announcement of the abolition of the Aboriginal and Torres Strait Islander Commission (ATSIC). The Shared Responsibility Agreement being a form of contract between the federal government, and sometimes state and territory governments, and Indigenous communities that link government funding and support to a list of performance indicators. A neoliberal technique and instrument of 'self-regulated regulation', the Shared Responsibility Agreement was deployed with the aim of inculcating a neoliberal ethic of 'enterprising' citizenship through extending and disseminating market values to Indigenous communities (Crawford 2003, 487–88).[10] [11] As the then Minister for Indigenous Affairs stated in announcing the Mulan Community Shared Responsibility Agreement: a petrol bowser ... gives

---

rather takes as its task the development, dissemination and institutionalisation of such a rationality' (Brown 2003, 3).

9   The targeting of the Indigenous population through a more authoritarian and interventionist approach differs from targeting the great majority of the population who have more or less been given greater market 'freedom' as a result of the dismantling of the 'nanny state' (Garland 2001, 100).

10   The rise of contractual and spatial governance has been particularly evident in neoliberal governmentality. Contractual governance has become a feature of state-centred governance of deviant behaviour in the United Kingdom. For example, the United Kingdom has moved toward contractual governing in the form of home-school agreements, and behaviour and attendance contracts that seek to regulate the anti-social behaviour of parents and pupils, setting out the responsibility of the school, the parent(s), and the pupil (Crawford 2003).

11   A whole barrage of carefully calculated tactics, such as audits, competitive tendering and outcome based performance indicators and contracts (Henman & Dean 2004, 4–5), operated as neoliberal technologies for governing the Indigenous population and providing for this government intervention.

them a chance for a bit of economic development' (Vanstone 2004a). The 'building [of] economically viable communities' and the adoption of neoliberal 'community capacity building' models to address social and economic dysfunction in Indigenous communities created a means in which the Indigenous citizen could become a responsible citizen through involvement in 'active consumption' and participation in the market economy, reducing dependency on 'passive welfare' (Vanstone 2004a,b). Yet, Shared Responsibility Agreements also operated as a mechanism for morally regulating the community space and a technology for disciplining and controlling of parties. For example, the Mulan Community Shared Responsibility Agreement stipulated that members of the Mulan community, particularly children, must shower daily, face and hands must be washed twice a day and the community must be kept rubbish free (Yaxley 2004, 1). Self-regulation and high levels of compliance worked through the adoption of invasive efforts to properly produce, manage, and discipline the Indigenous subject (Nadesan 2006, 8). Shared Responsibility Agreements operated as a combined mode of neoliberal and neo-conservative social control (Garland 2001, 98; Crawford 2003, 488).[12]

It was in this climate of combined neoliberal and neo-conservative reform that the state intervened in the affairs of the Northern Territory.

Political rationalities and technologies of governing violence, abuse and neglect in Indigenous communities in the Northern Territory

When confronted with a *failed society* where basic standards of law and order and behaviour have broken down and where women and children are unsafe, how should we respond? Do we respond with *more of what we have done in the past*? Or do we radically change direction with an Intervention strategy matched to the magnitude of the problem?

---

12   As Garland (2001, 98) writes: the often contradictory combination of what came to be known as 'neoliberalism' (the re-assertion of market principles) and 'neo-conservatism' (the reassertion of moral principles), the commitment to the rolling back of the state [in the sense of facilitating spontaneous market order] while simultaneously building a state apparatus that is stronger and more authoritarian than before … were the contradictory positions that lay at the heart of the Thatcher and Reagan regimes'.

We need to dry up the rivers of grog. We need to stop the free flow of pornography.

We need to improve living conditions and reduce overcrowding. More houses need to be built and we need to control the land in the townships for a short period to ensure that we can do this quickly.

We need to make sure money paid to parents and carers by the government for feeding children is not used for buying grog or for gambling.

We need to make sure local shops stock good, affordable food for growing children.

We need to show people that there is hope of a life beyond welfare so that going to school is seen to be worthwhile.

We need to show people that it is possible to own and control your own house, which can only happen when you have a lease over the land that it is built on …

With no work and no hope of getting a job, many Aboriginal people in these communities rely on passive welfare.

In an environment where there is no natural social order of production and distribution, grog, pornography and gambling often fill the void.

What do viable economies and jobs have to do with preventing child abuse? Unemployment and welfare dependency may not cause abuse, but a viable economy and real job prospects make education meaningful and point to a life beyond abuse and despair.

Currently, there are too few jobs in these communities and land tenure arrangements work against developing a real economy. The Community Development Employment Projects program has become the destination for far too many.

Banks will not lend money to start up small businesses because a committee decides what tenure arrangements will apply. People cannot even borrow to buy their own home because they cannot own or lease a block of land. And, to cap it all off, these towns have been closed to outsiders because of the permit system (Extract from the Northern Territory National Emergency Response Bill 2007 Second Reading Speech—Senator Scullion 2007, 1–17).[13]

As evidenced in the above extract from the Northern Territory National Emergency Response Bill 2007 Second Reading Speech, the governance of violence, abuse and neglect in the 73 Indigenous communities of the Northern Territory extends to wider ethical and moral imperatives in relation to the governance of social and economic behaviour in which the 'grammars of conduct', or what Rose (1999) refers to as the 'grammars of living', defined acceptable, correct and expected social and economic conduct (Flint & Rowlands 2003, 218). These ethical and moral imperatives worked to problematise Indigenous community governance, more generally (Rose 2001; Flint & Nixon 2006, 940).

The discursive construction of the failed society worked to define the crisis and shape its future in particular ways; for example, allowing violence, abuse and neglect to be constructed as symptomatic of 'extreme social breakdown' of the 'community', resulting from 'the scourge of passive welfare' and programs and the rationalities of autonomy and self-determination, which had 'failed' to facilitate economically viable Indigenous communities (Brough 2007; Howard 2007a, 2004b, 1; Scullion 2007, 11). This was apparent more generally in federal government discourses about the Intervention. For example, the then Prime Minister, John Howard, stated that the effect of welfare dysfunction, alcohol dependency and lack of economic viability were evidenced in

---

13   Senator Scullion (Northern Territory—Minister for Community Service) read, to the Senate of the Parliament of the Commonwealth of Australia, the Second Reading Speech—Northern Territory National Emergency Response Bill 2007. Senator Scullion introduced, into the Senate of the Parliament of the Commonwealth of Australia, the Social Security and Other Legislation (Welfare Payment Reform) Bill 2007, the Families, Community Services and Indigenous Affairs and Other Legislation Amendment (Northern Territory National Emergency Response and Other Measures) Bill 2007, the Appropriation (Northern Territory National Emergency Response) Bill (No.1) 2007–2008 and the Appropriation (Northern Territory National Emergency Response) Bill (No.2) 2007–2008.

the 'empirical fact' of 'children living out the Hobbesian nightmare of violence, abuse and neglect' (Howard 2007a).

The failed Indigenous society became a zone of governance; the failure of which gave the state the coercive license to govern. Violence, abuse and neglect, thus, became representative of Indigenous society's failure to self-govern, decontextualising family violence in Indigenous communities from the multi-causal factors, including the failure of government policies, identified in 30 years of Indigenous and non-Indigenous scholarship on this issue (see Howard-Wagner 2007a). Rather, it was put forward that, left to their own devices and given autonomy Indigenous communities had failed to maintain basic standards of law and order, and behaviour. Within such a logic, the failure of Indigenous communities to govern and the failure of Indigenous models of self-governance, including the failure of Indigenous models of land management to sustain Indigenous communities in this contemporary context, were evidenced in the breakdown of social order, which manifested in problems such as violence, abuse and neglect. Thus, the discursive construction of violence, abuse and neglect as representative of Indigenous society's failure to self-govern provided both a pretext for the rebuilding of the failed Indigenous society, allowing for the establishment of a new economic and social order in Indigenous communities of the Northern Territory, and a pretext for the moral regulation of social life in these Indigenous communities.

The constructing of a failed society within society allowed for the mapping out of zones of normalcy, the classifying and constructing of distinctions between the normal and the not-normal, and the establishing of a silent set of norms that positioned the Indigenous as 'Other' (Popkewitz 1996, 43). Yet, at the same time, it was a moral logic that denied the difference that historically figures in debates about relations of domination. Indigenous people were to be integrated into the mainstream—a mainstream that is epistemologically embedded in whiteness (Howard-Wagner 2007b, 5). An essentialising epistemological whiteness (Wiegman 2003, 22) operates here through the denial of difference and the elevated status of mainstream values (Howard-Wagner 2007b, 5).

Above all then, the Northern Territory national emergency response laws turned to the governance of social and economic marginality and the creation of a new social order. For the then Prime Minister, John Howard, the 'restoration of social order' in Indigenous communities was to be facilitated through participation in the Australia's prosperous economy, including real jobs and changes to land tenure (Howard 2007a, 11). This is evidenced too in the above extract from the Northern Territory Emergency Response Bill 2007 Second Reading Speech in which viable economies and jobs are deemed to give a 'point to life beyond abuse and despair' (Scullion 2007, 16). Social order within Indigenous communities is, therefore, morally structured around particular notions of citizenship; one in which the citizen has a duty and responsibility to participate in the processes of employment, home ownership and entrepreneurship (Flint & Rowlands 2003, 224).

The governance of social and economic marginality, and re-establishment of social order operates through the governance of the Indigenous citizen, the Indigenous community and the community space discernible in various interrelated technologies of governance identified in the five separate laws. The community and community space are, therefore, not only a territory of governance; they also become a technique for shaping the conduct of the Indigenous citizen. The community and community space become the objects of government through which the behaviours of the Indigenous citizen are governed, allowing for controls and norms to be instituted in various forms, and for these controls and norms to structure the field of action of the Indigenous citizen (Foucault 1982). The community and the community space are subject to a variety of regulatory mechanisms that manage the community population as a whole, prohibiting behaviour and instituting new mechanisms of social control through adopting pre-emptive mechanisms that 'socially engineer' the community and the community space, and the Indigenous citizen (Herbert & Brown 2006, 756). To demonstrate, technologies of governance target the community space; excluding alcohol, banning pornography, managing land and building houses, rather than disciplining offenders, punishing offences or dealing with the community/individual experience of violence, abuse and neglect (Engle Merry 2001, 6). In effect then, spatialised strategies, rather than individual sanctions, control alcohol consumption and access to pornographic material (Engle Merry 2001, 17).

The community space is not only a mechanism for regulating deviant behaviour within the Indigenous community though. It is also a mechanism for shaping, guiding and directing the conduct of the Indigenous citizen and community, more generally. For example, above and within the Second Reading Speech more generally, space-conquering imperatives promote logics of economic governance that work to shape, guide and direct the conduct of the Indigenous citizen and community (Havemann 2005, 68). Within such rationalities, the community space is defined as a mechanism for facilitating the Indigenous citizen's and the Indigenous community's transition into the market economy (Flint 2003, 615). In order for this to be achieved, though, the idea of Indigenous communal ownership and self-governance must be problematised first. The failure of Aboriginal communal systems of land ownership in the contemporary period was demonstrated in the existence of 'poor living conditions' and 'places of despair', as well as the existence of 'ghettos' and 'murder capitals' (Scullion 2007, 17). The discursive construction of the failed society, the attributing of social disorder within Indigenous communities to the lack of viable economies, and references to the economically and socially dysfunctional community, also served this end (Scullion 2007). So too did the idea that 'existing land tenure arrangements [worked] against developing a real economy' (Scullion 2007, 17). The significance of land is reconceptualised within entrepreneurial and market rationalities as a mechanism for bringing social and economic independence to Indigenous communities through individual land ownership; a logic that views land as an economic commodity to be parcelled, packaged and sold (Havemann 2005, 78). A restructuring of land usage and tenure, therefore, works to facilitate entrepreneurial initiatives through the move away from a community-based approach to land management and ownership to a model of individual housing/leasehold tenure (Scullion 2007). It is a modernisation logic that, as Havemann (2005, 68) argues, 'requires the conversion of place into commodified and controlled space to effect order, building and growth'. Thus, it is through the management and use of the community space that further shifts occur in the practices of the Indigenous citizen. Indigenous communities become more economically productive, incorporating Indigenous citizens into the market economy, which facilitates the Indigenous citizen's move from 'passive welfare' to the 'active entrepreneurship'. Yet, within this logic, certain rules, or what Foucault (1982) refers to as moral 'codes', are laid out that function to discursively construct a particular moral and social order. For example, here moral codes outline the basis of so-called productive citizenship.

As noted above, while the strategies deployed evidenced political rationalities and technologies of governing described as advanced or neoliberal in relation to the forms of conduct they sought to shape and regulate, they also involved an extraordinary level of social engineering in which the Indigenous citizen was compelled to morally comply with certain societal standards through participating in new forms of 'active' welfare. This was further exampled in the Social Security and Other Amendments (Welfare Payment Reform) legislation, which was designed to 'tackle the scourge of passive welfare and to reinforce responsible behaviour through the establishment of [the] mutual obligation framework' (Scullion 2007, 11). This is similar to the principles underpinning the Shared Responsibility Agreement scheme. The legislation provides that Income Management Regime (IMR) provisions will apply based on, for example, the child's attendance at school, mirroring mechanisms incorporated into the Shared Responsibility Agreement scheme.[14] As noted in the Second Reading Speech, the Welfare Payment Reform Bill was introduced with the objective of 'promot[ing] socially responsible behaviour aimed at protecting and nurturing the children in our society and offering them the opportunities that a supportive family, a solid education and a healthy and safe environment can provide' (Scullion 2007, 11). It is argued that: 'this broad-based approach is needed to address a break down in social norms that characterise

---

14   See Social Security and Other Legislation Amendment (Welfare Payment Reform) Bill 2007 Explanatory Memorandum, House of Representatives, The Parliament of the Commonwealth of Australia.

many of our remote Northern Territory communities' (Scullion 2007, 13). More specifically, the former Prime Minister John Howard noted that the new Welfare Payment Reform laws were: 'designed to stem the flow of cash going towards alcohol abuse and to ensure that the funds meant to be used for children's welfare are actually used for that purpose' (Howard 2007b). Howard further noted that:

> The principal approach here will be to quarantine as from now through Centrelink, to be supported by legislation, 50 per cent of welfare payments to parents of children in the affected areas … and effectively the arrangements will be that that 50 per cent can only be used for the purchase of food and other essentials (Howard 2007b).

He clarified how this would work, noting that:

> We're going to enforce school attendance by linking income support and family assistance payments to school attendance for all people living on Aboriginal land. We'll be ensuring that meals are provided for children at school with parents paying for the meals (Howard 2007b).

Pre-emptive mechanisms of neo-conservative social engineering withhold welfare payments to ensure that at-risk parents meet their parenting responsibilities and the needs of their children (Brough 2007). The Indigenous citizen is forced to engage with, and required to participate in, the functioning of civil society in the linking of welfare payments to requirement of school attendance (Rose 1999, 175). It is a moral rationality exercised on the Indigenous citizen to cultivate new Indigenous subjectivities.

So, while the neoliberal state remained committed to transforming welfare responsibilities through 'active' welfare and creating a level of economic viability within Indigenous communities, a neo-conservative government simultaneously builds a more controlling and repressive state apparatus (Garland 2001, 98). In this combining of neoliberalism and neo-conservatism, the state deployed the policies of entrepreneurship and mutual obligation combined with a more focused and specific demand for moral discipline and greater social control that targets not only the Indigenous citizen, but also the Indigenous community and community space (Garland 2001, 99–100).

Conclusion

The declaration of a state of emergency and subsequent changes to the governance of Indigenous communities in the Northern Territory involved implementing a qualitatively different form of state governmentality (Rodgers 2006, 325). New laws instituted advanced or neoliberal modes of governance that reflected associated changes in the governmentality of Indigenous affairs more generally.[15] This blueprint for the rebuilding of social order in 73 Indigenous communities of the Northern Territory was one in which viable economies, individual home ownership, and entrepreneurship were to be the new norm (Howard 2007c, 1). Social order was to be facilitated through the incorporation of these communities into mainstream society through participation in 'Australia's prosperous economy' (Howard 2007c, 11).

Yet, while the strategies deployed by the state through the Northern Territory national emergency response laws evidenced political rationalities and technologies of governing described as advanced or neoliberal in relation to the forms of conduct that they sought to shape and regulate in the Indigenous citizens and communities they acted upon, they involved an unprecedented level of social engineering. Community dysfunction provided a pretext for the moral regulation of social life in that it provided a means for programming and transforming social fields and a technique for shaping and managing the Indigenous citizen, more generally (Miller and Rose 1990, 24; Miller 1998, 71; Simon 2000).

---

15 The five new Acts were the *Northern Territory National Emergency Response Act 2007 (Cth)*, the *Families, Community Services and Indigenous Affairs and Other Legislation Amendment (Northern Territory National Emergency Response and Other Measures) Act 2007 (Cth)*, *Social Security and Other Legislation Amendment (Welfare Payment Reform) Act 2007 (Cth)*, the *Appropriation (Northern Territory National Emergency Response Act (No.1) 2007–2008 (Cth)* and the *Appropriation (Northern Territory National Emergency Response Act (No. 2) 2007–2008 (Cth)*.

Legislation

Appropriation (Northern Territory National Emergency Response) Act (No. 1) 2007 (Cth)

Appropriation (Northern Territory National Emergency Response) Act (No. 2) 2007 (Cth)

Families, Community Services and Indigenous Affairs and Other Legislation Amendment (Northern Territory National Emergency Response and Other Measures) Act 2007 (Cth)

Northern Territory National Emergency Response Act 2007 (Cth)

Social Security and Other Legislation Amendment (Welfare Payment Reform) Act 2007 (Cth)

References

Atkinson J (1990a). Violence against Aboriginal women: reconstitution of community law—the way forward. *Aboriginal Law Bulletin*, 2(46): 6.

Atkinson J (1990b). Violence in Aboriginal Australia: colonisation and its impacts on gender. *Refractory Girl*, 36: 21–24.

Atkinson J (1990c). Violence in Aboriginal Australia: colonisation and its impact on gender. *The Aboriginal and Islander Health Journal*, June/September Editions. Brisbane: University of Queensland.

Atkinson J (1991). Stinkin thinkin—alcohol, violence and government responses. *Aboriginal Law Bulletin*, 2(51): 4–6.

Atkinson J (1995). Aboriginal people, domestic violence and the law. In D. Lawrence (Ed), *Future directions: proceedings of Queensland Domestic Violence Conference* (p233), Rockhampton: Rural Social and Economic Research Centre, Central Queensland University.

Atkinson J (1996). A nation is conquered. *Aboriginal Law Bulletin*, 3(80): 10.

Atkinson J (2001). Violence against Aboriginal women reconstitution of community law: the way forward. *Indigenous Law Bulletin*, 5(11): 4–9.

Atkinson J (2006). To do nothing is tantamount to genocide. *Indigenous Law Bulletin*, 6(20): 20–22.

Behrendt L (2006). Indigenous policy: no quick fix. *Australian Policy Online*, 1 June 2006 [Online]. Available: www.apo.org.au/webboard/results.chtml?filename_num=80532. [Accessed 1 September 2007].

Blagg H (2000). *Crisis intervention in Aboriginal family violence: summary report*. Partnerships Against Domestic Violence, Office of the Status of Women, Canberra, ACT [Online]. Available: padv.dpmc.gov.au/oswpdf/blagg_1st_report.pdf. [Accessed 1 September 2007].

Brough M (2006a). Blueprint for action in Indigenous affairs. Speech given at the National Institute of Governance, Indigenous Affairs Governance Series, 5 December 2006, Canberra [Online]. Available: www.facsia.gov.au/internet/Minister3.nsf/content/051206.htm. [Accessed 20 February 2007].

Brough M (2006b). Brough outlines blueprint for action in Indigenous affairs. Ministerial Media Release, 5 December 2006 [Online]. Available: www.facsia.gov.au/internet/minister3.nsf/content/blueprint_051206.htm. [Accessed 20 February 2007].

Brough M (2007) Northern Territory National Emergency Response Bill 2007, Second Reading Speech 07/08/2007 [Online]. Available: www.facs.gov.au/internet/minister3.nsf/content/nter_bill_7aug07.htm. [Accessed 1 September 2007].

Brown W (2003). Neo-liberalism and the end of liberal democracy. *Theory and Event*, 7(1).

Butler J (2004). *Precarious life: the powers of mourning and violence*. London: Verso.

Commonwealth of Australia (2002). *Executive summary of the Commonwealth Government response to the Council for Aboriginal Reconciliation final report—reconciliation: Australia's challenge*. Canberra: Australian Government Printing Service.

Crawford A (2003). 'Contractual governance' of deviant behaviour. *Journal of Law and Society*, 30(4): 474–505.

Dodson M (2003a). Violence dysfunction Aboriginality. Speech presented at National Press Club 11 June 2003 [Online]. Available: law.anu.edu.au/anuiia/dodson.pdf. [Accessed 1 September 2007].

Engle Merry S (2001). Spatial governmentality and the new urban social order: controlling gender violence through the law. *American Anthropologist*, 103: 16–29.

Flint J (2003). Housing and ethopolitics: constructing identities of active consumption and responsible community. *Economy and Society*, 32(3): 611–29.

Flint J & Rowland R (2003). Commodification, normalisation and intervention: cultural, social and symbolic capital in housing consumption and governance. *Journal of Housing and the Built Environment*, 18: 213–32.

Flint J & Nixon J (2006). Governing neighbours: anti-social behaviour orders and new forms of regulating conduct in the UK. *Urban Studies*, 43(5/6): 939–55.

Foucault M (1982). Afterword: the subject and power. In HL Dreyfus & P Rabinow (Eds), *Michael Foucault: beyond structuralism and hermeneutics* (pp208–26). Chicago: Chicago University Press.

Garland D (1997). 'Governmentality' and the problem of crime: Foucault, criminology, sociology. *Theoretical Criminology*, 1(2): 173–214.

Garland D (2001). *The culture of control: crime and social order in contemporary society*. Chicago: University of Chicago Press.

Havemann P (2005). Denial, modernity and exclusion: Indigenous placelessness in Australia. *Macquarie Law Journal*, 5: 57–80.

Henman P & Dean M (2004). The governmental powers of welfare e-administration. Paper prepared for the Australian Electronic Governance Conference, Centre for Public Policy, University of Melbourne, Victoria, 14 and 15 April 2004.

Herbert S & Brown E (2006). Conceptions of space and crime in the punitive neoliberal city. *Antipode*, 38: 755–77.

Howard J (2005). Transcript of the Prime Minister the Hon John Howard MP address at the National Reconciliation Planning Workshop. Old Parliament House, Canberra, 30 May 2005 [Online]. Available: www.reconciliation.org.au/home/media/speeches. [Accessed 1 June 2005].

Howard J (2007a). *To stabilise and protect*. Address to the Sydney Institute, 25 June 2007. ,

Howard J (2007b). Joint press conference with the Hon Mal Brough, Minister for Families, Community Services and Indigenous Affairs Canberra, 21 June 2007 [Online]. Available: www.pm.gov.au/media/Interview/2007/Interview24380.cfm. [Accessed 30 June 2007].

Howard-Wagner D (2006). Post-Indigenous rights: the political rationalities and technologies governing Federal Indigenous Affairs in Australia in the contemporary period, PhD Dissertation, University of Newcastle.

Howard-Wagner D (2007a). Restoring social order through tackling 'passive welfare': the statutory intent of the *Northern Territory National Emergency*

Response Act 2007 (Cth) and *Social Security and Other Legislation Amendment (Welfare Payment Reform) Act 2007 (Cth). Current Issues in Criminal Justice,* 19(2): 1–9.

Howard-Wagner D (2007b). The denial of separate rights: political rationalities and technologies governing Indigenous affairs as practices of whiteness. In Public Sociologies: Trans-Tasman Comparisons, The Australian Sociological Association and Sociological Association of Aotearoa New Zealand Refereed Conference Collection, 4–7 December 2007, Auckland New Zealand.

Howard-Wagner D (2010). From denial to emergency: governing Indigenous communities in Australia. In D Fassin and M Pandolfi (Eds), *Contemporary states of emergency: the politics of military and humanitarian interventions* (pp217–40). New York: Zone Publishing.

Hunter E (1993). Demographic factors contributing to patterns of violence in Aboriginal communities. *Australasian Psychiatry,* 1(4): 152–53.

Jessop B (2007). From micro-powers to governmentality: Foucault's work on statehood, state formation, statecraft and state power. *Political Geography,* 26: 34–40.

Keel M (2004). *Family violence and sexual assault in Indigenous communities.* Australian Centre for the Study of Sexual Assault: Briefing No.4. Canberra: Australian Institute of Family Studies.

Lemke T (2007). An indigestible meal? Foucault, governmentality and state theory. *Distinktion: Scandinavian Journal of Social Theory,* 15: 43–64.

MacDonald L & Muldoon P (2006). Globalisation, neo-liberalism and the struggle for Indigenous citizenship. *Australian Journal of Political Science,* 41(2): 209–23.

McGlade H (2003). Our own backyards. *Indigenous Law Bulletin,* 5(23): 6.

Martin C (2006). Chief Minister orders inquiry into child sexual abuse. Press release, Chief Minister of the Northern Territory, 22 June 2006.

Martin DF (1992). Aboriginal and non-Aboriginal homicide: same but different. In H Strong & S Gerull (Eds), *Homicide: patterns, prevention and control* (pp167–76). Canberra: Australian Institute of Criminology.

Miller P & Rose N (1990). Governing economic life. *Economy and Society,* 19(1): 1–27.

Miller T (1998). *Technologies of truth: cultural citizenship and the popular media.* Minnesota: University of Minnesota Press.

Nadesan M (2006). The MYD panoptican: neo-liberalism, governmentality and education. Radical Pedagogy [Online]. Available: radicalpedagogy. icaap.org/content/issue8_1/nadesan.html. [Accessed 3 March 2007].

O'Malley P (1996). Risk and responsibility. In A Barry, T Osborne & N Rose (Eds), *Foucault and political reason: liberalism, neo-liberalism and rationalities of government* (pp189–208). London: University College London Press.

Popkewitz T (1996). Rethinking decentralisation and state/civil society distinctions: the state as a problematic of governing. *Journal of Education Policy*, 11(1): 27–51.

Rankin KN (2001). Governing development; neoliberalism, microcredit, and rational economic women. *Economy and Society*, 30(1): 18–37.

Robertson B (2000). *The Aboriginal and Torres Strait Islander Women's Task Force on Violence Report*. Queensland Department of Aboriginal and Torres Strait Islander Policy and Development.

Rodgers D (2006). The state as a gang—conceptualizing the governmentality of violence in contemporary Nicaragua. *Critique of Anthropology*, 26(3): 315–30.

Rose N (1999). *Powers of freedom: reframing political thought*. Cambridge: Cambridge University Press.

Rose N (2000). Government and control. *British Journal of Criminology*, 40: 321–38.

Rose N (2001). Community, citizenship and the third way. In D Merydyth & J Minson (Eds), *Citizenship and cultural policy* (pp1–17). London: Sage.

Rose N & Miller P (1992). Political power beyond the state: problematics of government. *British Journal of Sociology*, 43(2): 173–205.

Scullion N (2007). Northern Territory National Emergency Response Bill 2007, Senate Hansard, Federal Parliament of Australia: 10–18.

Shergold P (2004). *Speech to launch the Connecting Government Report* [Online]. Available: www.pmc.gov.au/speeches/shergold/connecting_ government_2004-04-20.cfm. [Accessed 14 November 2007].

Shergold P (2006). Indigenous economic opportunity: the role of the community and the individual. Speech delivered at the First Nations Economic Opportunities Conference, 19 July 2006 [Online]. Available: www.pmc.gov.au/speeches/shergold/indigenous_2006-07-19.cfm. [Accessed 1 September 2007].

Simon J (2000). Megan's law: crime and democracy in late modern America. *Law & Social Inquiry* 25(4): 1111–50.

Stanley J, Kovacs K, Tomison A & Cripps K (2002). *Child abuse and family violence in Aboriginal communities: exploring child sexual abuse in Western Australia*. Australian Institute of Family Studies [Online]. Available: www. aifs.gov.au/nch/pubs/reports/wabrief.pdf [Accessed 1 September 2007].

Stanley J, Tomison A & Pocock J (2003). Child abuse and neglect in Indigenous Australian communities. *Child Abuse Prevention Issues*, 19 [Online]. Available: www.aifs.gov.au/nch/pubs/issues/issues19/issues19. html [Accessed 1 September 2007].

Vanstone A (2003). Passive welfare – killing them softly. Paper presented at the CofFEE Public Policy Lecture Series, The University of Newcastle, 21 July 2003.

Vanstone A (2004a). Ministerial taskforce to focus on Indigenous families, Media Release vIPS 031/04, 16 June [Online]. Available: www.atsia.gov.au/ Media/media04/v04031.aspx. [Accessed 10 January 2005].

Vanstone A (2004b). New service delivery arrangements for Indigenous affairs. Media Release: vIPS 012/04, 15 April [Online]. Available: www. atsia.gov.au/media/media04/v04012.aspx. [Accessed 10 January 2005].

Vanstone A (2005). Address to National Press Club. Wednesday 23 February, Canberra.

Wiegman R (2003). 'My name is Forrest, Forrest Gump': whiteness studies and the paradox of particularity. In E Shohat & R Stam (Eds), *Multiculturalism, postcoloniality, and transnational media (pp227–55)*. New Brunswick: Rutgers University Press.

Wild R & Anderson P (2007). *Ampe Akelyernemane Meke Mekarle 'Little children are sacred': report of the Northern Territory Board of Inquiry into the protection of Aboriginal children from sexual abuse*, June 2007.

Wright A (1997). *Grog war*. Broome: Magabala Books.

Yaxley L (2004). Govt makes 'shared responsibility' deal with WA Indigenous community. Transcript of Report for *The World Today*, Radio National, 9 December [Online]. Available: www.abc.net.au/worldtoday/content/2004/ s1261373.htm. [Accessed 25 April 2005].

6

Colonial violence and postcolonial France

Robert Aldrich

It would be reductionist to argue that violence is the key to colonialism, or that all colonial encounters ought to be seen in terms of violent confrontations between imperialists and native peoples. There was also collaboration, complicity, even solidarity between the colonisers and the colonised. Colonialism, as present-day practitioners of the 'new colonial history' are well aware, presents one of the most complex topics in modern history (Aldrich 2007a). Numerous motives—economic gain, international rivalry, political positioning, ideological commitment, evangelisation and humanitarian efforts—combined in overseas expansion. The colonies provided the terrain for pursuit of individual, group and national objectives impossible to reduce to a simple equation or tally by a conclusive balance-sheet. Some of those involved in the colonies were moved by high-minded vocations justified as a 'civilising mission'; others were officials and officers carrying out their duties to the state; settlers, often of modest background, aspired for a better life; transported prisoners, among others, were implicated unwillingly in the colonial enterprise. Moreover, throughout colonial history, in addition to a current of violence, there appears a counter-current of opposition to violence. Anti-colonialists—a prominent voice in European politics—protested against conquest and colonial exactions. Journalists exposed incidents of awful violence, their reports sparking outrage even in colonialist circles. Many 'Indigenous' politicians promoted non-violent strategies to obtain reforms and wholeheartedly rejected violence. Decolonisation of some possessions occurred with little bloodshed.

Nevertheless, physical violence—sometimes excused or even celebrated, at other times bemoaned or condemned—provided an important component in overseas expansion and in the reaction to imperialism.[1] Violence of various sorts, of course, was a fact of life in European nations and other colonial *métropoles*, but differed in a colonial situation because of the racial cleavages that created or exacerbated antagonisms. Furthermore, the norms of the colonial context allowed a wider, often arbitrary and generally less constrained violence by the colonisers than authorities could practice at home. Colonialism also generally deprived the 'indigenes' of forms of peaceful protest—electoral politics, trade unionism—that increasingly existed for subalterns in Europe, on occasion pushing them into the use of violence as a primary tactic or a last resort in anti-colonial action.

This chapter will discuss some types of violence apparent in colonial situations, examine several particular episodes in the French empire, and suggest ways in which colonial violence left a legacy to postcolonial France.

The classic partisan discussion of colonialism and violence comes from Frantz Fanon's *The wretched of the earth*, written in the midst of the war for Algerian independence. Fanon's views are well known. He argued that violence is inherent in the relationship between the coloniser and the colonised: 'Their first encounter was marked by violence and their existence together—that is to say the exploitation of the native by the settler—was carried on by dint of a great array of bayonets and cannons' (Fanon 1963, 36). Moreover, decolonisation necessarily involved violence because of the intransigence of the colonial system: 'The naked truth of decolonisation evokes for us the searing bullets and bloodstained knives which emanate from it' (Fanon 1963, 37). One type of violence bred another: 'The violence of the colonial regime and the counter-violence of the native balance each other and respond to each other in an extraordinary reciprocal homogeneity' (Fanon 1963, 88). Only such anti-colonial violence could effect a break with the old order.

---

1 This chapter concentrates on physical and armed violence, though other types of violence—mental abuse, land dispossession, exploitative labour and a variety of other exactions and mistreatments—ought not to be minimised.

Violence, in the Martinican psychiatrist's analysis, was necessary for both the colonised society collectively and the colonised personally to shake off the shackles of domination: 'At the level of individuals, violence is a cleansing force. It frees the native from his inferiority complex and from his despair and inaction; it makes him fearless and restores his self-respect' (Fanon 1963, 94). It thereby provided a vital experience necessary for the evacuation of the old order and the foundation of new societies.

Fanon's revolutionary ideology offered provocative theories and powerful rhetoric. Most historians now reject his vision of colonial environments as composed of compartmentalised, motionless and Manichean divides between the colonised and the colonising. Present-day analysts see the two groups within the same situational and analytical field, and stress the social and cultural interchange, linkages and hybridities between the colonisers and those over whom they ruled (see e.g. Cooper & Stoler 1997). Fanon's own context was the war by the *Front de Libération Nationale* (FLN), composed of largely Muslim Algerians opposed to the settler community and the French state, which considered Algeria integrally a part of France. Such circumstances promoted the types of violence and counter-violence that Fanon evoked. Even so, he paid little attention to the murderous violence that pitted Algerian factions against each other, and the violence that ultimately (though largely after his death) turned diehard defenders of *Algérie française* against compatriots who accepted Algerian independence. Not all examples of colonialism, or all episodes of decolonisation, were so violent as Fanon hypothesised. Furthermore, violence often soiled newly independent states with continued blood-letting rather than symbolic cleansing. Indeed, Fanon's defence of violence probably promoted the valorisation and persistence of a culture of violence after the transition from colonial to postcolonial regimes.

If Fanon's views remain useful in underlining the presence of violence in colonialism and decolonisation, that violence was more manifold and multi-directional than he theorised, and its heritage proved longer lasting than he foresaw.

Violence in the French colonial world

A typology of violence in the French empire reveals multiple expressions of suffering endured by the peoples over whom Paris established colonial dominion, but also endured by the colonisers themselves. Violence was present, first of all, in the conquest of territory. Although a few countries came under French rule without great bloodshed—Laos, colonial promoters exulted, represented such an example—these proved the exception to a general rule of military incursion and occupation. The conquest of Algiers, inaugurating renewed expansionism in 1830, is a case in point. In sub-Saharan Africa and South-east Asia, France acquired a massive empire through the force of gunboats and an armed soldiery—sometimes arguing that this violence was necessary to save 'natives' from violence inflicted by Indigenous or foreign slave-traders, brutal potentates or local warlords.

Wars of colonial acquisition provided a proving ground for masculine valour and national accomplishment, with great generals and brave foot-soldiers lauded for their achievements. Colonial heroes—General Faidherbe, General Gallieni, Marshal Lyautey and a pantheon of others—won laurels in battle, pushing back the frontier of the empire, raising flags over remote hinterlands, defeating opponents who resisted their onslaught. A veritable doctrine of beneficent violence formed part of the imperial gospel. French troops must impose their rule, amicably if possible, through arms when necessary; enemies must be eliminated. For the French, extension of empire would provide, among other championed advantages, venues for garrisons, ports for the navy, and ultimately reservoirs of soldiers for the army. Imperial mettle would strengthen French manhood and counter modern degeneration. The benefits for the colonised populations—good governance, economic modernisation, access to Western science and technology, medicine and education—would be worth submission to French authority (Alrich 2007b).[2]

---

2 Paradoxically, colonialism also posed significant challenges to French manhood—disease and death, competition from natives to whom Frenchmen might or might not measure up, and the ravages of warfare.

Closely connected with the violence of conquest was the 'pacification' of rebels. Insurrections punctuated imperial rule: Abd el-Kader's campaigns in Algeria in the 1830s and 1840s the Tahitian wars of the 1840s, the Mokrani insurrection in Algeria in 1871, a rebellion led by the Melanesian chief Ataï in New Caledonia in 1878, widespread protests against conscription of troops for French armies in the First World War, then the Rif rebellion in Morocco and the Druze rebellion in Syria and Lebanon in the 1920s, and the Yen Bay uprising in Vietnam in the early 1930s. Putting down rebellions that challenged French overlordship meant defeating, capturing and punishing enemies of the colonial state, imprisoning or exiling their supporters, and clamping down on social dissent. Arms provided the guarantee of imperial sovereignty against subversion within the colonies and attacks by rivals from without, whence the importance of troops—*marsouins, zouaves, Légionnaires*—and their willingness to use their weaponry. Forts, barracks and garrisons arose as signs of military might, complemented by prisons and the guillotine as symbols of police power.[3]

Military service almost inevitably implied violence, with colonised men both victims and perpetrators. The *tirailleurs sénégalais*, forces of soldiers recruited across western Africa, became indispensable to the extension of French domains and the maintenance of colonial order, deployed throughout the empire down to the end of the imperial period. General Charles Mangin promoted the *force noire* of colonial soldiers as an auxiliary fighting force; in the First World War, 87,000 soldiers from the colonies were killed, including French citizens and 70,000 native men *morts pour la France*. Recruiters often used coercion to fill quotas of volunteers, and the rumour persisted that colonial soldiers were used as front-line 'cannon fodder' on European battlefields (Frémeaux 2006). Colonial troops were again deployed in the Second World War, a significant number either executed by the victorious Nazis in 1940 or sent to concentration camps. African troops also played a vital role— neglected in the public mind until the 2006 film *Indigènes* (shown in

---

3 Clamp-downs on dissidents, incarceration of rebels, execution of subversives and other sorts of violence helped stiffen anti-colonialist resolve. See Zinoman 2001.

English as *Days of Glory*)—in the Liberation of 1944. Colonial troops then formed a large contingent of French forces in the Indochinese war.

In addition to the violence of war, there was also the violence of daily life in colonised societies. Slavery existed in the French empire until 1848, succeeded in some areas by the use of indentured labour in conditions that opponents charged were reminiscent of enslavement. In many possessions, the *code de l'indigénat* made it possible for 'natives' to be disciplined by administrators, without judicial process, by corporal punishment, detention, confiscation of goods, even collective punishment of whole villages for infractions.[4] The *corvée* required native men to spend a certain number of days, without remuneration, labouring on public works projects. Back-breaking labour demanded of porters, miners and plantation labourers established a violent regime of employment. A few administrators and other colonialists were renowned for brutality,[5] and the rule of concessionary companies in equatorial Africa for a time institutionalised an almost untrammelled violence in the domination of local people. Violence formed part of an arsenal of coercive measures used by the colonisers, even when they hoped to win the hearts and minds of those under their rule.

A particular institution of violence in the empire was slavery and slave-trading, practised by the French from the 1600s until the mid-19th century. Space is lacking to say much here about the well-known violence of slavery: the capture and transport to distant outposts of Africans and Malagasy, overwork on plantations, the sexual violence committed on enslaved women, the punishments meted out to those who did not obey or to *marrons* who tried to escape. Memories of the violence of slavery lived on after emancipation in the West Indies, French Guiana and Reunion Island, as well as in the parts of Africa where slaves were taken (see Reinhardt 2006 and Cottias 2007).

---

4 Contrary to the implication given by the name 'indigenous code', this was not a specific law code but a series of administrative regulations that differed from colony to colony.

5 While congratulating soldiers on their bravery, and condemning enemy combatants for their brutality, metropolitan opinion did occasionally revolt against violence, as in denunciation of the excesses of the infamous Voulet-Chanoine expedition of 1898.

Violence, therefore, was thus regularly visited on subject populations by colonialists eager to conquer territory, suppress rebellion, gain maximum benefits from their new domains, and defend the *mère-patrie* against enemies at home or abroad. Violence, it should be added, affected Europeans and not just the colonised. Frenchmen were killed by those resisting invasion, memorialised for their sacrifice to the cause of expansion. Priests and friars—from the early missionaries in Vietnam to Charles de Foucauld, killed by Tuaregs in his hermitage in Algeria in 1916—achieved saintly martyrdom for spreading the Gospel.[6] Soldiers faced harsh conditions of service in uncongenial environments where death rates from battle and disease ran high. Offenders against military discipline incurred transfer to the notorious *Bataillons d'Afrique*. A cult of violence in the Foreign Legion, renowned for its stringent training and tough military campaigns, made that force legendary. Convicts transported to French Guiana perished in the 'green hell' of South America; those sent to New Caledonia fared somewhat better, but the penal regime and the difficulties of life for emancipists took a great toll (see Toth 2006). Europeans also committed crimes against each other, the difficult situations of colonial life inciting disputes resolved through fisticuffs and occasional murder. The macho, lawless nature of frontier societies—as portrayed in novels such as Loti's *Le Roman d'un spahi*—helped provoke and condone such episodes.[7]

In summation, a culture of violence existed among both the French and the original populations in the colonies. Settlers armed themselves against 'natives', rebels, foreigners and each other. Collective violence was officially sanctioned as the prerogative of military forces, police and penal authorities, but those resisting colonialism could see violence as a legitimate means of protest. An ideology of violence, among colonisers and colonised, endorsed the shedding of blood, celebrating the feats of conquest or resistance, mandating the maintenance of order or

---

6 Probably a larger number than those killed in warfare succumbed to endemic diseases—the death rate of soldiers in the campaign in Madagascar in the 1890s was particularly high.

7 One could also mention the prominence of violence in colonialist art, and the omnipresence of weaponry and 'trophies' in colonial-era museums.

the subversion of it. Weaponry exemplified the culture and ideology: military *matériel* developed for colonialists' use and then eagerly procured by the colonised, and the arms manufacturing and gun-running that profited from colonialism.

The multifarious nature of violence in colonial society can be illustrated in three incidents in West Africa at the time of the Second World War, as documented by Ruth Ginio. These played out against the background of the German defeat of France and a failed attempt to rally French West Africa to the Free French (Thomas 1998). Also in the background lay the violence committed against Jewish populations in the empire through the Vichy regime's application of anti-Semitic laws (including the internment of Jews), as well as stepped-up discrimination and closer control of the 'natives' by colonial governments loyal to Marshal Pétain (Cantier & Jennings 2004; Jennings 2001).[8]

The first incident occurred a month after the French capitulation in 1940. Although not an episode involving the colonial authorities, it illustrates the persistence of communalist violence despite the presence of a colonial regime that avowed the establishment of law and order as part of its mission. The 'Hamallist riots' took place in the Soudan (now Mali), involving an arcane liturgical dispute between rival Muslim confraternities and their leaders. An Islamic *notable* humiliated by a hostile group carried out a revenge vendetta in an attack at Mouchgag, in the Nioro region, leaving 400 dead. A year later, in August 1941, five Europeans were murdered, and eight injured, by a group of 25 Africans in Bobo-Dioulasso, in Haute-Volta (now Burkina Faso), as Sheika Amadou called for a holy war against the Europeans. The third incident, in 1945, concerned 1280 African soldiers serving with the French army in Europe who had been incarcerated by the Germans. After the liberation and the freeing of the soldiers, French officials sent the men back to Dakar, the capital of Senegal (though many were not Senegalese), and set them up in poor conditions at the Camp de Thiaroye 20 kilometres from the city. About 500 refused demobilisation

---

8 The Jews of Algeria had been the object of considerable anti-Semitic violence perpetrated by French settlers during riots at the time of the Dreyfus affair at the end of the 19th century.

until they received payment for their war service, including salaries accumulated while in German captivity. A group of soldiers mutinied, and the French troops opened fire. Thirty-five were killed (Ginio 2006). Although the incidents at Nioro, Bobo-Dioulasso and Thiaroye were isolated, they show how inflammable colonial conditions could be, with circumstances propitious for indigenous attacks on Europeans, for European use of violence against native peoples, or for violence between two groups in the colonised population that the Europeans could not control. Examples around the empire could be multiplied.

How and to what extent did the violence that permeated colonial life erupt in the *métropole*? One manifestation was the incidents involving colonial soldiers stationed in France. During the First World War, clashes often occurred implicating colonial soldiers or colonised people imported for work in the war industry; sometimes they started around questions of employment, at other times because of rivalries over women, or after racist attacks. One historian has characterised several confrontations as race riots (Stovall 1998). Violence also occurred behind the lines in the Second World War. In 1944, soldiers waited for demobilisation and return to their homeland while housed inadequately in transit camps and waiting, sometimes in vain, for money or supplies. Transit camps in Saint-Raphaël and Sète—as at Thiaroye—saw *tirailleurs sénégalais* refuse orders, demolish buildings for firewood, and beat up bakers and shopkeepers who would not supply them (Mann 2006).

Colonised people resident in France—who numbered around 150,000 in the early 1930s—were on occasion targets of violence, including random attacks motivated by racial hatred or class resentment, or more institutionalised violence under the auspices of the state. Authorities, seeking to control immigrant populations, used a plethora of techniques of surveillance, infiltration of migrant groups, arrests and heavy-handed police tactics to keep a check on those regarded as liable to be both criminal and subversive simply because of their colonial origins (Rosenberg 2006).[9]

---

9 See also Blévis et al. 2008, the catalogue of an exhibition at the new Cité Nationale de l'Histoire de l'Immigration (a museum located, somewhat curiously, in the former colonial museum).

Incidents of violence involving colonised people in France evidenced the racial tensions that existed in the *métropole*, while demonstrating the determination of the state to enforce order and retain imperial control. Most of the migrants from the Maghreb, black Africa and Indochina performed subaltern jobs and concentrated in poorer neighbourhoods of industrial cities or ports. They did not enjoy the full benefits of French citizenship until the late 1950s and had little legal recourse in the face of police or public harassment. Long before the large-scale arrival of 'guest workers', migrants lived in precarious situations where various types of violence could explode.

Violence and decolonisation

The wars of decolonisation brought colonial violence to a stage of paroxysm, and that violence spilled over into France itself (for an overview, see Clayton 1994). Violence ignited in North Africa immediately following the end of the Second World War. On 8 May 1945, protesters in the Algerian city of Sétif gathered to demand the release from detention of the nationalist leader Messali Hadj. The demonstration turned into a riot—Muslim rebels killed 102 Europeans, and the French military in response took the life of as many as 20,000 Algerians, an enormous reprisal intended to nip nationalism in the bud.[10] The next year, violence broke out in Indochina, as the French struggled to re-establish authority after the Japanese occupation and the success of Ho Chi Minh's Communist forces in gaining primacy in northern Vietnam. Several provincial uprisings targeted the French, and French warships bombed Haiphong, which was controlled by the nationalists. The actions touched off a war that lasted until 1954, resulting in the death of 20,000 French soldiers (many of them troopers from the colonies) and an unknown, but undoubtedly much larger, number of Vietnamese. Meanwhile, an insurrection broke out on the Indian Ocean island of Madagascar in 1947. Repression was quick and uncompromising, and the death toll of Malagasy rose to between 80,000 and 100,000 protesters (Liauzu 2007).

10　The number of dead in each of the incidents discussed here remains contested. These figures are taken from Liauzu 2007.

The most dramatic and painful decolonisation, of course, took place in Algeria, France's major colony of settlement and home to more than a million *Français d'Algérie* (also known as *pieds-noirs*) living amidst a population of nine million Muslims. The war began with a nationalist attack in the night preceding All Saints' Day, 1 November 1954: the killing of seven French settlers. By the time it concluded in 1962, at least 23,000 soldiers (of the two million Frenchmen who served) had been killed. Also dead were thousands of *harkis*, Muslims who served as auxiliaries in the French army. A conservative total estimated that 243,000 Algerians died. FLN nationalists killed 6000 Algerian rivals during the war and, after the ceasefire of 19 March 1962, killed between 10,000 and 150,000 Muslims—estimates vary widely—who had supported the French or were suspected sympathisers with *Algérie française*. Meanwhile, a French terrorist group, the Organisation Armée Secrète (OAS), determined to keep Algeria French, killed 1500 people, including many Frenchmen whom they accused of being willing to abandon Algeria. A police attack on an OAS demonstration in the Rue d'Isly in Algiers in 1962 (after the ceasefire) led to the deaths of 46 French people. Violence had thus erupted in all directions, targeting all manner of people, in attacks of revenge as well as in actual fighting—the 'reciprocal' violence of which Fanon spoke.

The death toll in the Algerian War was enormous, and the way in which many died particularly shocking. French newspapers highlighted the brutality of the Armée de Libération Nationale (ALN) with articles on the bombing of non-military targets such as the Milk Bar café in the Battle of Algiers in 1957. Photographs showed French soldiers and civilians with slashed throats, witnesses reported victims burned or buried alive, and there were images of cadavers with their amputated genitals stuck into their mouths. Opponents of the war also brought to public attention extra-legal French tactics, including torture of rebels. In 1957, the secretary-general of the French police in Algiers, Paul Teitgen, resigned because of the torture used by French soldiers, which he compared—and the strength of the statement is remarkable given France's experience of the German occupation in the Second World War—to that inflicted by the Gestapo. Henri Alleg's *La Ques-*

tion, published in 1958, represented one of a number of publications that revealed the extent of torture. Electric shock, 'water-boarding' and sensory deprivation figured among tactics said to be necessary to extract information about FLN terrorism and save the lives of innocent women and men.[11]

The variegated nature of violence in Algeria is worth underlining. The Algerians attacked the French—from the end of 1954 to mid-1957, authorities registered over 16,000 attacks against French civilians in Algeria as well as over 9000 against the French military. Over a thousand French civilians were killed in this period, and 3000 others disappeared. French soldiers and civilians attacked Algerians, in military exercises, random killings and revenge attacks (including the killing of 20 Muslims after the Rue d'Isly episode). Algerians attacked fellow Algerians. One directive issued by nationalists specified that any pro-French Algerian village should be burned, and that all males over the age of 20 should be executed. The ALN exacted a huge number of deaths from supporters of rival nationalist factions and among the *harkis*, whom they branded traitors. The French, though to a lesser extent, also turned violently on each other. One case that brought torture to public attention was the disappearance and murder at the hands of French authorities of Maurice Audin, a brilliant young mathematician, member of the Algerian Communist Party and supporter of independence, whose death in 1957 became a *cause célèbre*. The illegal OAS later assassinated supporters of Algerian independence (and practised scorched earth tactics, even burning the library in Algiers). Several supporters of the organisation were finally captured, convicted by French courts and executed by firing squad.

The violence spread from Algeria to France, even before the war 'officially' began. On 14 July 1953, Algerians protested in Paris to demand the freeing of Messali Hadj, who was again held under house arrest in Niort. The police interrupted the march, the situation

---

11 These figures and information in the following paragraphs are taken largely from Stora 1991. Literature on the war is voluminous, the number of dead and injured on both sides is highly debated, and the issues of torture, extra-legal executions and mutilations are objects of much disagreement.

degenerated, and the outcome was six Algerians dead and 44 wounded (Stora 1991, 134). Violence escalated rapidly after the All Saints' events of 1954, including incidents between Algerians. The Fédération de France of the FLN recruited members, extorted money and enforced obedience among the migrant population, and also sought to eliminate its still strong nationalist rivals. The war saw bloody confrontations between the FLN and rival nationalist organisations in Paris, Lyon, Lille, Marseille, Grenoble and elsewhere—in the first months of 1957, an average of eight Algerian victims a day, and then 119 in the single month of December. According to Benjamin Stora, 'in the years 1956–1957, one Muslim in eighty living in France was the victim of terrorism', and from 1956 through 1961, 3889 Algerians were killed (with 7678 wounded and 12,000 the targets of acts of aggression) in the settling of accounts between Algerian factions in the *métropole*. Similar violence occurred among Algerian communities in Switzerland, Germany and Italy (Stora 1991, 143–44).

French violence against metropolitan supporters of independence was also bloody, notably in the reaction to a demonstration on 17 October 1961. The prefect of police in Paris, Maurice Papon (later tried for deportation of Jews to death camps as an administrator in Bordeaux during the Second World War), had ordered a curfew on all Algerians in the city in the autumn, a period of particularly intense conflict in Algeria, and he stepped up measures to combat subversion in the French capital. In response, the FLN organised a peaceful protest with 20,000 marchers marshalled to converge on central Paris; the nationalists barred demonstrators from carrying any sort of weapon, and the march took place in silence. Police reacted violently. Several dozen protesters were killed, their bodies often dumped into the Seine, with over 11,000 arrested, and many manhandled in improvised detention centres in the worst incident of violence in metropolitan France since the Second World War. The repression, covered up and denied by the authorities, shocked many anti-war activists and traumatised Algerians in France. Jim House and Neil MacMaster, two British historians who have published the most comprehensive analysis of the incident, do not hesitate to speak of 'state terrorism' exercised against the Algerians in

France—by 1961 fully fledged French citizens—and which culminated in the October massacre (House & MacMaster 2006).

Despite growing opposition to the war, and a referendum in which a majority approved of self-determination for Algeria, some *pieds-noirs* and their supporters remained unreconciled to the end of *Algérie française*. A putsch by generals in Algiers failed in 1961. Diehard defenders of colonialism turned their ire against the state and its agents, including President de Gaulle who, having famously proclaimed 'Vive l'Algérie française!' on returning to power in 1958, was on the brink of ceding the country to the hated FLN. In the last months of the war and continuing after the ceasefire brokered in the Évian accords, the OAS undertook a campaign of violence in the *métropole*. One attack targeted the Minister of Culture, André Malraux; the minister escaped, but the bomb that exploded outside his apartment took the life of a four-year-old girl.

Such actions led to widespread outrage in France, and a protest against the OAS. On 8 March 1962, trade unionists and the Communist Party organised a march in eastern Paris near the Charonne Métro station. Security services locked the station doors and in the *mêlée* following a police charge on the demonstration, eight protestors were killed, crushed and trampled trying to escape. A crowd of half a million subsequently gathered to pay tribute to the victims. Despite condemnation of their activities, OAS violence continued, and on 22 August 1962, over a month after France had officially recognised the independence of Algeria, an OAS member tried to assassinate de Gaulle.

By this time, a bloody settling of accounts was taking place in Algeria. In the summer of 1962, a million *pieds-noirs* fled in scenes of chaos, agony and recrimination; the *rapatriés* arrived in a France hardly eager to welcome the erstwhile colonial compatriots. The victorious FLN was meanwhile engaged in exactions against the *harkis*, whom the French only belatedly allowed into the *métropole* despite their service to the French empire.

The legacy of violence in postcolonial France

Violence, thus, was a constant in many parts of the empire, rising to a crescendo in the Algerian War, and violence overseas infected the *métropole*. By the end of the Indochinese and Algerian wars, and other violent episodes in the decolonisation of Madagascar and sub-Saharan Africa, hundreds of thousands of colonised people were dead, some victims of their fellow countrymen, and well over 50,000 French men and women had also perished.

How does this violence lay in the background of present-day strife in France?

The record of colonial violence remains part of the collective memory and the heritage of the colonial epoch.[12] The relatively recent nature of decolonisation, and the violence that accompanied it, is pertinent. Benjamin Stora estimates that five million French people today claim a direct link with colonial Algeria—soldiers who served in North Africa, *pieds-noirs* and *harkis* 'repatriated' to France, children of migrants. Some *pieds-noirs* still harbour bitter resentment at their ejection from Algeria, the loss of their country, their land and life in *Algérie française*. Old soldiers have felt unacknowledged for the services they rendered, the deaths they mourned, and the wounds they bore (see Evans 1997). The *harkis*, who languished in resettlement camps until the 1970s, have searing memories of their treatment by the victorious FLN and perceived abandonment by the French. Migrants have lived with the wartime experiences and memories of their parents and grand-parents. The history of colonialism, in general, and of the painful and bloody war of 1954–1962, in particular, continues to inflect relations between Algeria and France, as well as the rapport between ethnic groups in France, despite efforts to breach the divides. And the Algerian War is not the only colonial memory that has festered. Other types of colonial violence—slavery, forced labour, imprisonment, arbitrary punishment, but also injury and death whether in heroic service to France or in opposition to imperialism—are imbedded in the genealogies, memories and history of both colonised and colonisers.

A second way in which this colonial-era violence affects France is in the occlusion or amnesia about the Algerian War (and colonialism

---

12 Philippe Franchini, in a book about métissage, made a prescient passing remark a decade before the violence of 2005: 'In the French banlieues, the memory of colonialism is revived by confrontations highlighted by ethnic grievances and demands that the steam-roller of History thought it had completely destroyed' (Franchini 1993, 130).

in general) common until recent years. Stora's 1991 *La gangrène et l'oubli* provides a detailed analysis of the way societies on both sides of the Mediterranean denied crucial aspects of the Algerian conflict. President de Gaulle created an orthodoxy in French ideology that elided colonialism to proclaim France the great decoloniser and the supporter of the Third World. Amnesties in 1962 and 1968 (eventually extended to OAS members) kept any French person who might have been accused of war crimes from being prosecuted. The 'operations for the maintenance of order' of 1954–1962 were a 'war that did not speak its name'—not until an act of parliament in 1999 was the conflict officially declared a 'war'. Not until 2002 was a national memorial to the soldiers in North Africa inaugurated. *Harkis* received little recognition until President Jacques Chirac held a *journée nationale d'hommage* for those who had served alongside the French. The issue of French torture remained a great taboo until it became a burning topic after the trial of Papon in 1998, followed by newspaper revelations to *Le Monde* in 2000. Louisette Ingilhariz, an aging FLN militant, recounted her torture at the hands of the French, and several generals, including Paul Aussaresses and Jacques Massu, responded with admissions about participation in torture and summary executions—Massu expressed regret, but Aussaresses justified the actions as necessary in the circumstances. Only with the opening of archives to such historians as Raphaëlle Branche and Sylvie Thénault did the French become cognisant of the broad extent and systematic nature of torture, and of the collusion of the administration and magistracy in a cover-up (MacMaster 2002; Branche 2001; Thénault 2004).

Similar censorship occurred in Algeria. The FLN maintained a 'party line' view of Algeria's history. Rival nationalist movements were written out of the chronicle of resistance to the French, just as their members were excluded from the government of Algeria. The narrative spoke only of an Algerian people completely united behind the anti-colonial FLN, ignoring both divisions within the nationalist movement and the support of some Muslims for the French. The orthodox version implied that the Algerians had won a military victory over the French, contrary to most outside historians' assessment. The violent exactions against FLN opponents and the massacre of the *harkis* after 19 March 1962 were ignored, and when the current Algerian president, Abdelaziz Bouteflika, visited Paris in the early 2000s, he still referred to *harkis* as 'traitors' and denied their right of return to Algeria (Stora 1991; Turquoi 2007).

Avoidance of the complex and conflicting memories and histories of the Algerian War and its aftermath has left its imprint on the population of France, both native Europeans and migrants from overseas. Lack of a more nuanced perspective on colonialism and the war perpetuates a binary view of right and wrong, colonised and colonising, hero and victim, martyr and traitor, with an avoidance of the multi-dimensional nature of the conflict, and the multi-directional targeting of the violence it encompassed. In these conditions, violence may appear to some, including a few disenchanted young French residents of North African background, as a legitimate reaction by the powerless to desperate situations (as Fanon theorised). Violence committed against migrants and their descendants may also be experienced as a metamorphosis of the violence endured by colonised people.

A third way in which the violence of the colonial period casts its shadow is the way that colonial and postcolonial issues have been manipulated in inflammatory contexts. The colonial-era basis of the anti-immigrant programs of the Front National and other extremist organisations is clear—the background of some members, such as Le Pen himself, in support of *Algérie française*, the targeting of Maghrebin migrants, the singling out of cultural specificities cast in racial terms, rhetorical insistence on an exclusivist and seemingly immutable French identity, the harking back to colonialist (and Vichyite) notions of Frenchness. More mainstream French politicians have also engaged in manipulation of the colonial past, most obviously in the 2005 adoption by the French parliament of a law paying homage to French soldiers and settlers and, most controversially, requiring the teaching of 'positive aspects' of colonial history, especially that of North Africa, in French schools. That law, a reaction against the debate on French torture of the preceding years, provoked great disquiet among historians as interference by politicians in the practice of their craft. Those holding a critical perspective on the colonial past lambasted a biased view of the imperial record. Faced with the outcry, President Chirac had the clause on teaching suspended, but the parliamentary action continues to rankle (Aldrich 2006a). More recently, Chirac's successor, Nicolas Sarkozy, has pronounced his refusal of any 'repentance' for French colonialism and emphasised the beneficial work done by colonists and soldiers.[13]

The colonial past and the violence of that era have been 'instrumentalised' by other groups as well. Pro-independence groups active in the 1970s and 1980s in the overseas territories remaining under French rule, such as New Caledonia, enumerated cases of colonial-era violence to justify their campaigns, and they sometimes borrowed as strategy the violent tactics pioneered by Algerian nationalists.[14] More recently, groups such as *Les Indigènes de la République*—the name is telling—have couched their grievances about the subaltern conditions of migrants, and discrimination against citizens and residents of Maghrebin or African ancestry in France, in terms of a continuation of colonial exploitation, racism and violence. Supporters of *sans-abri* (homeless people, frequently illegal migrants from Africa) have referred to the colonial sufferings of Africans under French rule, while they also recall the services of *tirailleurs sénégalais* to the state, in order to justify demands for inclusion of migrants into mainstream French society (Mann 2006). West Indians were active in persuading the parliament

---

13   See, in particular, President Sarkozy's letter to Denis Fadda of 16 April 2007, and his speech in Dakar, Senegal, on 26 July 2007, both reprinted on the website of the Ligue des Droits de l'Homme in Toulon (www.ldh-toulon.net). In response, see Gassama 2008. For a critical assessment, see De Cock et al. 2008.

14   The independence front in New Caledonia, the Front de Libération Nationale Kanak et Socialiste, took its name from the Algerian FLN; attacks on French targets, including kidnapping and assassination of settlers, marked the 'events' of the mid-1980s. The French replied with tactics developed in Algeria, including such violent measures as the killing of the nationalist Éloi Machoro and the storming of rebels' hideouts (notably on Ouvéa island, where indépendantistes held several kidnapped Frenchmen). There were also episodes of violent confrontation between the police and soldiers, on the one hand, and the Caldoches on the other. Internecine violence pitted one Melanesian faction against the other—the FLNKS leader Jean-Marie Tjibaou was assassinated by another Melanesian who rejected his negotiations with the French and the 'colons'

to adopt a law, in 2001, that declared slavery and slave-trading 'crimes against humanity', and the heritage of slavery is often evoked by organisations joined in the *Conseil représentatitif des associations noires de France*. In very different ways, and with varying ideologies and objectives, the colonial past thus for many groups becomes a platform for contemporary activism.

Opinions differ, among activists and historians, about the exact extent and role of violence in French colonialism. Violence was not the prerogative of the French; all of the countries involved in imperialism were also implicated in violence and in the violent reactions against expansion.[15] Furthermore, violence in the areas conquered by France did not begin with the French invasion—warfare was widespread among various tribes, clans and ethnic groups throughout the pre-colonial world.[16] Violence did not end with the lowering of the French flag, as the history of independent states has sadly shown. Tens of thousands of Vietnamese perished after 1954 in a second war—the war against the Americans from the early 1960s to 1975, which was also effectively a civil war. Under Pol Pot, the former French protectorate of Cambodia experienced genocide. Blood-letting occurred with *coups d'état* and under dictatorial regimes in much of former French West Africa and French Equatorial Africa. A decade-long civil war in Algeria in the 1990s pitted the military-based FLN against Islamists; approximately 100,000 Algerians died in the fighting, and episodic violence has continued. Few former French colonies have been exempt from bouts of postcolonial violence.

Though not confined to the age of *la plus grande France*, violence indeed formed a matrix of the period of colonialism and decolonisation.

---

15 On the British case, see Bayly & Harper 2008, and Elkins 2005. See also the essays comparing, for instance, Indochina and Indonesia, or Algeria and Cyprus, in Ageron & Michel 1995. Moses and Stone (2007) provide discussion of various cases of colonial genocide—and the issue of the applicability of the concept to colonial situations.

16 Warfare, of course, was not foreign to France—a generation of war during the Revolutionary and Napoleonic years, revolutions in 1830, 1848 and 1871, French troops engaged in nineteenth-century wars in Italy and against Germany, and sent overseas to the Crimea, to Mexico and to China in 1900 ...

One type of violence bred another, implicating both the colonisers and the colonised. The legacy passed from generation to generation, and was transmitted from the colonies to the *métropole*.

Over the past few years, the French (and other former imperialist powers) have 'rediscovered' their colonial past. The study of colonial history is booming. Historians have traced manifold links between the colonial age and the present in policy, demography and culture (see e.g. Blanchard & Bancel 2007). Debate has raged about the appropriate 'use' of the past, and what debts—moral or other—France may owe to those it colonised.[17] Commemorative gestures have proliferated (Aldrich 2005), including erection of a monument to slaves unveiled by President Chirac in Paris in 2007, and plans for new sites, such as a 'Mur des disparus' in Perpignan to commemorate *pieds-noirs* who disappeared in Algeria.[18]

As Stora has pointed out in *La gangrène et l'oubli* and later works, the 'rediscovery' of the colonial past since the early 1990s, and an 'acceleration of memory' since the end of the decade, is linked not only to historiographical developments but also to contemporary problems facing France (Stora 1991; Stora 2004). Has France come to terms with its colonial past—and indeed what would that mean? How does France intend to accommodate those of non-European ancestry who now live in the country? What is France's relationship with its former colonies? What is French identity today, and does that identity need to be recast to take account of the demographic, social and cultural changes wrought by, among other developments, larger-scale migration from the former colonies?

It would be simplistic to link colonial-era violence in a distinctively causal manner with civil unrest that has occasionally exploded into violence in France in the early 2000s, though theories of collective memory or trauma might provide insights into some connections. The

17 Among a growing stack of works, see Blanchard, Bancel & Lemaire 2005, Liauzu & Manceron 2006, Bertrand 2006 and Lefeuvre 2006.

18 A long-standing project to construct a Mémorial National de l'Outre-Mer in Marseille—part monument, part museum—was seemingly abandoned in 2007, largely because of disagreement about its purpose and content, and the role of various interest groups in setting up the institution.

violence in the Paris suburbs in 2005, and that experienced during the Algerian War of 1954–1962, are extremely dissimilar in magnitude, and the situations in which they occurred are hardly comparable. Much contemporary unrest has been linked, perhaps primarily, to issues of unemployment, disenfranchisement and marginalisation—issues of class as much as race, of today's urban problems more than the colonial problems of past years.[19]

However, the inheritance of colonial violence forms a substratum underneath tensions evident in France: the racial perspectives that underpinned colonialist attitudes and that have not disappeared, colonial domination over people whose descendants now live in France, violent campaigns for and against the maintenance of empire, incomplete understanding of the variegated nature of violence in the colonial and anti-colonial record, the abiding resentments and grievances of groups involved in colonialism. The very fact that questions are raised about connections between recent violent disturbances and the conflicts of the colonial period suggests that the former colonised and the former colonisers have not really come to grips with that past. A more concerted attempt to analyse and to work through the history of colonialism and its legacy may provide a way both to resolving conflicts of today, and to redefining French identity and France's national goals for a postcolonial present and future.

References

Ageron CR & Michel M (Eds) (1995). *L'ere des décolonisations*. Paris: Editions Karthala.

Aldrich R (2005). *Vestiges of the colonial empire in France: monuments, museums and colonial memories*. London: Palgrave Macmillan.

Aldrich R (2006a). Colonial past, post-colonial present: history wars French-style. *History Australia*, 3(1): 14.1–14.10.

Aldrich R (2006b). Coming to terms with the colonial past: the French and

---

19 Issues of gender are also present, notably in the debates about the wearing of Islamic head-coverings early in the 2000s, but also in the 2005 riots in the *banlieues*, the main participants in which were young men.

others. *Arts: The Journal of the Sydney University Arts Association*, 28: 91–116.

Aldrich R (Ed) (2007a). *Age of empires.* London: Thames & Hudson.

Aldrich R (2007b). Colonial man. In CE Forth & B Taithe (Eds), *French masculinities: history, culture and politics* (pp123–40). London: Palgrave Macmillan.

Bayly C & Harper T (2008). *Forgotten wars: the end of Britain's Asian empire.* London: Penguin.

Bertrand R (2006). *Mémoires d'empire: la controverse autour du 'fait colonial'.* Paris: Editions du croquant.

Blanchard P & Bancel N (Eds) (2007). *Culture post-coloniale.* Paris: Autrement.

Blanchard P, Bancel N & Lemaire S (2005). *La Fracture coloniale: la société française au prisme de l'héritage colonial.* Paris: La Découverte.

Blévis L, Lafont-Couturier H, Jacomijn Snoep N & Zalc C (Eds) (2008). *1931: Les étrangers au temps de l'exposition coloniale.* Paris: CNHI.

Branche R (2001). *La torture et l'armée pendant la Guerre d'Algérie.* Paris: Gallimard.

Cantier J & Jennings E (Eds) (2004). *L'empire colonial sous Vichy.* Paris: Odile Jacob.

Clayton A (1994). *The wars of French decolonization.* London: Longman.

Cooper F & Stoler AL (Eds) (1997). *Tensions of empire: colonial cultures in a bourgeois world.* Berkeley: University of California Press.

Cottias M (2007). *La question noire: histoire d'une construction coloniale.* Paris: Bayard.

De Cock L, Madeline F, Offenstadt N & Wahnich S (Eds) (2008). *Comment Nicolas Sarkozy écrit l'histoire de France.* Paris: Editions Agone.

Elkins C (2005). *Imperial reckoning: the untold story of Britain's gulag in Kenya.* London: Henry Holt.

Evans M (1997). Rehabilitating the traumatized war veteran: the case of French conscripts from the Algerian War, 1954–1962. In M Evans & K Lunn (Eds), *War and memory in the twentieth century* (pp73–85). Oxford: Berg Publishers.

Fanon F (1963). *The wretched of the earth.* Trans. C Farrington. New York: Grove Weidenfeld.

Franchini P (1993). *Métis*. Paris: J. Bertoin.

Frémeaux J (2006). *Les colonies dans la Grande Guerre: combats et épreuves des peuples d'outre-mer*. Paris: 14–18 Editions.

Gassama M (Ed) (2008). *L'Afrique répond à Sarkozy: contre le discours de Dakar*. Paris: Philippe Rey.

Ginio R (2006). *French colonialism unmasked: the Vichy years in French West Africa*. Lincoln: University of Nebraska Press.

House J & MacMaster N (2006). *Paris 1961: Algerians, state terror, and memory*. Oxford: Oxford University Press.

Jennings E (2001). *Vichy in the tropics: Pétain's national revolution in Madagascar, Germany and Indochina, 1940–1944*. Stanford: Stanford University Press.

Lefeuvre D (2006). *Pour en finir avec la repentence coloniale*. Paris: Flammarion.

Liauzu C (Ed) (2007). *Dictionnaire de la colonisation française*. Paris: Larousse.

Liauzu C & Manceron G (Eds) (2006). *La colonisation, la loi et l'histoire*. Paris: Syllepse.

Loti P (1896). *Le roman d'un spahi*. Paris: Calmann Lévy.

MacMaster N (2002). The torture controversy (1998–2002): towards a 'new history' of the Algerian War? *Modern and contemporary France*, 10(4): 449–60.

Mann G (2006). *Native sons: West African veterans and France in the twentieth century*. Durham, NC: Duke University Press.

Moses AD & Stone D (Eds) (2007). *Colonialism and genocide*. London: Routledge.

Reinhardt CA (2006). *Claims to memory: beyond slavery and emancipation in the French Caribbean*. New York: Berghahn Books.

Rosenberg C (2006). *Policing Paris: the origins of modern immigration control between the wars*. Ithaca, NY: Cornell University Press.

Stora B (1991). *La gangrène et l'oubli: mémoire de la guerre d'Algérie*. Paris: La Découverte.

Stora B (2004). 1999–2003, guerre d'Algérie, les accélérations de la mémoire. In B Stora & M Harbi (Eds), *La Guerre d'Algérie: 1954–2004, la fin de l'amnésie* (pp502–14). Paris: Robert Laffont.

Stovall T (1998). The color line behind the lines: racial violence in France during the Great War. *The American Historical Review*, 103(3): 737–69.

Thénault S (2004). *Une drôle de guerre: les Magistrats dans la Guerre d'Algérie*. Paris: La Découverte.

Thomas M (1998). *The French empire at war.* Manchester: Manchester University Press.

Toth SA (2006). *Beyond* Papillon*: the French overseas penal colonies, 1854–1952*. Lincoln: University of Nebraska Press.

Turquoi JP (2007). *Paris-Alger: couple infernal.* Paris: Grasset & Fasquelle.

Zinoman P (2001). *The colonial Bastille: a history of imprisonment in Vietnam, 1862–1940.* Berkeley: University of California Press.

5

The powerlessness of the powerful: riots as counter-violence

Justine McGill

An occasional and apparently marginal, but increasingly common, form of collective violence in contemporary societies is the riot that erupts in minority communities following the death of a young member or members of that community in connection with police intervention. A spectacular example of this is the series of riots that occurred in November 2005 in what we might roughly call African-French immigrant or 'post-immigrant'[1] communities living in the urban periphery or *banlieues* of France. In Australia, smaller-scale riots with the same trigger occur periodically in Aboriginal communities, ranging from highly urbanised communities like that of Redfern in Sydney to more remote country town and island communities, such as that of Palm Island in the Cape York Peninsula.[2]

In thinking about these riots, I have found myself insistently confronted with two broad sets of questions:

1. How can one interpret the violence of these riots? In particular, how does such violence relate, or fail to relate, to the language of politics and discourses about justice?

2. Why has all the intellectual and governmental work done with the aim of addressing the social problems in communities where

---

1 'Post-immigrant' in the sense that most participants in the riots were the descendents of immigrants from North and Sub-Saharan Africa.

2 Riots erupted in these communities in February 2004 (Redfern) and November 2004 (Palm Island) following the police-related deaths of community members.

these riots occur met with such little success overall? Why do we see problems of injustice linked to postcolonial racism intensifying rather than achieving resolution in modern liberal states like France and Australia? In particular, does this have something to do with the form of the modern state and the nature of its power?

In this chapter, I begin to shape a response to these questions by drawing upon Etienne Balibar's work on extreme violence and counter-violence. This work provides a powerful theoretical model which illuminates the structure of state-based violence and the unregulated explosions of violence it periodically provokes. I do not simply apply this model to give an interpretation of the riots, however. While Balibar's framework helps to make this kind of violence intelligible, the case of the riots simultaneously places a certain pressure on the model. In particular, it leads me to move from Balibar's focus on the way the violence of the state tends to cross over to become the violence of its victims, to an examination of how the *impotence* expressed in these cases of 'counter-violence' mirrors and infects the state, revealing or becoming its own weakness.

Before turning to this philosophical material, I shall begin by briefly explaining first, why I find it plausible and useful to compare the French and Australian cases of rioting, and second, the value of drawing upon a theory which, far from having been designed to deal with either of these particular cases, has its roots in yet another culture: that of ancient Greece. To begin with the Australian and French comparison, in spite of many obvious differences between the circumstances of the riots in these two countries, the stories of the deaths that provoke the riots are strikingly similar. Let me start with a case that is very close to home—a death that took place within easy walking distance of the University of Sydney.

A tale of two riots

> The inquest was a kangaroo court—that means there's no justice. TJ was chased to his death. I don't know when justice is going to happen. I don't know Mr Justice, I really don't know him. This is a cover-up by the police.

I don't know the system, but I know that TJ was murdered and I know there's a big cover-up in the justice system, as usual (Bowie Hickey, quoted in World Socialist Website 2004).

These are the words of Bowie Hickey, a relative of Thomas 'TJ' Hickey, a young Aboriginal man whose death sparked rioting in the Aboriginal community in inner-city Sydney in 2004. The circumstances of TJ's death were that he was riding his bicycle through an area in Sydney known as 'The Block,' when he encountered a police vehicle. He fled and ended up impaling himself on a fence. The police claimed after the event that they had not been chasing him, but were pursuing someone else at the time. Whether or not this is true, it seems fairly clear that it was fear of being caught by the police that led Hickey to his death. Many in the Aboriginal community of the Block certainly saw the police as responsible, and expressed their anger by rioting that night. The nearby railway station was briefly set alight, a car was torched and about 40 police officers were injured in a street battle in which Aboriginal youths threw Molotov cocktails and other objects at the police. These weapons had been stockpiled earlier, indicating that the intention to mount an attack on the police existed before Hickey's death. This incident was not the isolated cause, but rather the final trigger that led to a highly visible explosion of hostility toward the police—hostility that had developed over years of difficult relations between police and the Aboriginal residents of this area.

This story is one that has been played out, with the details altered but the essential pattern clearly recognisable, in a score of other Aboriginal and Torres Strait Islander communities scattered across Australia.

It can be compared with the narrative of events leading up to the outbreak of riots, or violent protests, throughout France in the autumn of 2005. Here, it was a case of three young men of North-African descent fleeing police in a *banlieue* of Paris. The boys hid in the compound of an electricity station, where two of them were electrocuted. Just as in the Australian case, the French police denied that they were chasing the youths, and no police responsibility was ever assumed or imposed for the deaths. Whether or not these particular police were chasing the boys who died that night, again it is clear that conflictual relations with the police were a significant element in the course of events that led the boys to their deaths.

More recently, riots briefly erupted in towns north of Paris (around Villiers-le-Bel) in November 2007. Again the catalyst for the riots was the death of two teenage men, although in this case there was no evidence of a police chase. Rather, the deaths were the outcome of a traffic collision between the boys' moped and a police vehicle, caused primarily by reckless driving on the part of the teenagers. However, the police involved were accused of contributing to the boys' deaths by failing to provide or call for timely assistance. In some respects, the riots that ensued resembled the Redfern riot more closely than the 2005 riots in France. They were short lived—lasting only two nights— but the level of violence was higher than in 2005, with youths using Molotov cocktails and other weapons to injure over 80 police officers. As in Redfern, commentators and members of the mixed immigrant communities in which this rioting occurred pointed to long-standing problems in the relations between youth and police in these areas as the underlying cause of the outbreak.[3]

This brief overview suggests that the pattern of events which leads to riots in Indigenous communities in Australia closely resembles that which has sparked larger scale riots in immigrant communities in France. In both situations we see evidence of troubled relations between youths and the state, represented most notably by the forces of order. In all cases, the police involved reject the claim that they are responsible for the deaths. In a certain sense, this refusal can be justified with reference to the fact that such deaths are not isolated incidents flowing from the misconduct or corruption of particular police. Rather, they are arguably the inevitable consequence, not only of certain patterns of policing, but even more broadly of what Gyanendra Pandey calls 'routine violence'

---

3   For example, Ahmed El Keiy, the news editor of Beur FM, a radio station popular among young French of North African origin, commented that 'The main problem is the relationship between police and young people. The police are seen as enemies. They don't know how to talk to these youths. They also have to produce results—they've been told they have to expel 25,000 illegal immigrants a year, so any Arab or African face they see, they think they're illegals and they do I.D. checks. It's very tense' (quoted in Heneghan 2007).

(Pandey 2006) that is to say, a multitude of mundane interactions which combine to create an atmosphere of oppression which affects all aspects of life for members of these minority communities, and not only their relations with the police. I would suggest that this is why these deaths have the power to provoke such violent reactions from a sector of the affected communities. The tragic loss of particular lives is only the most visible edge of the systematic loss of life opportunities in a social context which is saturated with the effects of racial discrimination. In both France and Australia, the roots of this racism can be traced to the violence and dispossession of colonisation.

Rather than trace the complex historical roots of this violence, or give a sociological account of the socio-economic factors that underlie it, I shall instead attempt a philosophical analysis of the structures of power and powerlessness that can be seen at work in the relationship between the state and the rioters. As indicated earlier, my chief resource in this task will be Balibar's theory of extreme violence and counter-violence. In large part, this model rests on insights drawn from an ancient source, since Balibar's work is inspired by Simone Weil's analysis of the understanding of power and violence to be found in the writings of the ancient Greeks.

To be a little more specific, in what follows I will be relying on Balibar reading Weil reading Homer and Sophocles to explain the structures of power and powerlessness that inform riots in places as far apart as Redfern and Villiers-le-Bel. Now at this point, you may well be wondering if the stresses and indulgences of academic life have sent me a bit mad. To compare Indigenous Australian communities with immigrant communities in France already requires some justification, but then to compare both of them with literary instances of violence in ancient Greece may seem unlikely in the extreme. What is to be gained by such a broad comparative sweep? Aren't these cases of violence and the cultures in which they occur more different from one another than they are similar? Wouldn't there be much more to be gained from a close study of any one case of rioting, in all its cultural specificity?

I do not question the value of close studies, and in particular of ethnographic and sociological work on particular instances and cultures of violence. On the contrary, the kind of analysis I am attempting could not be done without the existence of such work. However, I would argue that the value of comparing these far-flung instances of state-directed violence lies precisely in the fact that they are so different, in many ways. This is because the project of comparison forces us to jettison everything that is culturally and temporally specific. What remains, and even the fact that something does remain, is very striking. It suggests that there are structures of power and powerlessness that cut across cultural difference over space and time, at least within the broad confines of Western civilisation. Especially in the Australian context, this is very important. It means that violence in Indigenous communities cannot be explained simply or even primarily by reference to Indigenous culture. Instead the comparative project forces attention onto the opposite pole of the violent relation, that is, it lead us to consider the structure of the state in its relation to marginalised peoples.

I turn now to Balibar's theory of extreme violence and counter-violence as a starting-point—or limit-point—from which to understand this relation.

Extreme violence and counter-violence

What is extreme violence? Balibar emphasises the heterogeneous nature of the acts and experiences that can be described using this expression: from mass destruction resulting from social or natural causes to strictly individual cases of physical or moral suffering; from the sudden brutality of catastrophic events to forms of violence that are imposed quietly and relentlessly, even invisibly, through the indefinite repetition of social and cultural techniques of domination. As his discussion progresses, however, it emerges that his primary interest is in extreme violence as it is perpetrated by the state, for example the colonial or Nazi state.

To speak of extreme violence implies on the one hand an acknowledgement that violence is a part of human experience inextricably linked to politics, aesthetics, morality, and so on, and on the other, the need to establish thresholds beyond which violence becomes intolerable. In order to suggestively characterise this limit, beyond which violence becomes 'extreme,' Balibar turns to Simone

Weil's commentary on Homer's *Iliad*. This text provides a meditation on violence as annihilation of the possibility of resistance. It identifies three characteristics which, as Balibar puts it 'intertwine to support a tragic vision of the world':

1. 'the reduction of the vanquished to the state of powerless "thing" at the moment of violent death';

2. 'the illusion of total power, which passes back and forth from one camp to the other in war, and causes the participant to lose the opportunity he had to escape his destiny';

3. 'finally, the moral equity that makes one feel the suffering of the enemy as one's own' (Balibar 2004, 4; my translation).

The third element relates to the way extreme violence escapes the control of those who wield it. In the *Iliad*, those who make use of violence are not spared from experiencing its effects. 'For violence so crushes whomever it touches that it appears at last external no less to him who dispenses it than to him who endures it' (Weil 1957, 39).

Before considering how the effects of extreme violence are distributed between the powerful and the powerless, let me focus on the question of what these effects are, or of what it means to reduce a living human being to the state of a thing. Extreme force achieves this end, not only by killing and thereby literally reducing human beings to corpses, but even more effectively, by subjecting them to the constant anticipation of imminent death. As Weil puts it, the

> might which kills outright is an elementary and coarse form of might. How much more varied in its devices; how much more astonishing in its effects is that other which does not kill; or which does not kill yet. It must surely kill, or it will perhaps kill, or else it is only suspended above him whom it may at any moment destroy. This of all procedures turns a man into a stone. (Weil 1957, 25; translation slightly modified)

Those who suffer the effects of this kind of power 'are not men living harder lives than others, not placed lower socially than others, these are another species, a compromise between a man and a corpse' (Weil 1957, 28).

This definition makes it clear that we are not dealing here only with the harsh effects of a system of oppression and inequality which might nevertheless include escape routes in the form of opportunities to improve one's condition. Rather, Weil emphasises the idea that the constant threat of violence creates a situation in which the most basic aspirations become futile.

> That a human being should be a thing is, from the point of view of logic, a contradiction; but when the impossible has become a reality, that contradiction is as a rent in the soul. That thing aspires every moment to become a man, a woman, and never at any moment succeeds (Weil 1957, 29).

This is a description of what happens to people under conditions of war, a state in which the soul is constrained to 'mutilate' its own aspirations. The constant threat of death during wartime makes ordinary human goals futile, and ultimately inconceivable: 'In this way war wipes out every conception of a goal, even all thoughts concerning the goals of war' (Weil 1957, 41). The condition of servitude produces the same deadening effect. Weil describes it in terms of the loss of the ability to communicate: 'In contact with might, both the soldier and the slave suffer the inevitable effect, which is to become either deaf or mute' (Weil 1957, 44).

I would suggest that these effects of extreme violence can also be seen where the constantly renewed and repeated experience of institutionalised racism suppresses the capacity of a community or an individual to set and achieve goals for themselves, and to communicate effectively with others. Consider the words of Alexis Wright, an Australian Aboriginal writer from the Waanyi nation of the Gulf of Carpentaria in far north Australia: 'I have often thought that Indigenous people cannot break through the deafness caused by the walls of the status quo that surround our containment, even if we wanted to, because of the layers in the maze of institutional violence.' Wright explicitly links this form of violence to the reduction of human beings to the status of things, suggesting that in the Australian psyche, Aboriginal people are regarded 'as objects that are owned, while anyone outside is involved in the management of the contained area, e.g. the taxpayer' (Wright 2007, 29). For those trapped within such boundaries, the problem is not merely a matter of having to endure external living conditions that are harder, in material and social terms, than those of other Australians; in addition, it is a question of confronting violence that reaches within to create what Weil calls 'a rent in the soul.'

In the French context, Robert Castel, among others, has interpreted the lack of recognised leadership, structured organisation or precise claims or objectives—in short the lack of any meaningful goals or aspirations—associated with the riots as revealing an 'absence of any perspective on the future' (Castel 2006, 777; my translation). Castel sees the youth of the *banlieue* as occupying a social space that is neither within nor outside French society. It is, like the *banlieue* itself, a margin placed close to the centre.[4] By this, he means that the situation of these youth is at once the direct product of policies pursued by the state, and the overdetermination of its central activities, something which appears as an undesired excess, which needs to be suppressed or overcome. The individuals caught in this dynamic have a certain access to the goods and rights provided and guaranteed by their society, but nevertheless fail to occupy any recognised position within it, and seem unlikely to be able to create one. These are French citizens who share many of the values and aspirations that characterise mainstream French culture, but experience their membership of this society in the mode of impossibility or frustration—that is to say, with an awareness that the concrete realisation of many of the personal possibilities that liberal democratic society is designed to facilitate is barred to them (Castel 2006, 783). In concrete terms, they suffer high rates of failure in the school system, and subsequent difficulties in finding or keeping regular employment, associated with the repeated experience of discrimination. These failures then lead to high rates of delinquency. The result is a negative experience of citizenship, which takes the form of promises that are not kept, rights that cannot be exercised, shared goals that in their case

---

4   See Balibar 2007, 48–49 for a discussion of the significance and connotations of the term *banlieue*.

cannot be accomplished (Castel 2006, 788).[5] In short, the 'revolt of despair' that Castel sees in the riots flows from the conviction of these young people that for them the future is blocked. As Weil would say, the aspiration 'to become a man, a woman,' or to formulate meaningful goals, is wiped out.

Some might object that the situation of young people in the *banlieues*, and corresponding conditions in Aboriginal communities in Australia, is not so unremittingly dire as this account would suggest, and point out that this picture ignores the creative and constructive work done by young people and others within these communities. I do not wish to deny the existence or importance of such hopeful projects, and it must be admitted that the model of tragedy is not apt to draw attention to them. However, the tragic model does bring out another aspect of the lives of at least a sector of the youth in these communities, which is the fact that they are vulnerable, in a way that other young citizens are not, to being reduced to the state of 'things' by the 'routine violence' they endure—or fail to endure. In the more shocking cases, like those that spark off riots, young men are literally reduced to corpses. In more everyday cases, their sense of the future is curtailed by the experience and the expectation of institutional violence. From their perspective, this is a situation of extreme violence. If it is difficult for others to accept this perspective, this is because, as Weil puts it, the 'possibility of so violent a situation is inconceivable when one is outside it, its ends inconceivable when one is involved in it. Therefore no one does anything to bring about its end' (Weil 1957, 41).

This brings me to the second form of violence identified by Balibar: 'counter-violence.' The nature of extreme violence makes it impossible for its victims to 'respond,' in the sense of making a proportionate response, which is to say a political response. Even extreme violence cannot, however, exclude certain modalities of resistance. These

---

5   Cf. Senator Aden Ridgeway's description of an Australian Aboriginal community: '"The Block" has its share of drug, alcohol and dysfunction problems, just like any other community where poverty is rife. What is exceptional here is that we have a community of Aboriginal people living in Australia's largest and wealthiest city. They have life's entire infrastructure at their fingertips—and yet the opportunities of life in the big city are not within their reach.' (Ridgeway 2004)

fundamentally include silence, but may also take the form of 'counter-violence.' The latter is often said to be 'suicidal.' Since the nature of extreme violence is to reduce individuals and groups to powerless 'things,' it is predictable that counter-violence on their part will lead to their own harm or destruction, rather than to the ending of violent relations in favour of more peaceful ones. In this sense, the emergence of counter-violence is compatible with Weil's remark that in situations of extreme violence, no one does anything to bring about its end.

Nevertheless, Balibar's analysis suggests that counter-violence is not properly interpreted as a sign of suicidal impulses. On the contrary, drawing on Spinoza, he sees it as evidence of an incompressible minimum in the human being that even extreme violence cannot abolish or turn against the individual's efforts to live and to think. Here, it is important to note that for Spinoza, individuality itself has a transindividual character, and that it is this which gives individuals the capacity to resist violence. Transindividuality means that the 'being' of individuals consists in the collection of relations that they always already hold with other individuals, who make up part of themselves, just as they participate in the being of others.

In the Greek worldview which informs the theory of extreme violence, transindividuality might be said to take on a particular form in situations of conflict, a form that might be dubbed 'tragic transindividuality.' To explain this concept, let me supplement the analysis of violence that Balibar draws from Weil's reading of Homer with a brief discussion of the Sophoclean tragedy *Antigone*. I would argue that an appreciation of this text is vital to understanding Weil's reading of Homer. *Antigone* was a play Weil passionately loved, and which, in my view, strongly influenced her understanding of the ancient Greek worldview as it appears in Homer. Her own account of the relation is that the Homeric understanding of violence as a limit-case of human relations is then re-elaborated by the tragedy, to which she also adds Christian theology, in relation to the moral identification of the other. However, the framework Weil uses to articulate the structures of power and violence in Homer is arguably more clearly visible in Sophoclean tragedy, and I would suggest that her reading of Homer's epic is one informed by her understanding of tragedy rather than the other way around. (It is also possible that this order of reading has been introduced or at least reinforced by Balibar's exegesis of Weil.) In any case, as we shall see, the story of Antigone perfectly illustrates the second and third elements of tragedy as they emerge in Weil's reading of the *Iliad*, that is the movement of 'the illusion of total power' from one side of the conflict to the other and back again, and the final result that each side comes to experience the suffering of the enemy as its own. The drama of Antigone also lends itself to a suggestive comparison with the experiences of young rioters in Australia and France, bringing us back to the contemporary situations which have provoked this discussion of extreme violence and counter-violence.

Tragic transindividuality: Antigone and the rioters

Antigone is a famous symbol of defiance of state authority, carried out in the name of justice. The form of justice she seeks is one that exceeds and contradicts the laws (or the 'justice system') of the polis, and therefore has an air of the impossible about it. Her struggle with authority begins with a decision to honour her dead brother, Polynices. He is no hero; he has died attacking the forces of Thebes, forces led by another brother who, also dead, has received the honours due to one who died defending his city. By contrast, the body of the traitor, Polynices, has been left unburied, as a warning to others. When Antigone learns that this has been done by decree of Creon, who is her uncle and the new ruler of Thebes, she is incensed with grief and anger. Despite knowing that the published penalty for contravening Creon's order is death, she impulsively tells her horrified sister that she intends to defy the decree by carrying out funeral rites for their brother. Shortly afterwards, when guards find the corpse of Polynices covered with a layer of dust, Antigone proudly, even jubilantly, claims responsibility: 'I say that I did it, and I do not deny it.' This declaration does nothing to achieve an honourable burial for Polynices, but due to the rigidity of Creon's response, it leads with fateful logic to a new series of deaths. Although Creon finds himself confronted, not by the political enemies whose uprising he fears, but by the suffering and pride of his own niece, his anxiety about defending his position of power prevents him from responding with compassion or moderation. Neither pity nor any trace of humour or humility tempers his reaction to his niece's youthful passion and her desperate appeal to an authority higher than his. His only concession is to order that Antigone be buried alive, rather than executed. His moment of doubt about the wisdom of this course of action comes too late, and by the end of the play, the number of corpses has multiplied: Antigone, her fiancé who is also Creon's son, and Creon's wife all lie dead by their own hands.

To come back to the case studies with which I began, there are some obvious parallels between Antigone's story and those of contemporary youths who react with reckless passion and defiance of state-imposed order to the news that a brother has died an early and ignominious death, in the context of long-term hostile relations between their community and the police. Like Antigone, these people are young, and feel they have little to lose. And like Antigone, they may find themselves buried alive within what we call the 'justice system.' There, the loss of freedom and the end of any lingering conventional hopes may turn out to be a devastating price to pay for a jubilant display of defiance. In Australia, the incidence of Aboriginal people dying while in prison or police custody has been high enough to warrant a governmental inquiry.[6]

On the other side, there are also some notable parallels between the behaviour of Creon, and that of contemporary governments faced with youthful rebellion from within communities suffering entrenched disadvantage, the roots of which can be traced back to the repression of colonisation. Both the French and Australian governments have responded to such challenges with displays of force that are arguably out of all proportion to the threat posed by their relatively disorganised, weak and politically unambitious opponents. In Australia, the riot in the Block, which lasted nine hours, led to the creation of a full-time riot squad and a dramatic increase in the number of police officers working

---

6 The Royal Commission of Aboriginal Deaths in Custody found that the clearest and most enduring reason for the high rate of Aboriginal deaths in custody is 'the grossly disproportionate rates at which Aboriginal people are taken into custody, of the order of more than twenty times the rate for non-Aboriginals.' (Royal Commission of Aboriginal Deaths in Custody 1991, preface)

in the area. In France in 2005, the Villepin government responded to the riots that spread across the country by declaring a state of emergency, relying on a law passed in 1955 which was designed to curtail support for the nascent Algerian war of liberation. Since the end of that war, the law had been used only once before, to suppress an uprising in New Caledonia by the Indigenous movement for independence. In 2005, it allowed a large number of arrests, summary hearings and court convictions to take place, but it also generated considerable internal criticism and resistance on the part of mayors of all parties who considered its use inappropriate, especially given that these riots involved almost no attacks upon persons.

As in the story of Antigone, the level of apparent insecurity demonstrated by dramatic responses from government is flattering to the egos of the young rebels, and means that the effects of their acts is magnified, providing dramatic scope for media coverage. The hyperbolic demonstration of the coercive resources of state power encourages an interpretation of the violence of the riots as a direct and serious threat to state authority, and a challenge to the principle of the state's monopoly on the legitimate use of force, as if the young rioters were literally at war with the state. Balibar has observed that 'this is a dangerous game, prone on the one hand to ridicule, on the other to slipping dangerously out of its instigators' control ...' (Balibar 2007, 49–50) We might add that in this respect, the state's tactics closely resemble those of the young people whom it recognises as its enemies. On both sides we see impulsive and dramatically exaggerated self-affirmation, and sense an undercurrent of fear and uncertainty.

This identity of opposites is the basic structure of tragedy, and more generally of the ancient Greek understanding of conflict. According to Nicole Loraux, the Greek taste for symmetry leads to a tendency to equalise the two parties to a conflict, 'to the point of rendering them interchangeable in their being and their speech' (Loraux 1997, 104; my translation). It is typical of the Greek language to repeat the same word to describe two antagonistic forces, 'as if, in the heart of the division, there were only one possible language' and in the two camps 'the same process at work, only redoubled (unless it is quite simply split)' (Loraux

1997, 105). In this singular language of violence and split identity, the terms 'power' and 'powerlessness' tend to shade into one another and make sudden reversals of reference.

It may seem strange to suggest that the distribution of power and powerlessness between government and governed is one that is unstable and reversible, especially if this hypothesis is to be extended from its ancient origins to the relations between modern liberal governments and some of the most dispossessed, but also intensely governed of their subjects. Whilst there are limits to the application of this analysis, it appears that at least in moments of flagrant confrontation, when the tensions created by less visible, continuous, repetitive forms of violence linked to institutional racism break out in the form of rioting and dramatically repressive reactions to it, we do witness two parties that, like the antagonists in Greek tragedy, tend to become interchangeable in their being and in their speech.

Balibar makes use of the Greek idea that in situations of extreme violence, the one who wields violence and the one who suffers it are ultimately merely two parts of a single 'tragic transindividual', to explain how victims can become contaminated by the violence that is inflicted upon them, for example in the case of the Sonderkommando, the Jews who assisted the Nazis in the concentration camps. The example of riots in marginalised communities leads me to lay emphasis instead on the opposite direction of identification between the state and those who suffer and resist its authority. Rather than focus on the way the violence of the state crosses over to become the violence of its victims, I am interested in how the *impotence* expressed in 'counter-violence' mirrors and infects the state, revealing or becoming its own weakness. Balibar describes counter-violence as a form of resistance which takes place 'at the limit of powerlessness and the illusion of total power' (Balibar 2004, 7), and which redoubles the play of this illusion. In my interpretation, this means that counter-violence reflects or makes visible the illusory quality of the claim to total power which is projected in the violent actions of the state.

If the contemporary violence of the riots in France and Australia (and similar outbreaks of violence in many other countries) is interpreted as 'counter-violence', provoked by the extreme violence of the state, this implies that the violence of the rioters might be said to illuminate not so much their own powerlessness, which is constantly reinforced and requires no illumination, but rather the impotence of the state. This is to say that these riots highlight the failure and apparent inability of the state to take effective responsibility for addressing the social problems and the legacy of historical injustice that provide the background conditions for the periodic eruption of such 'counter-violence.' The momentary illusion of total power that is created in the spontaneous outbreak of violence holds up a mirror to the illusory sense of total power created by systems of social control (and authoritative theoretical discourses).

This helps to explain why governments in both France and Australia have responded to riots on the part of visibly powerless youths with exaggerated displays of quasi-military strength. They are responding, not to a minor threat of physical damage, but to a highly potent threat of symbolic damage: the threat of having the state's own impotence exposed. To claim that the state is impotent is not, of course, to imply that it lacks force. Like the rioters, the state certainly has force at its disposal, and on a much greater scale. This greater magnitude of force, however, cannot mask the fact that, also like the rioters, the state lacks the positive power to create the social and political conditions for justice and flourishing human lives. It is this impotence that is exposed in the highly visible exchange of violence that occurs between rioters and the state.

Conclusion

Where to from here? Clearly an impotent and violent state is undesirable, and not only because it exists in a condition of 'tragic transindividuality' which binds it inexorably to impotent and violent marginalised communities within its borders. And yet, from within this perspective on violence, even the conception of a way forward to a state which would be powerful in a positive, socially just and effective sense seems impossible. Nothing, it seems, can be done to bring about the end of relations of violence. As Weil puts it, 'The man who is faced with an enemy cannot lay down his arms. The mind should be able to contrive an issue; but it has lost all capacity for contriving anything in that direction. It is completely occupied with doing itself violence' (Weil 1957, 41–42).

This is the case, I would suggest, so long as each pole of this transindividuality remains focused on combating and controlling the force which threatens it, and fails to recognise the intertwined, interdependent nature of the identity that binds it to its opposite. In particular, the state will not overcome its own impotence in this domain so long as it reacts to violence from the marginalised with attempts to assert total control, whether this is via the crude exercise of armed force or the more nuanced coercion of social control mechanisms. While it is the impotence of the other that is the focus of efforts to manage or ameliorate the situation, change in the basic structure which keeps the two parties locked in a relation of violence cannot occur. This analysis suggests that the way out of this tragic bind would be for the state, or its representatives and agents, including the intellectuals who think on its behalf, to shift attention from the problems, failures and powerlessness of marginalised communities to the question of what underlies the interlinked and equally enduring impotence of the state. To do this would mean turning to the marginalised, not as objects to be studied and controlled, or problems to be solved, but as interlocutors in an investigation of the state's own failures. For it is more than likely that members of marginalised communities are in the one of the best positions to observe and gain insight into the reasons for what I have called the impotence of the state. This implies that for the state to recognise and begin to investigate and address its own impotence in relation to the social problems within its jurisdiction would be the turning point which might allow a truly political response to the violence of young rioters, here in Australia, in France, or in any state which exhibits a relation of tragic transindividuality with the most marginalised of its citizens.

At the outset of this paper, I posed two sets of questions. In response to the first problem of how to interpret the violence of the riots and their relationship to the language of politics, Balibar's theory of extreme violence and counter-violence supports a reading of this violence as a form of resistance that emerges where political means are unavailable due to the level of state-sanctioned violence that shapes the social environment in which the riots occur. Such 'counter-violence' is not political as such, but it operates to expose the impact and failure of political processes: we might say that it emerges out of the political, or is founded in the political.

The second set of questions concerned a particular failure of politics in asking why, in spite of so much scholarly and governmental work aimed at resolving the problems flowing from postcolonial racism, we have not seen more progress in this area. On this point, we may say that a tragic vision of the riots suggests that this failure is not circumstantial. Rather, it would be linked to the very identity of the state, insofar as this depends on an illusion of total power of which the inevitable underside is a destructive form of powerlessness. This perspective suggests that if the powerlessness of the powerful is to be overcome, the first thing which must be sacrificed is this illusion of total power. Recognition and investigation of the *impotence* of the state would be the condition for the emergence of a less violent future, both for the liberal state and the marginalised youth who oppose and mirror it.

References

Balibar E (2004). Violence et civilité. Sur les limites de l'anthropologie politique. In A Gomez-Muller (Ed), *La question de l'humain entre l'éthique et l'anthropologie*. Paris: L'Harmattan.

Balibar E (2007). Uprisings in the *banlieues*. *Constellations*, 14 (1): 47–71.

Castel R (2006). La discrimination négative: le déficit de citoyenneté des jeunes de banlieue. *Annales HSS*, 4: 777–808.

Heneghan T (2007). Why we don't call them 'Muslim riots' in Paris suburbs. Filed November 29 [Online]. Available: blogs.reuters.com/faithworld/2007/11/29/why-we-dont-call-them-muslim-riots-in-paris-suburbs/ [Accessed 21 December 2007].

Loraux N (1997). *La cité divisée: l'oubli dans la mémoire d'Athènes*. Paris: Payot & Rivages.

Pandey G (2006). *Routine violence: nations, fragments, histories.* Stanford, California: Stanford University Press.

Ridgeway A (2004). The underlying causes of the Redfern riots run throughout Australia *The Australian*, 18 February.

Royal Commission of Aboriginal Deaths in Custody (1991). National Report Vol I [Online]. Available: www.austlii.edu.au/au/other/IndigLRes/rciadic/national/vol1/ [Accessed 21 August 2007].

Sophocles (1947). *The Theban plays: King Oedipus, Oedipus at Colonus, Antigone.* Trans. EF Watling, Harmondsworth, Middlesex: Penguin.

Weil S (1957). The 'Iliad', poem of might. In E Chase Geissbuhler (Ed & Trans). *Intimations of Christianity among the Ancient Greeks* (pp24–55). London: Routledge & Kegan Paul.

World Socialist Website (2004). There's 67 percent poor people—we need our own government. July 28 [Online]. Available: www.wsws.org/articles/2004/jul2004/tjh2-j28.shtml [Accessed 21 December 2007].

Wright A (2007). Trapped in a cycle of fear. *Sydney Morning Herald*, 30 June–1 July: 28–29.

7

Violence, identity and the postcolonial French state

Elizabeth Rechniewski

For the last 20 years, the issue of violence in the *banlieues*—the suburbs of extensive housing-estates (*cités*) mainly inhabited by populations of recent immigrant origin, including from France's former colonies in Africa—has been a constant topic of newspaper headlines and political point-scoring, with academic and media attention paid in particular to rates of crime and delinquency and violent forms of anti-social behaviour on the streets. More recently, however, it is violence against women in the *banlieues* that has increasingly occupied the front pages of newspapers. Two high-profile cases drew attention to this phenomenon during 2002. The first was revealed by the publication of *Dans l'enfer des tournantes* [In the hell of gang-rape] by Samira Bellil (Bellil 2002), in which she recounted her life as a girl growing up under the 'loi des cités'. Gang-raped more than once, the first time at the age of 13, but intimidated by the 'loi du silence' from speaking out, seen only as a sexual object by the young men and shunned by family and some friends, she took ten years to recover from this trauma and to write the book which she hoped would encourage other women to recount such experiences. The second case was that of Sohane Benziane, 17, burnt alive by a Muslim gang leader in the *cité Balzac*. These and other cases awoke public opinion to the situation of some young women in the *banlieues* (the question of how representative such incidents are remains a matter of contention), as the cases became *causes célèbres* and were covered, some might say sensationalised, in the media. These incidents incited some women from the *banlieues* to capitalise on the awakening public opinion, notably Fadela Amara, principal animator of the campaign that became the movement *Ni putes ni soumises* (Neither whores nor submissive). Founded in 2002, it campaigns against violence and other forms of discrimination and exclusion exercised against women, particularly in the *cités*.

It was a rare movement of women in the *cités*: until that point there seemed to have been little presence of women in the increasingly heated debate over the young generations growing up in the *banlieues* that was taking place in the late 1980s–90s. Occasionally it would be stated that— in contrast to young men of immigrant origin—the young women were doing rather well. They studied at school because they saw education as a way of escaping from rather constricted roles at home; they were far less likely than young men to be involved in gangs, delinquency and crime and so did not pose a problem to the authorities. But here was a grassroots organisation of women from the suburbs arguing that the incidents that made the headlines were not terrible exceptions but the extreme expression of generalised oppression and even violence against women.

The movement points to a paradox: it would be easy to suppose that young women from cultures that traditionally imposed strict religious, cultural and social constraints on their behaviour, would have moved over the last 50 years of the presence of migrants in France from a situation of confinement and surveillance within the domestic sphere, towards greater exercise of personal and social freedom; and that through education and the impact of French secular values, such women would gradually have attained greater independence, visibility, and autonomy. In short, that they would have moved out of the private sphere into the public, urban spaces of work and sociability. And yet there is evidence that the situation of the women and girls born into ex-immigrant families in the *cités* has actually deteriorated over the last 15 or so years; such at least is the thesis of Fadela Amara, herself born and brought up in the *banlieues*, in the suburbs of Clermont-Ferrand, one of ten children of illiterate parents born in Algeria. She acquired a political education through her association with movements such as the *Marche des beurs* (1983); the *Maisons des potes* of which she was president from 2000—a network of youth centres that was the outcome of an earlier attempt by the young inhabitants of the *banlieues* to demand rights and recognition; and above all *SOS racisme* since 1986.

In her book of the same title, Amara set out the analysis that inspired much of the positioning of *Ni putes ni soumises* under her leadership. Particularly interesting are her arguments that the situation in the 1990s actually worsened for women, and the explanations she offers, citing socio-economic, sexual and cultural factors, and the role of the state. The long-running economic crisis with accompanying unemployment, affects, in particular, adult and young unskilled workers and therefore the first and second generation of immigrants. The resulting alienation and powerlessness have led to a breakdown, she argues, in generational authority. Fathers in immigrant families who are unemployed tend to lose their authority over their children, particularly over their sons. The position of head of the family is then occupied by the eldest sons who, although they may not be able to find legal employment, can provide for the family through the parallel economy. With this increased authority in the home they seek to exercise their control over women, repository of their 'honour'; and to prove their authority amongst their peers by performing violent sexual acts against those women who do not conform to the code of 'modesty' demanded of them. This situation is compounded by what Amara describes as 'sexual misery': the lack of sex education; the association of the sexual act only with pornographic videos; the pressure of male peers who scorn and mock romantic liaisons and consider the proof of masculinity to lie in brutal sexual encounters (Amara 2003, 51–55).

Amara points also to the influence of the rapid rise of Islamic fundamentalism, *l'islam des caves* [islam of the cellars], in the years 1990–95. But significantly, she argues that the influence of the imams was fostered by the state itself: radical imams were recognised, even welcomed as privileged intermediaries in the 1990s by local authorities, thus displacing the representatives of secular associations and earlier militants (Amara 2003, 74–75). Authorities—and some parents—no doubt thought that the moral influence of these imams on the young men could only be for the good. Their radical interpretation of Islam was, however, centrally based on the question of the relationship between the sexes and the subordination of women. They offered young men a morality, but one that involved imposing strict rules on women; they offered the young men an identity, but one that involved exercising control and authority over women as an essential feature of Islamic faith (again, one might argue, the only sphere where power actually lay with these men).

In the last 25 years, the *cités* have been increasingly abandoned by the state, with the withdrawal of educators, youth workers and public services under the pressure of cost-cutting and neoliberal reforms.[1] Further ghettoisation has occurred because of the housing policies of successive governments and local councils who have refused to apply social *mixité* in the attribution of apartments. Amara adopts deliberately the term 'ghetto' to describe this concentration of poverty (Amara 2003, 67). Little financial or organisational support has been provided for local neighbourhood associations. All these factors have led to what she describes as 'la désertification culturelle et sociale' [the creation of a cultural and social wasteland] (Amara 2003, 64).

The movement seeks to represent women of all faiths and ethnic origins who find themselves trapped by poverty and the ghettoisation of the *cités*. The program of *Ni putes ni soumises* demands the application of the 'values of the Republic', which they define as liberty, equality, *mixité* and *laïcité*. *Mixité* (the free association of the sexes) and *laïcité* (secularism) are 'the sine qua non of the equality of the sexes', states their website: the segregation of men and women leads to ignorance of one another and inevitable inequality; *laïcité* is the guarantor of the 'common space'.[2] They raise issues that concern women in particular: *les tournantes*—gang rape; pressure to wear the hijab, to drop out of school

---

1 This situation was extensively analysed by Bourdieu as early as 1992 (Bourdieu 1992).

2 Citing Ferry's School laws, the law separating Church and State of 1905, and the preambles to the constitutions of 1946 and 1958, the website declares that laïcité is the 'pierre angulaire de notre pacte républicain, la laïcité est le garant de la cohésion sociale et de l'égalité de toutes et de tous devant la loi'.

or further education, to marry early and/or accept arranged marriage. They are strongly in favour of the law banning the wearing of ostensible religious signs at school. They reject the *droit à la différence* [the right to be different] which too easily becomes *la différence des droits* [difference of rights].

Their Appeal and their manifesto pose questions of citizenship, including the importance of civic education and of *la démocratie à proximité* [local democracy]. Taking up issues first raised by Henri Lefebvre 40 years ago, relating to the unequal distribution of the 'right to the city', which he defined as the citizen's right to use, enjoy freely, work in, the city (Lefebvre 1968), they demand the access of women to the public sphere and their freedom of movement. They affirm that women in the *cités* are *citoyens de seconde zone*—second-class citizens—who live in *un état de soumission*—a state of submission. The movement raises more general issues of urban planning such as the need to improve the access between periphery and centre and to provide places of sociability in the *banlieues* (Amara 2003, 138). It is the responsibility of the state and state institutions to provide these services, they argue, and to further and protect women's rights in accordance with the values of equality enshrined in the Republic.

Ni putes ni soumises now has 60 local organisations in France, 60,000 members and sister organisations in other countries, such as Belgium and Spain. Amara has not only become a media personality but her advice and the collaboration of the movement has been widely sought by government and advisory bodies. In 2007 she was appointed by the new president Nicolas Sarkozy to the position of Secretary of State responsible for urban planning[3] under the authority of the minister Christine Boutin.[4] This is a particularly interesting tandem: it would be hard to imagine two women of more divergent background, formation,

---

3 Sarkozy's 'politique de l'ouverture' [policy of openness] has seen socialists and independents included in his cabinet.

4 After a career as a journalist, Christine Boutin rose steadily through the political ranks of the UDF, then the UMP and became political advisor to Nicolas Sarkozy in late 2006. A devout Catholic, she is a social conservative on issues such as abortion, the morning-after pill, gay marriage and adoption.

and attitudes and the tension between the two has already become apparent in disagreements over the recently announced *Plan-banlieue*.[5]

From its inception, *Ni putes ni soumises* was accused by some in the *banlieues* communities of playing into the hands of racists, by stigmatising the young men of immigrant background (Guénif & Macé 2004) and by painting the *cités* in the direst colours. As the marchers travelled through France in 2003, they organised meetings at each stop where they encouraged women to come forward and discuss their situation; and many women did so, and joined the march for a while, or joined it for the final march through Paris, some 30,000 strong, to deliver their petition to the government. But the marchers would also frequently be met with hostility from the audience for attracting negative publicity about the *banlieues*, areas which had experienced much negative media coverage over the years. The most virulent criticism of Amara and of *Ni putes ni soumises* has come from a rival movement: *Mouvement des Indigènes de la République* (MIR). Indeed the founder, Houria Bouteldja, in a television program on 21 June 2007, described the nomination of Fadela Amara to the government as *une promotion à l'islamophobie et au racisme* [a move designed to encourage islamophobia and racism]. Launched with the Appeal of 2005, provoked in part by the law banning religious symbols at school, in part as a critical response to *Ni putes ni soumises*, this movement has in its turn provoked much controversy, which has cut across traditional political fault lines.

The deliberate adoption of the term *indigènes* [natives] reveals the basis of their perspective and analysis: the problems from which the *banlieues* suffer are mainly the result of the 'colonial continuum'. In other words, the present can be understood as the survival of the past, in particular of the representations of these populations in terms of prejudices inherited from colonial mentalities and practices. *La France a été un état colonial, La France reste un état colonial* [France has been a colonial state', 'France remains a colonial state] declares their first Appeal. *Les Indigènes* make an immediate and direct connection not only to past oppression but also to contemporary political issues, in particular to Palestine, and the war in Iraq and in Afghanistan, which

---

5 Announced by Nicolas Sarkozy on 8 February 2008.

are seen as expressions of a continuing mindset and policies of neo-colonialism.

The terms liberty and equality are often used by MIR only in a critical context or with implied inverted commas: these *principes abstraits* ('abstract principles') obscure the reality of oppression. Since *La République de l'égalité* is a myth, to appeal for protection to republican values would be to share in an illusion; rejection and discrimination are systemic and structural, are an integral part of the institutions of the nation.[6] *La laïcité* is dismissed as a tool of oppression and exclusion. Unlike *Ni putes ni soumises*, *Les Indigènes* are vehemently opposed to the law banning the veil. They reverse the arguments of *Ni putes ni soumises*: it is the state that oppresses women (specifically Muslim women) by forcing them to uncover their heads. The question of women, though, is less central to their platform, and the emancipation of women and feminism may be suspect, Western, neo-imperial ideas which turn women against their own culture and community, and against their men. They do use the term 'feminist' in certain contexts: Houria Bouteldja founded the feminist movement *Les Blédardes* (bled is the word for the North African 'bush'), now dissolved and replaced by the *Collectif des féministes pour l'égalité*.[7] However both the Collective and *Les Indigènes* are suspicious of the attention given by *Ni putes ni soumises* to violence against women in the *banlieues*, arguing that such violence is no more typical of the *banlieues* than of other places. The May 2006 issue of the Collective's broadsheet *Inch'Allah l'Egalité!* includes a scathing denunciation of *Ni putes ni soumises*, accused of being the ideological mouthpiece of a ruling class panicked by a range of 'anti-colonial' demands and protests (Collectif des féministes pour l'égalité 2006, 3).

The first *Appel des Indigènes* called for a conference to foster 'the struggle of all the oppressed and exploited [populations] for a truly

---

6 'dans les organisations, les procédures d'embauche, l'organisation des concours, les mécanismes d'orientations, les implicites des attributions de logement' ('Qui sommes-nous', article 5). Their Appeal of January 2005, and the clarifying text 'Qui sommes-nous?' can be found on their website: www.indigenes-republique.org. [Accessed 18 October 2007].

7 The French feminist Christine Delphy was the first president of the Collective.

egalitarian and universal social democracy'[8] and defined itself as standing alongside other social movements that are working towards equality. In the text on their website, *Qui sommes nous?*, however, their call is more specifically for 'the end to the unequal treatment of those people who originate from colonisation'.[9] Existing political parties and trade unions have failed to represent the interests of these populations, hence they argue the need for an autonomous movement, to construct alliances on a more equal footing. Their interventions on political and social issues will be decided on a case by case basis, according to whether they concern *l'oppression particulière des indigènes* [the specific oppression of 'natives'].

As is the case for *Ni putes ni soumises*, the movement's leaders have gained considerable media attention, particularly Houria Bouteldja who has appeared on many television programs (Giesbert's *Cultures et dépendances*; *Ce soir ou jamais!*) as a representative of what is widely presented as being a radical, even extremist position. She has in turn been attacked by left-leaning journals such as *Marianne* for offering her own brand of racism. The controversial inclusion of the issue of Palestine (with some positive references to Hamas) in the movement's platform adds a touch of sulphur. There seems as yet to be little risk of the movement being 'recuperated' by mainstream power structures or political parties.

Axes of comparison

In order to better understand these two movements, this chapter will examine them as actors in the French political 'field', struggling for legitimacy, in the context of the decline of the traditional parties of protest, and in particular the French Communist party, to represent the populations living in the *banlieues*. Moreover these movements offer a way of re-examining three problematic concepts: identity, violence and the state, through considering the limitations of self-identification and

---

8 'un combat commun de tous les opprimés et exploités pour une démocratie sociale véritablement égalitaire et universelle' (Appeal of January 2005).

9 'la fin du traitement exceptionnel des personnes issues de la colonisation' ('Qui sommes-nous?').

identity politics; the types of violence, and the forms we are perhaps failing to recognise; and the role attributed to the state and to the republic by these two protest movements.

Alain Touraine, Ronald Inglehart and other sociologists identified a number of distinguishing characteristics of the 'New Social Movements' (NSMs) which emerged in the 1970s in the context of disillusionment with traditional political parties and solutions and the failure of May 1968. NSMs were considered to differ from earlier class-based movements in terms of their 'ideology, origins, structure, style and goals' (Dalton & Kuechler 1990, 10). They campaigned around values and cultural issues; the origin of their discontent lay not (primarily) in economic disadvantage but in the lack of respect and rights accorded to a cultural community: 'that is, cultural understandings, norms and identities rather than material interests and economic distribution' (Williams 2004, 92). *Ni putes ni soumises* and *Mouvement des Indigènes de la République* may be considered to belong to this type of movement through their particular relationship to the political field, their innovative forms of action and protest, and the nature of their demands.

For NSMs, autonomy and independence from traditional organisations such as trade unions and political parties are seen as essential to be taken seriously as authentic movements. However, as Bourdieu would argue, these two movements can only be fully understood through their relation to one another and to the minor and mainstream parties: they occupy antagonistic but complementary positions within the political 'field' (Bourdieu 2000). Both these movements can be seen as positioning themselves to speak with an exclusive voice for the populations of the *banlieues*, in a field left largely vacant by mainstream and alternative political parties.

The two movements adopt and adapt the 'non-institutionalised' forms of action characteristic of NSMs (Snow, Soule & Kriesi 2004, 7): for example the march across France of *Ni putes ni soumises* which organised meetings and gathered support along its route. Both movements use the new technological means of creating virtual communities of protest, which Palczewski terms 'counterpublics' (Palczewski 2001), through websites and online petitions, and are attuned to the power of the media in attracting attention. Indeed Amara has been accused of exploiting violent incidents such as the death of Sohane Benziane for media coverage (Marteau & Tournier 2006). The ability to create 'virtual movements' through the internet raises an additional problem for analysts of social movements in determining the extent of support and degree of commitment of its members.

NSMs are movements that campaign for values and less tangible qualitative demands, rather than for traditional quantitative demands, such as the redistribution of wealth and resources. Often described as undertaking identity politics, NSMs are centrally concerned with the self-identification of its members: they do not identify themselves by class or socio-economic status but by beliefs ('Muslim'); origin ('Welsh nationalist'); gender or sexual orientation ('homosexual'). The very names of our two movements reveal the question of identity to be central. This has implications for the leadership of NSMs: they must be able to demonstrate their legitimacy to lead or speak for the movement, usually by claiming to share the identity assumed. Moreover, the charisma of the leaders becomes particularly important in the era of mass media. Both movements have dynamic, attractive, articulate women leaders, from immigrant background, whose very names and appearance accord them legitimacy to speak for 'their community'[10]. But what is the community that each claims to represent?

Identity

To try to answer this question I will examine the claims each movement makes to identity and self-identification—which in turn determine the problems they point to; who they consider responsible for the problems; and the solutions they propose.

Ni putes ni soumises seeks to recategorise and redefine the inhabitants of the *banlieues* by drawing a distinction between women and men, a distinction which sees women as having different interests, experiences and needs, and by asserting that they are the victims of violence by the men amongst whom they live. In response to this situation, they

---

10   The current president of *Ni putes ni soumises* is Sihem Habchi.

claim their primary identity as citizens of the Republic, and demand state protection of its principles. They assert the principle of the direct relationship of the citizen to the state, wherever she may live, whatever may be her origin, independently of race or religion, because such is the nature of citizenship that the Republic upholds: republican universalism. They assume that all women share in common a secular identity and seek emancipation from constricting roles; they want the same access as men to work and education, to be on an equal social footing, to be able to play similar roles in society. They therefore claim to represent all women whose rights as full citizens are restricted. However, although originating in the *banlieues*, it is not clear how representative they are of all women—and certainly not of the views of men—living there. And their claim to do so is challenged by the *Mouvement des Indigènes de la République*.

Les Indigènes, as their name suggests, define themselves primarily as the descendants of France's colonised; they focus on the injustices perpetrated against the populations from the former colonies by the majority population, by the state and by the Republic. In a provocative interview, Bouteldja referred to *Les Blancs'* as 'souchiens—an ambiguous term which might be understood as stemming from the expression *Français de souche* (used to refer to long-standing French citizens) but which might also be transcribed as *sous-chiens*—under-dogs.[11] Moreover, on their website, a page entitled *Front blanc de soutien* [White support front] suggests that the *Indigènes* do not include 'whites'.

However, in their clarification text of June 2005, *Qui sommes-nous*, they assert: 'The "We" of the Indigènes de la Republique is neither ethnic, nor religious, nor cultural, nor dependent on origin. We define ourselves in opposition to the cultural and ethnic readings of social reality ... Our identity is secular and political'.[12] And later in the same document they add that their name indicates a coming-to-consciousness

---

11 'Il faut rééduquer le reste de la société, la société occidentale. Nous, on les appelle les souchiens (ou sous-chiens?), parce qu'il faut bien leur donner un nom: les Blancs!' Quoted in Jeanpierre (2007).

12 'Le "Nous" des Indigènes de la République n'est ni ethnique, ni religieux, ni culturel, ni à base d'origine. Nous nous construisons en opposition avec les lectures culturalistes et ethnicistes de la réalité sociale. Ce "Nous" s'oppose donc à un "Eux"

not only of those populations stemming from postcolonial immigration but 'by association, those that share their material living conditions and are perceived, treated, constructed as natives'.[13] A similar ambiguity can be seen in the very first lines of their Appeal where, on the one hand, they refer to themselves as people who have 'come from past and present colonies', while on the other, they claim to include all those who, 'whatever may be their real origins', have become 'indigenised'.[14] They seem, therefore, to hover between a social, a cultural and a political definition of their status: Are they 'indigenised' because of their current social position of disadvantage, a position which they might share with other marginalised groups? Or are their specific origins and appearance a defining characteristic? (so poor whites could never share this status). A related question might be: Does the term *indigènes* apply only to those who voluntarily assume this identity? Or is it a label applied from outside, by the movement, on the basis primarily—it would seem—of ethnic origin?

It has been suggested, moreover, that their analysis relies heavily on the Algerian experience. Certainly the examples they give, their frequent reference to themselves as victims of islamophobia, their use of illustrations from French-Algerian history, the origins of the leadership—all suggest a certain bias towards a specifically Maghrebian experience. Very few migrants of Asian background seem to have signed the Appeal or joined the movement, although Indochina was of course also colonised by the French Republic.

---

qui n'est pas non plus ethnique ou culturel ou religieux. Notre identité est séculière et politique.'

13 'L'expression "Indigènes de la République" signifie la prise de conscience que les populations issues de l'immigration postcoloniale, et par contamination, celles qui partagent avec elles leurs conditions de vie matérielle, sont perçues, traitées, construites comme indigènes.'

14 'Discriminés à l'embauche, au logement, à la santé, à l'école et aux loisirs, les personnes issues des colonies, anciennes ou actuelles, et de l'immigration postcoloniale sont les premières victimes de l'exclusion sociale et de la précarisation. Indépendamment de leurs origines effectives, les populations des «quartiers» sont «indigénisées», *reléguées aux marges de la société.*'

A sociological response to the question 'Who are they?' might point to the fact that the leaders of the movement tend to be well educated with qualifications of Bac+3 to 5, i.e. with three to five years of university study. Houria Bouteldja was not born in the *banlieues* but in Algeria in 1974. She came to France to study and has a Bac+5 in *arabe-anglais appliqué au commerce*; Said Bouamama has a Bac+5 in history; Youssef Boussoumah is *professeur d'histoire-géographie.* These advanced levels of education make them untypical of the populations of the *banlieues* whose experience they claim to interpret. Clearly there is an intellectual, even a professional component to their ideology: they have access to the knowledge, books, histories, afforded by their education and their current professions. Youssef Boussoumah appears to recognise their limitations when he states: 'we have never claimed to speak for the urban quarters'.[15]

His comment points to some of the paradoxes implicit in identity politics. If for some 20 years, post 1968, identity politics became the grounds on which movements were founded—claiming recognition of rights for mainly ascribed characteristics such as gender, ethnicity and sexual orientation—the limitations of these identifications have more recently become apparent, both on a practical/political and on a theoretical level. The campaign of *Les Indigènes* for recognition of their subordinate status, and the confusion that seems to exist concerning the basis on which this status should be defined, illustrate this problem. An individual possesses many identities, overlapping and often contradictory. Does the possession of one characteristic (Maghrebian origin for example), allow one to speak for others of the same origin, whatever other sources of difference may exist? What is the relative importance in the life of an individual of a certain identity; and does the nature and importance of that identity not evolve in the course of a lifetime? On a theoretical level, Patchen Markell has called attention to the limitations of calls for recognition of identity as a solution to social injustice: 'the pursuit of recognition involves a "misrecognition" of a different and deeper kind: not the misrecognition of an identity, either

---

15 'nous n'avons jamais eu la prétention de parler au nom des quartiers.' From the interview quoted in Robine 2006.

one's own or someone else's, but the misrecognition of one's own funda-mental situation or circumstances'. The characterisation of the problem as one of failure of recognition may: 'mislead us about the structure of this sort of injustice, and, consequently, about what it would mean to overcome it' (Markell 2003, 4).

Violence

To understand these movements and their demands it is also neces-sary to problematise the concept of violence, in order to avoid accepting unquestioningly the definition adopted by the social actors of what con-stitutes violence against them. In the table below I have attempted to draw an analytical distinction between various types of violence: physi-cal, symbolic and distributive; and the originators of violence: state/society and communal. (I emphasise that these types are often inter-related and inter-dependent in reality).

An additional dimension is the degree to which the forms of violence are 'visible' or 'invisible'.

A few comments on symbolic and distributive violence.

Symbolic violence involves undermining or denigrating culture and identity and includes stereotyping, racism, discriminatory attitudes. Axel Honneth's concepts of moral and evaluative disrespect offer a further gloss on this type of violence (Honneth 2006). For Pierre Bourdieu, the state holds the monopoly of 'legitimate' symbolic violence[16] since, via institutions such as schooling, administration and law, it imposes and reproduces the fundamental categories of social life and fosters the incorporation of norms of thought and behaviour.[17] Through its agents (doctors, public servants, psychiatrists, statisticians) it controls the identification and thus the identity of the members of society: whether, for example, they are to be classified and treated as disabled, members of a caste or ethnic etc. The state's capacity to name and categorise determines whether the individuals concerned can gain

---

16 The state is the 'détenteur du monopole de la violence symbolique légitime' (Bourdieu 1997, 202).

17 Bourdieu (1997, 205): 'un pouvoir inscrit durablement dans le corps des dominés sous la forme de schèmes de perception et de dispositions'.

access to social goods and services and to various kinds of capital, not only economic but social and cultural. The political struggle, writes Bourdieu is a struggle over the principles of vision and division which are current in a given society (Bourdieu 1997, 206–10).

Types of violence	State/society wide	Community
Physical: public/private Domestic Sexual Imprisonment Assault	'Legitimate' monopoly of violence by state via army, police and other agencies	Violent communities, tribes, subcultures, families.
Symbolic Denial of cultural identity Categorisations Stereotyping Disrespect	Imposition of cultural norms, and 'principes de vision et de division' through institutions such as school, admin and law, the role of 'experts' and bureaucrats	Systems of belief represented by priests, and other leaders and sanctioned by charisma or tradition
Distributive Health services Education Welfare Place	Unequal access to state-provided goods and services, 'structural violence'[18]	Unequal access to privately or community-controlled goods and services

Bourdieu extends the notion of symbolic violence to community authority figures and the belief systems they impose: 'le guérisseur, le sorcier, le prêtre, le prophète ...' (Bourdieu & Passeron 1970, 11) [the healer, the sorcerer, the priest, the prophet ...], in other words, to those who exercise traditional authority and charismatic figures.

---

18 A term which was first used in the 1970s and which has commonly been ascribed to Johan Galtung.

The brainwashing operated by the leaders of cults is only the most extreme example of the symbolic violence that charismatic figures can exercise. For their part, traditional male authority figures have typically promoted chauvinistic ideas; in contemporary society their attacks on the reputation of women who wear or do not wear certain clothing can lead to ostracism, exclusion and worse for those criticised. Masculine domination is the purest form of symbolic violence, writes Bourdieu: '[la] forme par excellence de la violence symbolique' (Bourdieu 1997, 204).

Distributive violence refers to the unequal access to or distribution of goods and services, such as food, education and health, between individuals, social categories, and communities, an inequality that often profoundly affects life chances, morbidity and mortality rates (Leclerc et al. 2000). The state plays a key role in modern societies in the distribution of such goods and services. I would argue the need to include under this heading access to public spaces, to transport and the right to use all the spaces and facilities of the city, a right which, Thierry Paquot argues, is 'a common good' (Paquot 2002).

Identifying the diverse forms of violence that may be experienced by individuals and communities within the modern state is a first step in revealing an implicit hierarchy within the ideology of the two movements as to what constitutes violence, and who is responsible for it. *Ni putes ni soumises* campaigns primarily against the incidence of physical, symbolic and distributive violence perpetrated against women in the suburbs, by men from the same locales. Thus they argue that a subculture of physical violence and threats of violence, including at one extreme the burning of Sohane, at the other, confinement and forced marriages, affects the way women, in particular, live their lives. They identify symbolic violence in the denigration, the lack of respect shown towards girls and women by young men in particular: one of their most successful initiatives has been the publication of *Le guide du respect*, a pocket-sized and cheap (1 euro) guide to relationships in general, and between the sexes in particular, which has been very widely distributed. They draw attention to the distributive violence that limits women's access to education, and the restrictions on their use of public spaces and facilities. Women's use of the *cités* has, *Ni putes ni soumises* claims, been constrained over the last 15 years not only because of a subculture of harassment and threats of violence, but because of negative representations of women who go out alone or to certain places, which might be described as symbolic violence to their reputation.

Although they point to the involvement of particular forms of Islam in constricting the choices of women and dictating certain behaviours, their explanation of this violence does not exclusively focus on traditional cultures imported from overseas; rather they blame the culture that has arisen over the last 15 years, that builds on ideas of honour and patriarchy. The state has contributed to the development of this culture by withdrawing from the *banlieues*, and by privileging dialogue with radical imams, who have interpreted Islam in such a way as to give young men a sense of identity based on control over women. Therefore the state also holds the solution to the problems of the *banlieues*: *Ni putes ni soumises* appeals to the state to protect the rights of women, to enforce law and order, to offer protection to women through safe houses, to undertake education campaigns etc.

Les Indigènes, in contrast, focus on the symbolic and distributive violence exercised against 'the indigenised' by the Republic and its administrative arm, the state and its institutions. The Republic, they argue, perpetuates the repressive, discriminatory and exploitative relationship with descendants of the former colonised and enslaved that they sum up in the phrase: *le continuum colonial*. As objects of symbolic violence, they are categorised and stereotyped, and their culture denigrated or undermined by the wider community, including by private institutions and enterprises. They are also the victims of systematic and systemic state discrimination, which is a form of distributive violence, denying them equal access to schooling, housing and other benefits.

They focus hardly at all on physical violence against women in the *banlieues*. Indeed they contest the categorisation that sees women in these areas as the victims of men and in need of protection from them. Rather it is the Republic itself that victimises women who wish to wear the veil. They define the law banning the wearing of the veil as an example of state-sponsored symbolic violence—an attack on the cultural identity of young Muslim women. They cite the historical precedent of the French colonialists who encouraged Muslim women to bare their heads and burn their headscarves in 1958, in Algeria, as an illustration that such a gesture is not emancipation but playing the colonialists' game. (A photograph of this incident is displayed on their website and commented in these terms). This might be described as an example, from the perspective of *Les Indigènes*, of what Gayatri Spivak refers to as 'White men [...] saving brown women from brown men' (Spivak 1988, 296). The law banning religious signs could also be considered a form of distributive violence, since the state excludes girls from school, if they refuse to give up the headscarf.

The state and the Republic

Both movements define themselves very centrally by their relationship to the state and the Republic: in a general sense, their argument and actions are directed at the state, they seek a response from the state; in a specific sense, they seek a redefinition of their categorisation from which many consequences should follow. In the case of *Les Indigènes* they seek recognition of their difference, as a special category whose historical and cultural needs should be addressed; while *Ni putes ni soumises* seek to be defined as universally and inclusively citizens of the Republic. The significance they both attach to the role of the state is certainly a consequence of the importance that the state and the Republic historically acquired in the French nation.

However both movements tend to see the state and the Republic as monolithic, homogeneous entities, which is a form of essentialism and a-historicism. These are in fact, I would suggest, profoundly ambiguous, Janus-faced entities. The Republic has been a force for liberation, its ideals have inspired dominated groups both within France and beyond, to struggle for their rights. The Second Republic abolished slavery. On the other hand the Third Republic oversaw and pursued colonisation, often citing the ideals of the Republic as a justification of the 'duty' of the French to bring rights and enlightenment to foreign people, as the speeches of Jules Ferry demonstrate. And yet colonisation was also opposed by French people who cited the same ideals. While *Ni putes ni soumises* discounts the past and present violence perpetrated by the Republic, *Les Indigènes* have targeted indiscriminately all the manifestations of the Republic, as if they formed a totalitarian block.

The state too is not a monolithic entity: 'the State is an ambiguous reality'; 'the State in every country is to some extent the trace in reality of social conquests' (Bourdieu 1998, 33). The state is both repression and restitution, both the police and the welfare agencies. But the young men in the *banlieues* sometimes target indiscriminately all the figures associated with and employed by the state, not just the police, but employees such as firemen and bus drivers.

Conclusion

Each movement adheres to an implicit hierarchy of the significance to be attached to different kinds of violence and this determines their priorities and the solutions they propose. Social scientists may also be influenced by implicit definitions of what constitutes violence that determine the kind of studies undertaken and the victims identified. The definition of violence is, I would suggest, always problematic and potentially controversial. In prioritising the forms of violence that must be addressed, we cannot avoid making tendentious choices that are often influenced by the political agenda and the media hype of the day. For example, there tends to be an emphasis on the experience of the young men in the *banlieues*, no doubt because they pose a visible 'problem' to the authorities. In such a context, the violence suffered by less visible and more vulnerable groups may be ignored.

Moreover, in seeking to implement solutions to one kind of violence, we may overlook the implications and effects of the solutions on others. Nicolas Sarkozy argued in *La République, les religions, l'espérance* (Sarkozy, Collin & Verdin 2004) that it may be necessary to revoke the 1905 Law of Separation of State and Religion, in order to enable the state to fund, hopefully moderate, Islamic mosques that would exert a religious influence over the young men of the *banlieues* and, by providing them with a moral code, reduce violence on the streets. But what if this strategy encourages other forms of violence that stem from this code, against women notably? The search for understanding of and solutions to violence necessitates a balanced and complex approach that takes into account the diverse experiences of all the actors in the *banlieues*.

References

Amara F (2003). *Ni putes ni soumises.* Paris: Editions La Découverte.

Bellil S (2002). *Dans l'enfer des tournantes.* Paris: Folio.

Bourdieu P (1992). *La misère du monde.* Paris: Seuil.

Bourdieu P (1997). *Méditations pascaliennes.* Paris: Seuil.

Bourdieu P (1998). *Acts of resistance.* Oxford: Polity Press.

Bourdieu P (2000). *Propos sur le champ politique.* Lyon: Presses Universitaires de Lyon.

Bourdieu P & Passeron JC (1970). *La reproduction: éléments pour une théorie du système d'enseignement.* Paris: Editions de Minuit.

Collectif des féministes pour l'égalité (2006). *Inch'Allah l'Egalité*, 2(4).

Dalton RJ & Kuechler M (Eds) (1990). *Challenging the political order: new social and political movements in western democracies.* Oxford: Oxford University Press.

Guénif N & Macé E (2004). *Les féministes et le garçon arabe.* Paris: Editions de l'Aube.

Honneth A (2006). *La société du mépris: vers une nouvelle théorie critique.* Trans by O Voirol, P Ruschet & A Dupeyrix. Paris: La Découverte.

Jeanpierre L (2007). Houria Bouteldja, un racisme de moins en moins voilé. *La Gauche républicaine*, 3 July.

Leclerc A, Fassin D, Grandjean H, Kaminski M & Lang T (Eds) (2000). *Les inégalités sociales de santé.* Paris: La Découverte.

Lefebvre H (1968). *Le droit à la ville.* Paris: Anthropos.

Markell P (2003). *Bound by recognition.* Princeton NJ: Princeton University Press.

Marteau S & Tournier P (2006). *Black, blanc, beur … La guerre civile aura-t-elle vraiment lieu?* Paris: Albin Michel.

Palczewski CH (2001). Cyber-movements, new social movements, and counterpublics. In R Asen & DC Brewer (Eds), *Counterpublics and the state* (pp161–86). Albany: State University of New York Press.

Paquot T (2002). L'urbanisme comme bien commun. *Esprit*, 288: 75–86.

Robine J (2006). Les 'indigènes de la République': nation et question postcoloniale. *Hérodote*, 120 [Online]. Available: www.herodote.org/spip.php?article211. [Accessed 7 July 2009].

Sarkozy N, Collin T & Verdin P (2004). *La République, les religions, l'espérance.* Paris: Éditions du Cerf.

Snow DA, Soule SA & Kriesi H (2004). Mapping the terrain. Introduction to *The Blackwell companion to social movements*. Oxford: Blackwell Publishing.

Spivak G (1988). Can the subaltern speak? In C Nelson & L Grossberg (Eds), *Marxism and the interpretation of culture* (pp271–313). Urbana: University of Illinois Press.

Williams R (2004). The cultural contexts of collective action. In *The Blackwell companion to social movements* (pp91–115). Oxford: Blackwell Publishing.

8

Violence and disrespect in the French revolt of November 2005

Emmanuel Renault

In France, the topic of the *banlieues* provokes a lot of prejudices and phantasma, and because of the 'ghettoisation' that is going on and the violence of the interaction between *banlieues* and inner cities, it is very rare that intellectuals, politicians or journalists know what they are talking about when they talk about the *banlieues*. That's one reason why, on this issue, it's important to make one's standpoint explicit from the outset. I personally come from a Parisian *banlieue*, but from a middle-class suburb that is quite different from what we usually call *banlieue*, i.e., poor and disadvantaged parts of satellite suburbs. Nevertheless, I know the *banlieues* we are dealing with from several points of view. First, from my experience as a teacher at the beginning of the 1990s; second from having participated in the political mobilisation that followed the death, at the hands of the police, of two young men in Damary Les Lys in 2002 (Renault 2002), and from having attended and participated, in 2005, in political interventions and discussions during the revolt and its aftermath, in Paris and in Lyon, with organisations close to the MIB (*Mouvement pour l'Immigration et la Banlieue*); third, from having conducted research on the meaning of the claim for 'respect' in some of the high schools of the *banlieues* around Lille, Paris, Lyon and Marseille (Renault 2007a). In brief, I am interested in the situation of the *banlieues* for biographical and political reasons, as well as scholarly ones.

During and after the November 2005 revolt, the debate among sociologists displayed a wide range of political positions, as well as conflict between various methodological claims: the claim of the 'expert' trying to meet the social demand for explanation coming from the government and the media, the claim of detached scientific objectivity, and the claim of a critical sociology making its own social and political commitment explicit (see Cohen & Renault 2008). The fact that the last option is assumed in what follows, is the second reason why I had to start by making my standpoint explicit.

During the revolt of 2005, a lot of journalists and politicians denied that the riots had any political content, arguing that no explicit claim was made, and that the behaviour of the young protesters was either a kind of emotional reaction, or a revenge against police that was orchestrated by drug dealers, or a competition between *cités*.[1] By contrast, various sociologists have tried to make explicit the political content of the riots, arguing either that it was a reaction against social and geographical marginalisation, or against police abuses, or against ethnic or racist discrimination. This conflict of interpretation raises a double problem. The first one is that of the political threshold: are the riots prepolitical, protopolitical, or political? The second problem is that of the interpretation of the political content of collective violence.

In regard to the first problem, it is worth noticing that the denial of the political content of subaltern insurgency is a constant feature of the social judgment of these kinds of insurgencies. Subaltern studies have provided much evidence of this in the context of colonial India, and Gayatri C. Spivak has pointed out that this social denial demonstrates that the definition of the threshold between the political and the prepolitical is in itself a matter of political conflict (Spivak 2000). The French revolt of 2005 gives a good illustration of this denial and of the necessity of tackling the problem of the political threshold in a context other than colonial India.

But if one admits that the political threshold has to be displaced so that the political content of subalterns' insurgency becomes visible, then the problem of the description of this political content emerges. If no political claims are explicitly made, all political ascriptions run the risk

---

1 Editor's note: the *cités* are large public housing developments located in the *banlieues*.

of hermeneutic arbitrariness. One way of reducing this arbitrariness is to seek the political meaning of the revolt in the discourse that has accompanied it, or that has been used just after it by young protesters to justify it. In so far as the issue of 'respect' has been evoked both in the revolt and in its post-justifications, various sociologists have been tempted to identify its political content with a refusal of social disrespect and humiliation. But they have disagreed on the nature of social disrespect, highlighting either the social situation (Mauger 2006; Castel 2007; Beaud & Pialoux 2006; Mucchielli & Le Goaziou 2007), or the problem of relationships with the police (Mohammed & Mucchielli 2007; Jobard 2006), or the conflict between French republicanism and the multicultural situation (Lagrange 2006), or the postcolonial situation (intellectuals supporting the movement *Les Indigenes de la République*).[2]

In order to discuss these two problems, I proceed in three stages. First, I argue that a theory of recognition inspired by Axel Honneth is able both to describe the moral content of violent reactions to social disrespect and to displace the political threshold so that the political dimension of these violent reactions becomes visible. Second, I discuss the various interpretations of the motivations of the protesters. Third, I present social disrespect as the moral context of the revolt.

Denial of recognition and protest action

First, let me say why it seems to me that Honneth's theory of recognition could be useful for our discussion. Sociologists such as Mucchielli and Lagrange have often described lack of recognition as a cause of the revolt, and the revolt has then been described as a struggle for recognition (Mucchielli & Le Goaziou, 2007; Lagrange & Oberti 2006). But these ideas remain vague as long as the notion of recognition and the dynamic of resistance to denial of recognition are not more clearly articulated. In this respect, Honneth's theory offers us a very interesting

---

2 Even if he is not part of this movement, one finds in Castel (2006, 2007) an interesting attempt to recast this interpretation in light of the long-term history of the ways of naturalising social inequalities.

model that is able to take into account the various aspects of social disrespect and the various dynamics of its refusal.

According to Honneth, in all cases of injustice, a denial of recognition is at stake. And since social and political movements are reactions to feelings of social or political injustice, a theory of recognition can be conceived of as a 'normative grammar of social conflicts.' Such a theory works toward different goals. It aims to show that social movements have not only utilitarian motivations, but also moral ones, and that the latter play a primary role in their emergence. This theory asserts that normative incentives are not only found in moral or legal rules, in moral consciousness or practical reason, or in individual or collective deliberation—rather, they are driven by the normative content of specific feelings (Honneth 1995). It is worth noting that in Honneth, the struggle for recognition only has a loose link with what is usually called 'politics of recognition' understood as 'politics of identity.' Struggle for recognition is understood as a reaction against all form of social disrespect and not as a claim oriented toward respect of cultural difference or cultural survival. This notion of recognition does not support a multicultural policy, but it is nevertheless able to interpret ethnic and racist disrespect as particular forms of social disrespect (Renault 2007b).

One is often tempted to refuse to give protest actions (such as riots or other forms of collective violence) any kind of political dimension or moral legitimacy. However, it would be wrong to conclude that a feeling is always irrational when it is not rationally articulated, or that legitimacy depends only on universal rights and social justice, separate from individual motivations and psychological factors. The ethics of recognition can be used to elaborate a normative framework at the very level of motivation for protest actions in order to describe its normative dynamic and its specific claims to validity (Deranty & Renault 2007). It can be used to show how various forms of social denial of recognition can lead individuals to react in various ways and with various means against the social injustice they experience. And it provides a means to describe the continuity between prepolitical and political protest actions (Renault 2004, ch.1) and to disclose the political content of some apparently prepolitical protest actions.

The demand for 'respect' in the French revolt of the *banlieues*, can benefit from such disclosure. There is a lot of sociological evidence that the social disrespect that young habitants of the *banlieues* are constantly facing (unemployment, geographical marginalisation and racism) is experienced as social injustice. Since violence has been consciously justified by the fact of injustice, and since it has been oriented towards what the rioters identified as symbols of social injustice, such as school, police, and buses, it can be said that it has a political content and, in this respect, a kind of legitimacy.

The Honnethian framework also helps to distinguish various recognition claims. In the revolt, violence has at least three meanings. First, violence is an attempt to come out of social invisibility, and to prove through one's deeds one's existence to those who considered that one could be ignored. In this sense, violence is part of a struggle for social visibility. Second, it is an attempt to transform the social conditions of disrespect (disrespect of police and of government). In this sense, violence is part of an agonistic struggle of recognition. But, third, and paradoxically, violence is also an attempt to have the validity of a claim for justice acknowledged. After the death of the two young immigrants, this involved asserting the right to be considered as victims, as well as an attempt to gain recognition as full citizens, having the same rights to legal and social justice as any other French citizens. In this sense, violence is part of a consensual struggle of recognition, or of a struggle for recognition,[3] although it is an ineffectual way to obtain positive recognition, since violence and consensus are antonymic. In a way, this paradox is explained by the historical context of riots in the French *banlieues*: from the 1970s on, immigrants had to fight both against rejection and solicitude, and riots probably appeared as an appropriate way to work simultaneously toward these two ends.

Motivations of revolt

What are the motivations for revolt? According to the protesters, they are extremely diverse. For example, in interviews made by Mucchielli and his team, a young man says, 'all the guys that had rage against

---

3   On the distinction between struggle of and for recognition, see Renault 2007b.

something found a way to express themselves' and other guys were there only for their reputation (Mucchielli & Le Goaziou 2007). But what is important to explain is not so much the various motivations but the fact that so many young men were involved in the revolt and that they benefited from real support, tacit or explicit, from other inhabitants of the *banlieues*. To explain this large mobilisation and support, one must admit the existence of something like a collective experience of injustice that justifies the revolt in the eyes of a large group of the inhabitants.

Here, a first problem is to decide whether or not such a shared social experience is possible. The sociologist Nathalie Kakpo rejects this idea arguing that there are very heterogeneous social trajectories among protesters (Kakpo 2006). But this argument seems quite scholastic and offers no alternative interpretation of the fact that protesters as well as their implicit or explicit supporters gave moral meaning, linked with respect and injustice, to the revolt.

A second challenge is to define the content of this shared experience. Here, as I have noted, three interpretations are possible: explanation by reference to social situation (Beaud & Pialoux 2006; Mauger 2006; Castel 2007; Mucchielli & Le Goaziou 2007), to multicultural situation (Lagrange & Oberti 2006), or to postcolonial situation (Castel 2007). The first interpretation highlights the social conditions of young inhabitants of the *banlieues*: school failure due to a lack of cultural capital, unemployment due to geographical and ethnoracial discrimination, and the centrality of relations with the police due to the withdrawal of the social services and to the criminalisation of the social question. The second interpretation stresses the ethnoracial discrimination, which translates into discrimination at work, police discrimination, and is the origin of the ghettoisation of the *banlieues* (white French only being supposed to be able to escape the *banlieues* because of ethnoracial prejudices). The third interpretation highlights the conflict between official French republicanism and the multicultural reality of French society: according to that interpretation, the feeling of injustice results from the fact that the Muslim religion is not sufficiently taken into consideration and the multicultural claim coming from the *banlieues* is not satisfied. It seems to me that the third explanation is not convincing: in the *banlieues*, the issue of ethnoracial discrimination is framed as denunciation of discrimination and racism, that is, as the claim for equal treatment more than as the claim for a multicultural society. The two other interpretations are significant as long as they are combined with one another (Balibar 2007). It would be absurd to reduce the revolt to a reaction against postcolonial racism, since in Lille's suburbs for example, a lot of protesters (and victims of juridical prosecution) were of Polish origins (Mauger 2006; Castel 2007). And the fact that no riots took place in Marseille is probably explained by the fact that the working-class and 'immigrant' areas are inside the city, so that geographical discrimination does not have the same impact. Conversely, it wouldn't make sense to reduce police or employment discrimination to class discrimination, without taking racism and ethnic prejudices into consideration. It is an analytical mistake to reduce the social problem of the *banlieues* to a mere metamorphosis of the social question, or to reduce it to the mere effect of the postcolonial structure of the French nation-state. Such reductionist approaches also lead to political shortcomings. Both the social and postcolonial analysis must be articulated, for example as the MIB has attempted to do since the end of the 1980s. It seems to me important to notice that the postcolonial reductionism of *Les Indigenes de la République* would have the disastrous consequence of excluding from political attention young prisoners whose parents or grandparents have come from Poland. It is also worth noting that, even more than the MIB, *Les Indigènes de la République* have difficulty recruiting activists in the *banlieues*.

The third problem is to define the structure of this experience of injustice and to explain how it can lead to revolt. The collective experience of injustice can be conceived of as community of experience (Beaud & Pialoux 2006; Castel 2006), or as shared moral experience (Mucchielli & Le Goaziou 2007; Marlière 2006; Lapeyronnie 2006). According to Mauger, Beaud and Pialoux, who adopt a Bourdieusian approach, it is the shared experience of social violence, derived from all forms of symbolic violence and denial of recognition, that introduces violence into the *habitus*, a violence that is therefore always on the verge of exploding. According to Mucchielli, Marlière and Lapeyronie, who adopt the point of view of a sociology of moral experiences, it is the feeling of injustice and humiliation that turns into struggle against injustice when it becomes unbearable. These two explanations seem to me more complementary than in contradiction with each other.

Disrespect in a subaltern context

In order to try to describe social disrespect more precisely as a moral context, one approach is to investigate what young inhabitants of the *banlieues* have in mind when they demand respect. I turn now to the results of my questionnaire and discussions with schoolboys and schoolgirls (Renault 2007a).

In these results and discussions, the meanings given to the term respect are clearly associated with dynamics of refusal of experiences of social disrespect and disrespect is described as a moral wound that justifies violent reactions. This political dimension of the demand for respect and its link with the psychological dimension of negative social experiences seems to be better taken into account by a Honnethian model than by any constructivist Bourdieusian or Foucaldian moral sociology: the core of the meaning of 'respect' is reducible neither to the expression of a 'popular culture', nor to a possibility defined by a contemporary grammar of legitimate claim; nor can it be reduced to a 'moralisation' or 'psychologisation' of politics. Important to note is also that, in this questionnaire, the experience of disrespect is associated not only with singular interactions, but also with general social relations. This macro-social dimension of the experience of disrespect provides a reason for preferring a Honnethian model to interactionist approaches such as that of Goffman—although the institutional part of the theory of recognition remains underdeveloped in Honneth's writings (Renault forthcoming).

In the questionnaire, disrespect is associated with relationships with social hierarchies such as school and police, and also with general structures of class domination (through poverty and class contempt), gender domination and ethnoracial domination, and even with society as a whole. These schematic results speak in favour of a combination of the social and postcolonial approaches, as I have just argued. But this questionnaire also complicates the picture. Schoolchildren sometimes consider that justice is more important than respect. As one of the schoolboys said: 'When you have nothing left but respect, then, it is normal that you demand only respect'. Maybe it is because there is no longer any hope for justice that respect comes to the fore. And sometimes also, schoolchildren say that the discourse of respect is a discourse that journalists have given to protesters rather than their own discourse. Instead of considering this last complication as an objection, I would be tempted to understand this as a characteristic feature of what Spivak defines as subalternity when she asks if the subaltern can speak: because of the failure of legitimate political discourses to tackle their problems, young inhabitants of *banlieues* may have no other way of making political claims about their experiences of injustice than by demanding respect, even if they know that this demand is not taken seriously in the public political sphere.

The language of respect, indeed, cannot be reduced to a language imposed by another social group (journalists) that is taken up in a simply strategic manner, for it clearly appears as a means to make explicit certain problems met in social experience: problems linked with the various forms of social and ethnoracial disrespect the school students constantly talk about in the questionnaire and the related discussions. Attempts to make these negative social experiences explicit and to express the specific claims that arise from them are precisely what explain the original meaning that young inhabitants of the *banlieues* give to the term 'respect'. But they also know that their demand for respect can be interpreted in terms of ordinary meanings of 'respect' (as politeness and moral requirement) and thus, be deprived of all its political meaning (as protestation against social disrespect). In order to struggle against the invisibility, or denial, of this political meaning, they then have no other solution than to stress its agonistic dimension, transforming a *demand* into an *accusation*. In the questionnaire, as well as in many other reports, one can notice a shift from 'respect' as claim ('I want you to respect me') to 'respect' as conflictual issue and justification of violence ('You haven't respected me'). Hence, 'respect' becomes the matter of a struggle *of* recognition that is no longer a struggle *for* recognition: as such, violence can't provide positive recognition.

Typical of subalternity is the situation where one has to use a normative language that one knows to be inappropriate to the goal that is to be achieved, or a situation where one has to use means, such as violence, whose effects one knows to be paradoxical. In such a situation the definition of the political threshold and of the political content of actions and discourses is not only a problem for observers, but also for agents of protest action and producers of claims.

References

Balibar E (2007). Uprisings in the *banlieues. Constellations*, 14(1).

Beaud S & Pialoux M (2006). La 'racaille' et les 'vrais jeunes': critique d'une vision binaire du monde des cités. In C Belaïd, C Autain, S Beaud, P Chemetov & Collectif, *Banlieue, lendemains de révolte* (pp11–28). Regards/La dispute.

Castel R (2006). La discrimination négative. Le déni de citoyenneté des jeunes de banlieue. *Annales HSS*, 4: 777–808.

Castel R (2007). *La discrimination negative: citoyens ou indigènes?* Paris: Seuil, coll. La République des idées.

Cohen D & Renault E (2008). La révolte des banlieues. (Review) *Actuel Marx*, 43: 210–14.

Deranty JP & Renault E (2007). Politicising Honneth's theory of recognition. *Thesis Eleven*, 88(1): 92–111.

Honneth A (1995). *The struggle for recognition: the moral grammar of social conflicts*. Cambridge: Polity Press.

Jobard F (2006). Sociologie politique de la 'racaille.' In Lagrange H & Oberti M (Ed). *Émeutes urbaines et protestations. Une singularité française* (pp59–80) Paris: Les Presses de Science Politique.

Kakpo N (2006). Communauté d'expérience et diversité des trajectoires. In Lagrange H & Oberti M (Ed). *Émeutes urbaines et protestations: une singularité française* (pp81–104).Paris: Les Presses de Science Politique.

Lagrange H (2006). La structure et l'accident. In Lagrange H & Oberti M

(Ed) (2006). *Émeutes urbaines et protestations: une singularité française* (pp105–30). Paris: Les Presses de Science Politique.

Lagrange H & Oberti M (Ed) (2006). *Émeutes urbaines et protestations: une singularité française*. Paris: Les Presses de Science Politique. Collection of essays, no pages.

Lapeyronnie D (2006). Révolte primitive dans les banlieues françaises. *Déviance et société*, 4: 431–48.

Marlière E (2006). Sentiment d'injustice chez les jeunes d'une cité HLM. *Société et jeunesse*, 2: 1–22.

Mauger G (2006). *L'émeute de novembre 2005: une révolte protopolitique*. Bellecombe-en-Bauges: Editions du Croquant, coll. savoir/agir.

Mohammed M & Mucchielli L (2007). La police dans les 'quartiers sensibles': un profond malaise. In L Mucchielli & V Le Goaziou (pp104–25).

Mucchielli L & Le Goaziou V (2007). *Quand les banlieues brûlent*. Paris: La découverte.

Renault E (2002). L'ordre règne à Dammarie-Les-Lys. *Le Passant ordinaire*, 42 [Online]. Available: www.passant-ordinaire.com/revue/42-451.asp. [Accessed 30 March 2010].

Renault E (2004). *L'expérience de l'injustice*. Paris: La découverte.

Renault E (2007a). Le discours du respect. In A Caillé (Ed). *La quête de reconnaissance: regards sociologiques* (pp161–83). Paris: La découverte.

Renault E (2007b). What is the use of the notion of recognition? *Revista de Ciencia Politica*, 27(2): 195–205.

Renault E (forthcoming). Theory of recognition and critique of institutions. In D Petherbridge (Ed), *The critical theory of Axel Honneth*. Leiden: Brill.

Spivak GC (1985). Subaltern studies: deconstructing historiography. *Subaltern Studies*, 4: 197–221. New edition in *In other worlds: essays in cultural politics* (1988). New York: Routledge.

Spivak GC (1999) *A critique of postcolonial reason*. Cambridge Mass.: Harvard University Press

Spivak GC (2000). The new subaltern: a silent interview. In V Chaturvedi (Ed), *Mapping subaltern studies and the postcolonial* (pp324–40).London: Verso.

9

The violence of racialisation: the 2005 riots as event[1]

Didier Fassin

When the urban riots occurred during the autumn of 2005 in France, I had been involved for several months in two research programs. The first one, theoretical, was entitled: 'From the social question to the racial question?' It consisted of international seminars, through which we explored the *racialisation* processes in contemporary societies, especially France. The second research program, named: 'The social meaning of racial discrimination' was empirical. It involved different fieldwork in schools, enterprises and administration, but was mainly focused on the police.

The outburst of the riots had two notable effects on my work. On the one hand, it reversed my theoretical proposition about the dialectics between racial and social issues. When we started our seminar we had to demonstrate, against the reluctance of many colleagues who thought that we were importing these categories from elsewhere (such as, the United States and South Africa—where we had previously done research), that racialisation processes did exist in France as well.[2] It is not merely a coincidence, we argued, that a significant number of the people in France who were segregated in poor housing estates and

---

1 This paper is based on an investigation conducted within a scientific program entitled 'The new frontiers of French society' founded by L'Agence nationale de la recherché.

2 With Eric Fassin at the Ecole Normale Supérieure and the Ecole des Hautes Études en Sciences Sociales. The book that resulted from it is Fassin & Fassin 2006.

excluded from the labour market are Arabs and Blacks. In other words, we asserted that the *question sociale*, as the problem of inequality and disorder has been phrased since the 19th century, is also a racial issue. But after the riots, as we were preparing our book, we suddenly faced the symmetrical situation. The presence and visibility of the children of postcolonial immigration among rioters was so overwhelming and the accusations formulated against them and their families by intellectuals and politicians so overtly racialised and often racist that the vocabulary of race started to impose itself as obvious in the public sphere, and without any further reference to the pauperisation of the French *banlieues*. Now we had to affirm that the *racial* question, as we had named it, was also a *social* issue.

On the other hand, the riots provided empirical evidence supporting my initial hypothesis that confrontation with the police is for the Arab and Black adolescents and youth of the *cités* (housing estates) the most ordinary experience of humiliation and powerlessness. When the 2005 revolt started, while going around at night with the *brigades anti-criminalité* (anti-crime squads), I was witnessing for weeks the provocations and harassment that these adolescents and youth were exposed to and were now responding to, and the occasional repressive interventions, which were disproportionately brutal and uselessly stigmatising in these neighbourhoods.[3] Through interviews with the police, the judiciary and the inhabitants, I tried to reconstitute the genesis of these episodes and the chain that led to these confrontations. During the riots—at least, until the declaration of the state of emergency by the government—I had the opportunity to see these events through the eyes of the police, in real time so to speak, and this confirmed my preliminary findings about the sort of interactions that the police have with the inhabitants of the *banlieues*. Although complex in their determination and diverse in their expression, these interactions were often explicitly racialised and sometimes overtly racist.

What makes an event significant is that it draws a temporal divide distinguishing in the flow of historical time a 'before' and an 'after'.

---

3 Research conducted in the disadvantaged neighbourhoods outside of Paris from April 2005 to June 2007. For a preliminary presentation see Fassin 2006.

It introduces a radical transformation in the way social realities are represented and configured: 'things will never be the same', one often says. But the condition of possibility of this rupture is that what is revealed was already there, although unseen or untold: 'things were waiting to happen', one sometimes hears. From this perspective, the event produces a new *problematisation* of society (see Foucault 1994; Rabinow 2003); in other words, a new way of considering what poses problems, as well as how and why.

If one accepts this definition, then the 2005 riots certainly constitute one of the most important events of the past decades in France, not for the violence which was, in fact, very limited in spite of its spectacular character, but for the process of racialisation that they suddenly made visible. Of course, other events took place in the same period which both facilitated the consciousness of the racialisation phenomenon and brought more complexity to the picture (see Bowen 2007; Thomas 2007): one could refer in particular to the affair of the 'Islamic veil' which led to legislation against external manifestations of religion, to the vote on a law which asserted the 'positive effects' of colonisation and gave rise to a protest from historians, to the celebration of the end of the slave trade for which the choice of the date became quite controversial, and finally to the birth of a black movement with the creation of the CRAN, Representative Council of Black Organisations.

I am interested here in the problematisation of the racial issues in France and am concerned with the 'problems' that it reveals. I will first analyse the emergence of a racial question against the background of colour-blindness or, more precisely, the displacement from denial to recognition and denegation. I will eventually bring empirical findings based on my fieldwork on the police in order to show how the racialisation process occurs in this specific context. I will thus present elements of a genealogy, on the one hand, and of ethnography, on the other. Put in a different manner, I will try to go from the problematisation to the problem itself.

The end of colour-blindness?

Until very recently, France has seen itself and was often seen by others as colour-blind. The French took this absence of racial differentiation for granted, whereas an increasing number of foreign intellectuals and scholars, particularly from the United States, saw in this lack of a race line a type of mystification that was not even working any more as a self-fulfilling prophecy. For the French, colour-blindness was the consequence of a politics of universalism, which has been entrenched in the modernity of the nation since the 1789 Revolution; while for commentators, universalism was a rhetoric used to eschew lucid analysis of racial issues. French social scientists have themselves contributed to the perpetuation of this situation by systematically maintaining in their discourses a confusion between prescription and description: for a long time sociologists, anthropologists and historians avoided speaking of colour line, because of what they considered would be the performative effect of its acknowledgement. It has been repeated in the social sciences—and it is still the most common argument opposed to the revelation of the colour line—that talking about race makes race real, as if it were not already real in the social world where people are discriminated against because of their origin and phenotype. This intellectual self-intimidation was so effective that I myself only dared qualify discrimination as 'racial' in the late 1990s, when the problem was officially recognised as such, and only named people as 'black' in 2005, when a social movement qualified itself with this adjective.

This difficulty of giving race and racial issues an explicit translation in our language is obviously not unique to France. Even in Britain and the United States many underline the risk of the routinisation of such categories. In South Africa, where I have been doing research for seven years, talking and not talking of race, using and not using racial identifications in statistics and referring to Blacks or Africans in public discourses remain highly problematic: the classical paradox being that to fight racial discrimination one needs to use racial instruments, such as ethnic statistics and affirmative action.

However, the French case is somewhat unique for its insistent consensus on colour-blindness. How is it possible to explain this specificity? Of course, one should not see it as essential, that is, cultural in essence, but on the contrary, as entirely historical, that is, cultural as a process. Three historical concepts may be convened here: Republic, Nation and Class. Of course, they are abstract words, often grandiloquent, sometimes empty, but they may still help us to understand this—relative—French singularity.

Firstly, since the 1789 Declaration of Human Rights, the Republican model is founded on equality as one of the three fundamental principles—with liberty and fraternity (see Rosanvallon 1992). It was reasserted in 1848 when it was repeated that the Republic does not make any differentiation within the human family. It was inscribed in the 1958 Constitution, which proclaims no distinction of race, a formulation that was intensely discussed, as it seemed to presuppose the existence of races. This principle of equality should not be considered as merely rhetorical, as one often tends to do, even if it is easy to demonstrate that such 'distinction' existed in relation to slavery during the first half of the 19th century, the colonies over a long period, and even in France during the first half of the 20th century, and hence that equality was not respected and racism was underlying the political treatment of slaves and colonial subjects under the Republican rule. Until now, the principle of equality has had juridical as well as social consequences in French society, such as when, for instance, the law prescribes equal access to health care or to school for all.

Secondly, the Nation has worked as a potent instrument to produce colour-blindness at the very moment when it was defining whiteness (see Noiriel 1991). The colonial subjects, later the immigrant workers, and today the non-European foreigners had, and still have, for their natural destiny, if one may say so, to be culturally, and somewhat organically, assimilated if they want to participate in the national community. This obsession with cultural, and sometimes organic, assimilation, which is less present in Britain for instance, has had juridical consequences, particularly for the administrative process of naturalisation. Naturalisation is much more accessible in France than it is in countries like Germany, where the model of nationhood is much more biological. Through cultural assimilation and administrative naturalisation, otherness is thus incorporated in the national project.

Thirdly, Class has functioned as a remarkable obstacle to the thinking of racial issues (see Beaud & Pialoux 1999). The only visible difference for many French intellectuals has long been the economic one. Race, no more than gender, was an eligible cause of inequality. The influence of Marxist theory and of the Communist party on intellectual life, including the social sciences, is obviously a key factor here. Class has been effective as well in the ideology and the administration of the state: significantly, the only social differentiation in French statistics has always been professional categories, which is a bureaucratic version of class. In the studies of health inequalities for instance, the origin or colour of persons was never analysed; the sole significant difference has always been economic, which was the only one tested (see Fassin 2001). In fact in the 1990s some statisticians started to include nationality and even parents' nationality, previously absent from surveys, but obviously it was only a very distant proxy for race.

This representation of a colour-blind French society succeeded until the 1980s and even the early 1990s, not only for the ideological reasons just mentioned, but also for social reasons. Arabs and Blacks in France were kept at the margins of French society: after decolonisation, families, mainly Algerians, lived in *bidonvilles* (slums) on the outskirts of large cities like Paris and Marseilles, whereas in the context of the need for cheap labour, immigrant workers from Northern and Sub-Saharan Africa resided in *foyers* (collective homes). They were thus invisible to the rest of society. Children, still relatively few in number, were going to special schools and workers were transported back and forth from the collective homes to the factories. For trade unions and leftist parties, the situation was merely analysed in terms of exploitation, and racial issues were all the less evoked, especially since unionists themselves were not exempt of racist attitudes and communists even started to develop nationalist and xenophobic discourses. Moreover, this was a context in which their illegitimacy was constantly recalled, not only by right-wing politicians but also by their supposedly natural allies on the left side. Immigrants themselves were not inclined to protest and, if a few strikes and demonstrations did occur, the majority of African workers and their families more or less interiorised their illegitimacy, as testimonies demonstrate. So for all these complex but convergent reasons, both ideological and practical, on the side of French society as well as on the side of its immigrants, there was little space for naming racial issues and combating racial discriminations.

This situation started to change in the 1980s with the first riots in Vaux-en-Velin (near Lyons) and the social movement known as the *Marche des Beurs* (protest of first- and second-generations immigrants against racism), and even more significantly in the 1990s with the increasing success of the *Front national* (far-right-wing party) especially in local elections and with the official, although timid, recognition of discrimination by the government of Lionel Jospin (of the Socialist party). In the 1980s, France had rediscovered racism. In the 1990s, she invented discrimination (see Fassin 2002). The shift is not merely rhetorical, since it displaces the problem from the individual to the collective, from prejudices to practices, from the question of racist intentions to the issue of systemic discrimination, in other words since it opens the possibility of a new politics of race based not on isolated acts of racism but on social contexts producing discrimination. This evolution has two series of determinants which may be differentiated as structural and circumstantial.

On the one hand, the structural dimension corresponds to the displacement from an immigration of labour to an immigration of settlement, paradoxically fuelled by the increasingly restrictive policies of immigration from 1974 onwards. Afraid of not being able to go back and forth to visit their families as they did until then, many African workers decided to stay and bring wives and often children. This old and new population resided in the large housing estates that were built in the 1960s but, as the economic crisis developed in the 1970s, the installed immigrants had fewer and fewer possibilities of moving away from this housing. Unlike the French working class, who had bought small houses and apartments, precisely because of the discrimination that became more obvious as competition on the job market increased: in the 1990s, among comparable blue-collar workers the unemployment rate for Northern and Sub-Saharan African men was twice that of the

French. Thus not only racial discrimination in the labour market but also in the private housing system, which closed itself to new African families, determined the spatial segregation that led to the large *cités* and their predominantly Black and Arab populations.

Until the late 1990s, however, racial discrimination was not recognised as such in France. The only legitimate discourse among policy-makers, pro-immigrant organisations and even social scientists was that of *intégration* (see Schnapper 1991; Sayad 1999): on the right side of the political and intellectual spectrum, it was considered that immigrants had to make more efforts to integrate themselves; on the left side, it was said that the state and society as a whole were to be held responsible for the difficulties experienced by immigrants to become integrated. But both sides, whatever opposition they had to one another, agreed on the fact that the issue was that of integration, which meant that, in the last instance, it only concerned immigrants and not the host society.

This is precisely what adolescents and youth today disagree on: most of them are French or will become French at the age of 18, most of them were born in France or at least spent all their school years in France. 'We don't have to be integrated, they say. We have been here since we were born or children, we live here, this is our country, why should we still have to integrate ourselves—and to what?' Whereas the parents, as foreigners and immigrants, had accepted a certain level of racial discrimination as the price they had to pay in order to stay, their children, often born in France, not only do not accept racial discrimination but for the first time also name it as such, that is not only as discrimination but also as racial. This includes Blacks from the Caribbean who have been French for many generations. The increased vote for the far right in the 1990s—when in the former 'red belt' of Paris that had been traditionally composed of the Communist working class the National Front became the second party with 30 to 40% of voters— is a symptom of this evolution. Its leader, Jean-Marie Le Pen, perversely maintained the confusion around immigration by calling Moroccans or Algerians those youth who are actually French but remain stigmatised— and racialised—as immigrants.

On the other hand, the more circumstantial dimension of the revelation of racial discrimination is related to two factors. One is the necessity of harmonising French policies with European policies in terms of discrimination and race: France could not remain the exception, regularly criticised or even condemned by European institutions. The other is the increasing mobilisation of the French civil society with, in particular, social scientists making effective alliances with trade unions and non-governmental organisations, thus producing data, reports, and books, but also lobbying among policy-makers, at that time Socialists, under the government of Lionel Jospin. The Geld, French Study Group Against Discrimination was created in 1999. A national Conference for Citizenship and against Discrimination was held in 2000, with three ministers in attendance. A law making it easier for victims of discrimination to sue the perpetrators was passed in 2001.

In this new favourable context however the game was far from being won. Although racial discrimination is now common language in the media, with frequent references to anecdotes, statistics, surveys, trials, resistance to its full recognition remains strong (see Fassin 2007). If we consider the three ideological elements which had been obstacles to acknowledging racial issues in France—Republic, Nation and Class—we see that they now play a more subtle and complex part. 'Republicans', whether right, centre, or even left, whether in the social sciences or in the political arena, minimise discrimination (seen as a too negative vision of France) and reject any racial interpretation of society (in the name of universalistic principles). 'Classists', evidently on the left side, denounce the new consensus against discrimination, which would hide underlying economic inequalities (thus missing its real logic). 'Nationalists', often on the far right, but also on the right and sometimes on the left of the political spectrum, are actually the most open to speaking of race, either with racist intentions (the National Front) or with clientelist views (especially in the Presidential party to get the vote of the minorities). Ideological confusion is then at its peak when language becomes too complex to decipher.

It is in this context that the 2005 riots occurred. The racialisation of the riots may be seen at three distinct levels. Firstly, sociological: the great majority of the adolescents and youth involved, and even more obviously those arrested and condemned, were Arabs and Blacks, a fact that was not unnoticed, as for the first time some started to talk of 'racial riots', this talk emerging from both ends of the political spectrum. However, contrary to the common accusation of *communautarisme*, when interviewed the adolescents and youth always demanded more—and not less—Republic; that is equality. Secondly, ideological: by way of a symmetric paradox, in the intellectual world, it is the so-called Republicans of yesterday who have become the nationalists of today using racialised vocabulary; among others, the director of the weekly *Le Point* talked of the 'failure of the long work of social biology which is required by a felicitous integration' and a member of the Academy of Moral and Political Sciences spoke of a 'proletariat from outside of hardly French populations'. Thirdly, political: the lessons of the riots and their practical consequences, beyond the obvious problem of public order, were drawn by the French president; actually Jacques Chirac interpreted the riots as the result of uncontrolled immigration (which was to be restricted from then on) and of the 'poison of discrimination' (which was to be combated). Of these three dimensions—sociological, ideological, and political—one fact above all should be retained: the link systematically established between immigration issues and race issues. But let us go back to the events.

The discovery of racial policing?

When it became evident at the end of October 2005 that the burning of cars in the Northern *banlieues* had turned out to be a symptom of unprecedented riots, which had rapidly spread to the whole country, the interpretations multiplied. On the one hand, in order to account for the spontaneous explosion of violence, the Minister of the Interior, Nicolas Sarkozy, preferred the much more politically profitable explanation of local manipulations, alternatively by radical Muslim networks or by drug dealing mafias—both soon contradicted by the investigations of his own intelligence services (which did not prevent him, as well as other political commentators, from continuing to use this line). On the other hand, media experts and social scientists suggested deeper causes, either on the right side considering that the involvement of Black and Arab adolescents was the result of the insufficiently controlled immigration of African families, which were described as impossible to integrate within the French society (the Permanent Secretary of the French Academy thus asserted that polygamy was the cause of the riots), or on the other side of the political spectrum, unveiling structural phenomena, such as spatial segregation and economic inequalities, with the concentration of the jobless population among first or second generation immigrants (which is the typical left-wing interpretation: from Neo-Marxists as well as social-democrats).

Neither spontaneous explosions nor Machiavellian manipulations, neither polygamy nor inequality is an adequate explanation of what happened from 27 October 2005 onwards. In his study on peasant riots in 18th-century England, E.P. Thompson has shown that this kind of social violence always has immediate causes related to a rupture of the tacit contract which underlies the local moral economy (see Thompson 1971). Up to a certain point social injustice is tolerated by its victims but there is a limit to it. On 27 October this limit was reached when two adolescents died in an electric plant where they had hidden to escape the police who were chasing them for an act that they had not committed. Here the whole sequence of events is crucial to recall if one wants to understand the meaning of the riots.

Instead of expressing compassion towards the dead children and their families, the Minister of the Interior immediately asserted that the adolescents were delinquents, although they had never had any affairs with criminal justice. Instead of asking for a public investigation into the case, he protected the police, who were proved to have nevertheless been aware of the deadly danger that the adolescents were exposed to without intervening. The death of the two children thus appeared as mere collateral damage of the enterprise of cleansing the poor suburbs of its *racaille* (scum) with effective instruments such as *kärcher* (high-pressure hose) in Nicolas Sarkozy's vocabulary. In an interview I did with the head officer of the police in the *banlieue* where I was at that time precisely doing my fieldwork on anti-crime squads at night, my interviewee commented with a smile: 'This often happens. When our police get in a neighbourhood, very often kids run away. The police go after them. When they catch them and arrest them, they often discover they haven't done anything wrong. But why did they run then? It's like a Pavlovian reflex', he concluded laughing. I could not refrain myself from sharing with him my comment that the police running after them might also correspond to such a Pavlovian reflex. I guess he did not appreciate the irony of it.

In fact the question should rather be: why should Black and Arab adolescents and youths think that they have to flee when they see the police entering their neighbourhood if and when they have done nothing? The answer is their everyday experience of the police, the permanent checks and constant humiliations, the frustration of being verbally or physically abused, often in front of their friends and relatives without having any possibility to reply. One of the usual practices of the members of these squads is to drive slowly besides a walking Black or Arab youth and to provoke him by insulting comments, which are sometimes overtly racist. In one case I studied, a 14-year-old adolescent of African origin, at some point of this cruel game, burst out: 'Leave me alone', he said, 'I have done nothing'. Immediately the car stopped and the child was surrounded by three threatening policemen who only renounced taking him to the police station after being implored by a woman of the neighbourhood.

But the reaction of the adolescent, who ended scared and crying, is somewhat unusual. One of the first things a male child is taught by his older brothers or parents in the *cités* is to never talk back to the police, whatever 'provocations' they might have ('provocations' is the word they use). Actually, in the many night rounds I have done, the only youth I have heard responding arrogantly to the police were white middle-class ones. Conversely, however harshly they were treated, young Blacks and Arabs remained silent without any physical reaction or any emotional expression. This was their only way to avoid losing face in front of others but above all to prevent spending several hours at the police station, at the least, or being charged for rebellion, which often meant prison. When asked, in a recent survey, what is the main problem that they are confronted with and would like changed, a majority of these youth mentioned police misconduct and brutality.

If we thus go back to the riots, although the death of Ziad Benna and Banou Traore in Clichy-sous-Bois was not a direct consequence of police misconduct or brutality, it was inscribed in a context of police harassment in these *cités*. Moreover, this harassment is not oriented in just any direction: the adolescents who died were of immigrant origins. Just like Aissa Ichich and Youssef Khaïf in 1991, Makome M'Bowole in 1993, Abdelkader Bouziane in 1997, Habib Ould-Mohammed in 1998, Ryad Hamlaoui in 2000 and Mourad Belmoktar in 2003: in all of these cases the death had been the starting point of riots; reciprocally, all significant riots during the past 15 years in France have occurred after the death of Arab and Black youth directly or indirectly related to police interventions (see Jobard 2002). Clearly if one is looking for an explanation of the riots, it is in the relation of these youth to the police—or rather in the racial policing of the lower-class youth—that the answer is to be found.

The moral economy of the dominated (see Scott 1976) includes a set of values and norms, but also of justification and legitimisation of the social order, however unjust it is. It is when these values and norms are violated and when justifications and legitimisations become inefficient that violence occurs. From this perspective, racial discrimination probably involves the individual more deeply than spatial segregation and economic inequality. Segregation and inequality can be related to general and abstract circumstances, whereas racial discrimination is related to what the individual is physically and what the individual represents genealogically. In this sense, it goes beyond the normally accepted injustice. However, this is not sufficient to provoke a riot: if it were, the *banlieues* would be permanently on fire. What makes racial mistreatment definitely intolerable is when it leads to death.

In the two aborted riots I have studied during my fieldwork, police violence that was oriented toward Arab and Black families could only be described as a politics of punishment. In one case, two Black youth seeing friends of theirs being checked by the police had greeted them in Arabic; one of the officers told them to speak French since they 'were in France' and called them 'dirty Blacks'; the youth talked back and ran away; an impressive charge of 20 policemen from all the squads of the area ended up surrounding their house, doors and windows were broken, his mother was hurt, and the youth arrested. All this happened in front of a growing mob of indignant neighbours; interestingly, this episode, which was filmed and later shown on the news, occurred in a residential area and the family belonged to the middle class; this probably explains why the Black youth dared to talk back to the police; they actually did not know the social cost of doing so. In the second case, a young Arab was chased by the police as he was illegally driving a quad bike. He fell down and as the two policemen tried to catch him, several other youths came to help their friend and started to hit the police. The retaliation was impressive, with dozens of officers surrounding the neighbourhood, various apartments being damaged, and several adults and children being hurt. In this *cité* I had witnessed everyday harassment of youth by the police. Indeed, there was drug dealing in the neighbourhood but the racially profiled stopping and checking was not oriented towards finding drugs and the dealers, whom the police knew and never bothered. The violence of the youths was thus a reaction to the brutality of the police, which had consequently alienated the local population, including the adults who had been trying for months to act as mediators and whose efforts were not only annihilated but also discredited.

In seeking to interpret this racial policing (see Rowe 2004), two main explanations may be given. When asked by the Socialist mayor about this phenomenon, the head of the local police answered: 'It's not my fault if you have only Blacks and Arabs in your city'. The argument has some relevance: in sociological terms, it refers to the racial segregation that has led to the concentration of immigrant families in overcrowded housing. This phenomenon is a consequence of racialised housing policies and labour market inequalities that have displaced African families to the far outskirts of Paris. In this context, adolescents and youth for both material (space at home) and social (street lifestyle) reasons are statistically more exposed to being stopped and checked. But the structural argument is only part of the story. When interrogated about racism in the police force, the same head officer told me: 'Of course we have some cases but not more than anywhere else—and even probably less than in the rest of society'. Yet, the few surveys conducted on the topic and my own observations show the contrary. Some local police officers of the anti-crime squads confirmed my impression when they confided to me that they had decided to change their working hours to day shifts because of the racism of their colleagues, who were much less under the control of their superiors at night.

Racism in the police force includes a relatively sophisticated ethnic characterisation of youth. Roma and Romanians are the lowest in the moral evaluation of the police, because of their living conditions (poverty, nomadism) and economic resources (supposedly theft and trafficking); but the police often have a surprising degree of connivance with them, which they explain by saying that Roma and Romanians 'play the game'; if arrested, 'they don't protest or resist'; they just consider that 'the police have won this time'. Blacks and Arabs, on the contrary, are a little less despised but hostility towards them is much stronger; they are often referred to as 'bastards who always cheat', the distinction between the two groups being that 'Blacks are like Arabs except they have no brain', as one policeman told me. This racism has many practical consequences in terms of racial policing: on the selection of candidates to physically search, on the decision made when confronted by small delinquent acts, and above all on the way that people are talked to and treated, handcuffed and humiliated in everyday situations. In fact, if the checking of youth—often several times a day—is useless in terms of the repression of delinquency and crime, as most police experts admit, including the heads of police that I interviewed, and as was confirmed to me by the local Superintendant, it is quite obvious then that racial profiling is more about demonstrating power and implementing domination than about maintaining security and order.

These ethnographical fragments on the French police may seem caricatured or biased. In fact, my observations are limited: two years spent with different anti-crime squads in the suburbs of Paris. However when I presented my research to the heads of police in the National School of Magistracy, they came up to me afterwards to congratulate me for understanding so well these squads, which they referred to as 'a necessary evil'. And when, sometime after the end of my research, I had a private conversation with a high administrator of the national police who had precisely tried to reform these squads a few years before—when he was in a *département* near Paris, he compared the squad that he found when he arrived to a 'hound causing more damage than it was solving problems'. In fact the conduct of these squads, who have everyday contact with the youth, is well known by their superiors but it is often accepted in order to avoid conflicts and mistrust within the group.

Conclusion

Modern policing, Michel Foucault argues, is a pastoral power disciplining populations through different activities and devices, which include public health missions as well as public order obligations. In the French *banlieues*, as in many racially and socially segregated areas in the world, its role has been restricted to the latter dimension and even more precisely to the exercise of an unmediated power of control and castigation of marginalised youth, who are constantly stigmatised by public declarations and in the media coverage as enemies of the nation. In a society where social inequality seems increasingly related to racial discrimination, social welfare tends to be replaced by racial policing, more profitable in economic terms and highly beneficial for political reasons. This reality had long been dissimulated or avoided, since it was neither satisfying for the image of the Republic and its administration nor for the potentially ambiguous consequences that may result from discovering the high proportion of Blacks and Arabs having problems with the police. It is this reality that the 2005 riots brutally revealed or rather the consciousness that many had of it in the *banlieues*—maybe less through the action of the minority of rioters than through the silence of the majority of their neighbours and friends who said they disapproved of violence but admitted that they understood its authors.

References

Beaud S & Pialoux M (1999). *Retour sur la condition ouvrière*. Paris: Fayard.

Bowen J (2007). *Why the French don't like scarves. Islam, the state, and public space*. Princeton: Princeton University Press.

Fassin D (2007). Du déni à la dénégation. Psychologie politique de la représentation des discriminations. In D Fassin & E Fassin (Eds), *De la question sociale à la question raciale ?* (pp133–57). Paris: La Découverte.

Fassin D (2006). La force de l'événement. Réflexions sur les émeutes de l'automne 2005 en France, *Geste*, 3: 104–09.

Fassin D (2002). L'invention française de la discrimination. *Revue Française de Science Politique*, 52(4): 403–23.

Fassin D (2001). Qualifier les inégalités. In D Fassin, H Granjean, M Kaminski, T Lang & A Leclerc (Eds), *Les inégalités sociales de santé.* (pp123–44). Paris : La Découverte.

Fassin D & Fassin E (Eds) (2006). *De la question sociale à la question raciale? Représenter la société française*. Paris: La Découverte.

Foucault M (1994). *Dits et écrits 1954–1988. Vol 4*. Paris: Gallimard.

Jobard F (2002). *Bavures policières ? La force publique et ses usages*. Paris: La Découverte.

Noiriel G (1991). *La tyrannie du national*. Paris: Calmann-Lévy.

Rabinow P (2003). *Anthropos today: reflections on modern equipment*. Princeton: Princeton University Press.

Rosanvallon P (1992). *Le sacre du citoyen*. Paris: Gallimard.

Rowe M (2004). *Policing, race and racism*. Cullompton: Willan Publishing.

Sayad A (1999). *La double absence*. Paris: Seuil.

Schnapper D (1991). *La France de l'intégration*. Paris: Gallimard.

Scott J (1976). *The moral economy of the peasant: rebellion and subsistence in Southeast Asia*. New Haven: Yale University Press.

Thomas D (2007). *Black France: colonialism, immigration, and transnationalism*. Bloomington: Indiana University Press.

Thompson EP (1971). The moral economy of the English crowd in the eighteenth century. *Past and Present*, 50: 76–136.

Enacting half-positions: creative disrespect in the 2005 French riots

Craig Browne and Phillip Mar

The large-scale youth riots of late 2005 in France were powerfully non-discursive actions that embodied the frustrations of those with least access to a public voice. We examine the riots in a way that distinguishes between the lived experience of collective violence and the larger structural dimensions of the discontent. Although the lived experience and the structural dimension of the conflict cannot be reduced to each other, it is necessary to address how they intersect with pre-existing histories of discontent, which are anchored in experiences of social vulnerability and the denial of social recognition. In this paper, we initially provide a schematic analysis of the 2005 riots that draws on Charles Tilly's (2003) classification of types of collective violence and established research into riots in order to sketch the processes that transformed a single incident into a wave of violence. Following this event analysis, we argue that a crucial context to the French riots arises from a fracturing of the welfare state's channels of social integration and the corresponding creation of the contradictory 'half-positions' of citizens without the full entitlements of employment and workers without the full entitlements of citizenship. In light of the subjective experiences of half-positions, we then develop an account of the specificity of the French riots of late 2005 as a type of 'tongueless' action embodying the frustrations of those with the least access to a public voice. It is our contention that a close analysis of the actions of the riots discloses how these practices of contestation involved aspects of *creative disrespect*. This account of the structuration of the riots differs from some other explanations of them and, more generally, several influential perspectives on collective violence. Finally, we consider whether the aggressive actions of the young people should be regarded as an outcome of collective pride in which young French citizens exercised a new kind of retributive justice in a situation characterised by a lack of 'speech rights'.

Event analysis

The actions of the November 2005 riots belong to a longer established pattern of urban contestation concentrated in the specific French suburban environments, the *cités* and *banlieues*. This was very much a youth uprising: participants were mainly young males, with an average age of sixteen, according to some police reports (Donzelot et al. 2006). A schematic analysis of the types of actions 'on the ground' points to the highly bounded and ritualised nature of these actions, grounded in specific 'repertoires of contention' (Tilly 2003). A core activity was the 'rodeo', in which a car is stolen, a chase with police takes place, and the car is burned (Wieviorka 2005; Silverstein & Tetreault 2006). In the terms of Charles Tilly's typology of forms of interpersonal violence, such activities would seem to fall into the category of 'violent rituals' in their grounding in very particular social games involving well-defined participation roles and well-defined destructive means.[1] Such skirmishes also correspond somewhat to 'scattered attacks' i.e. damaging acts such as 'sabotage, clandestine attacks on symbolic objects or places, assaults of governmental agents, and arson' (Tilly 2003, 14–15) performed by small groups which would include expert car thieves and supporters who would engage in a fight with police. In other words, these acts were relatively strategic rather than random or 'riotous' acts, although grounded more in a working sense of 'street tactics' than in formally planned operations. Perhaps because of this, such encounters rarely

---

1 Tilly defines violent rituals as 'damage-dealing interactions involving public scripts, known scorecards, fixed and finite stakes, defined perimeters, stylised enactment of us–them boundaries, clear delineation of proper participants and targets, and sharp distinctions between those participants and either monitors or spectators.' (Tilly 2003, 101)

spilled over into 'opportunistic violence' and the pursuit of such normally forbidden ends as looting and rape. Considering that the rioting affected over 250 urban locales and involved numerous pitched battles with police and emergency workers, it is remarkable how few casualties were reported. While the tactic was to attack property (principally private cars and public buildings) to trigger an engagement with police, participants adopted a tacit strategy of reducing risk through a cat-and-mouse game with the authorities—torching cars or property to attract police then disappearing—which actually limited conflict from spreading. Hence, these acts of violence also entailed a self-protective strategy of containment and non-escalation. Rather than thinking in terms of explosive spasmodic and uncontained 'riot' (see Thompson 1991, 185), we can perhaps see the multitude of belligerent and destructive acts as having occurred within a framework of civility, at least in relation to respective local communities.[2] Hence situations were rarely as 'out of control' as they seemed, operating through quite limited repertoires involving engagement with front line authorities, principally police and fire-fighters.

Even the aggressive actions taken in relation to battles with police had a ritual or customary air. Nevertheless, there can be no doubting the fury and intensity of the actions on the frontline. Like many other violent outbreaks, a precipitating policing incident symbolically condensed a welter of discontent. For groups that feel disenfranchised, the interface with police comes to represent the boundary separating them from the rest of society and the oversights of the state (we can think of Australian examples such as the 2004 Redfern riots). As is well-known, the rioting began in response to a local event, the death by electrocution of two youths in an electrical substation in the Paris suburb of Clichy, apparently while hiding from police on 27 October 2005. Escalation to a nationwide phenomenon has been widely imputed to the provocative threats by the then interior minister, Nicolas Sarkozy,

---

2 'The young rioters, for instance, are violent but they are rather careful with ordinary people. They burn cars or buses, they fight with the police, but they don't attack people. They have an impressive capacity in meeting somewhere very quickly and disappearing as quickly, with the use of mobile phones much more than internet' (Wieviorka 2006).

to clear out or forcefully cleanse (*netoyer au Kärcher*) *cité* areas perceived as crime problems, and to deal with the rogues and scum (*racaille*).[3] Yet these immediate discursive 'triggers' were only the obvious headliners of a wider symbolic violence encircling urban underclass youth, *banlieue* dwellers and immigrant citizens most particularly of Arab and African origin from former colonies. The rapid escalation in the scale of the response occurred with the convergent perceptions of bodily attack at the local level (violent deaths on the ground and the prospect of increasing surveillance and law and order) and, of symbolic attack on the collective honour of young *banlieue* dwellers coming from the centre of national power.

If the events initially followed a similar trajectory to earlier conflicts between *banlieue* youth and police that went beyond a certain tolerable threshold (typically the violent death of young men), what was more surprising and of greater analytical interest was the speed at which localised events were transformed into a 'wave' of violent response of 'crisis' proportions for the nation. What were the preconditions for such actions to take 'extra-institutional' forms rather than being channelled and mitigated through local social and political networks, enabling them to escalate to a larger and qualitatively different phenomenon? (Turner 1994, 313).

As mentioned, the actors in the violence were largely young males, and it can be seen as an escalation of typical patterns of ongoing and endemic violence between police and youth of *cités* and housing projects areas (Balibar 2007, 50; Wieviorka 2005). Active participation did not spread to the broader *banlieue* population, within particular geographical locales, but laterally through networks of similar groups of young people in numerous locales in urban France. As we have seen, the policing and justice spheres were the immediate zones of conflict on the ground as well as at the executive level—Sarkozy's threats entailed

---

3 Both comments were staged 'live' by Sarkozy in *banlieue* settings, perhaps further amplifying their challenge through networks on the ground. The first comment was made on 20 June 2005 following the death of a child by stray bullets in the *cité* at La Corneuvre; the second much closer to the time of the riots on 25 October at Argentuil after being booed by young residents while announcing a program of urban rehabilitation.

further discriminatory 'law and order' initiatives, and the state of emergency laws brought into play by Prime Minister Villepin drew on legislation enacted during the Algerian War, a fact that only underlined the colonial legacy of the governmental framework. Escalation of violence is more likely where the state has inadequate channels to mediate effectively between adversary groups and the centres of state power. Clearly, antagonistic messages from the executive level inflamed the tensions, rather than facilitated mediation or negotiation. At the same time, state endorsed migrant associations, which had emerged in part in response to an earlier wave of discontent in the 1980s, had either withered away over time or had become less effective in their representation of migrant communities. In general, community organisations or Islamic organisations did not have any marked effect in either preventing or promoting the conflict (See Roy 2005, Donzelot et al. 2005) Social movements arguably tend to divert and re-channel violent actions. The absence of a broad-based social movement of relevance to the aggrieved young people meant that there was little opportunity for channelling of feelings and resentments in more peaceful directions, to 'give legitimacy to the group's grievances and thus help to justify an emergent norm' (Turner 1994, 313). Anti-racism movements which had earlier taken this role had lost relevance for this generation of young immigrant descendants: November 2005 has been strongly contrasted with the marches in 1983 which had crystallised in the wake of similar violent confrontations in the Minguettes area of Lyons (Beaud & Masclet 2006).

The actions of the rioters were not 'coordinated' in the usual sense: they were not programmatic in the traditional political sense and in this respect they were quite unlike the student-led protests that happened several months later. Many descriptions of the November 2005 riots noted the absence of slogans, religious, ethnic, class-political or otherwise. The riots undoubtedly constituted a powerful form of symbolic action and were laden with meaning, yet, as has been widely noted, it is problematic to define or attribute a particular objective to them. They were hardly 'issueless riots' (Marx 1970): in fact, there were abundant issues, which were not put forward in a 'political' form. If there was a politics it was built upon the blockage of political possibility and of self-representation (Balibar 2007, 62). Sociologist Michel Wieviorka (2006) has further underscored the rioters' lack of articulation of either identity or specific demands: 'they are not at all organised, they produce no discourse, they don't have any leader, any principle of structuration, they are typically crisis behaviours, and not at all a movement.'

While Wieviorka is correct in emphasising the absence of conventional political discourse, formal organisation or leadership, in asserting the lack of 'any principle of structuration' he denies the very sociological 'thing' that would account for the relatively homogeneous nature of the rioters' actions. It is this structuration that constituted their ability to constitute a sustained and significant (if not coherently signifying) political event. We would argue that the high degree of coalescence or unplanned 'coordination' in the widespread actions of young people in November 2005 was only possible due to the multitude of similarities in settings, locales, practical routines and intersubjective roles. Nevertheless, our examination of the 2005 riots maintains a distinction between the lived experience of collective violence and the larger structural dimensions of the discontent. In the following section we focus on these structural dimensions of French society and emphasise the way in which certain French citizens, especially the children of immigrants in *banlieue* settings, are located in contradictory positions in relation to the national polity, economy and welfare state.

Half-positions: on the dynamics of exclusionary integration

The main issues that underlie the rioting are neither unprecedented nor unfamiliar. France has periodically experienced riots, protests and civil disobedience relating to the situation of migrants, youth and police surveillance. The 2005 riots were probably unique in the diverse contexts of their mobilisation and their persistence over several weeks, but what had no less significantly changed is the perception of the French state and its capacity to deal with many issues underlying the discontent. In general, the state's policy options appeared to have diminished as a consequence of the restraints on budget deficits imposed by the European monetary union. Similarly, segments of the French immigrant population have experienced sustained high rates of unemployment, itself a reflection of the introduction of less labour-intensive methods of production and a decline in traditional manufacturing industries. In these respects, the backdrop to the riots is a fracturing of the welfare state's channels of social integration and the genesis of contradictory half-positions that lie at the margins of the state and the economy. Following Habermas' analysis, half-positions develop at the interchanges between the public and private spheres of the system and the lifeworld in advanced capitalist welfare states (Habermas 1987, 320). At the same time, the social structural characteristics of half-positions involve forms of social exclusion and marginality that were largely absent from Habermas' initial analysis, but which have been significantly consolidated by subsequent transformations in the relationship of the state, market and community.

Habermas argued that in modern societies social integration and system integration become 'uncoupled' and that bourgeois civil law institutionalises a series of interchanges between them. In the case of the economy, labour power and income intersect with the relationship between demand and the provision of goods and services, while, in the case of the state, political decision-making and mass loyalty are coordinated with the interchange between taxes and organisational accomplishments. Of particular importance from the standpoint of our analysis are the legally institutionalised positions and roles that correspond to these various channels of interchange, like those of consumer and employee in relation to the economy and those of citizen and welfare recipient in relation to the state. These positions institutionalise rights of participation and membership that are at the same time founded, in principle at least, on legitimate expectations and democratic public will-formation. Yet, the changes in the political and economic systems that are often associated with globalisation have resulted in these channels of interchange coming increasingly into contradiction with one another and, as a consequence, the social structural positions that some individuals occupy incorporate elements of contradiction. The prototypes of these contradictory half-positions are those of citizens without the full entitlements of employment and workers without the full entitlements of citizenship. Indeed, analyses of French immigration patterns have noted that the structural basis of inequality has undergone something of a generational change from the latter half-position to the former (Wieviorka 2005; Lagrange and Oberti 2006). Nonetheless, there are actually a number of intersecting processes that have consolidated types of half-positions and many of these reflect developments in system integration, like the changes in the international division of labour and the realignments in the relationship of the state to the economy.

In all cases, half-positions entail some reduction in the ability to effectively access those forms of social protection that had limited the subjective experience of structural transformations and social subordination more generally. For this reason, half-positions are by no means randomly distributed, but tend to coalesce with the markers of negative discrimination, like race and spatial location (Castel 2006). In particular, due to the pattern of twentieth-century French economic and urban development, the current high levels of unemployment are concentrated in the outer suburbs, especially in housing projects known as *cités* and *banlieues*. Although there are undoubtedly variations in their class composition, it is these outer suburban *cités* and *banlieues* that have acquired some of the negative connotations common to localities that have experienced the departure of the socially mobile, such as American inner city 'ghettoes'. Further, the deterioration in local suburban economies due to high levels of unemployment has been coupled with stigmatising of inhabitants of the *banlieue* and *cité*. In line with social science findings (*The Economist* 2006, 12), even the then President Chirac acknowledged in a response to the riots that job applicants from the *banlieues* had been subject to discrimination as a result of this stigmatising. The marginalising of communities like Clichy can be partly attributed to deficiencies in public infrastructure and the long-term decline of urban environments. Bourdieu described the latter as the outcome of the 'abdication of the state' and the sociopolitical struggle over spatial segregation, which acquired new dimensions with the undermining of notions of public service and the shift in the principle of the state's distribution of housing resources from the collective to private individuals (Bourdieu 1999, 181–88).

The manner in which unemployment is addressed in France has likewise changed and this has equally underlined the decline in the integrative capacity of the welfare state. In a sense, the corporatist dimension of the comparatively quite effective French system of welfare can function to the disadvantage of those in half-position, because the level of unemployment benefits is tied to past labour market participation (Esping-Andersen 1996; Smith 2004). However, the recent policy changes highlight the tendency for marginal groups to 'accumulate damages' (Offe 1996) in spite of positive policy intentions. Over the past decades, the social policy of the French state has shifted from active job creation through industry sponsorship to the more market-enhancing position of funding labour market training programs. Despite the considerable state resources that have been deployed, the emphasis on training has led to negative perceptions of 'warehousing' the unemployed in courses that have limited future employment prospects. In short, this compounds the sense of exclusion and lack of opportunity that the children of migrants from the *banlieues* and *cités* have experienced in relation to the education system. The children of non-European migrants are largely unrepresented in the advanced and prestigious educational institutions, severely limiting their range of career options and improving social status. There can be little doubt that a sense of indignation can be promoted by a social order that distributes opportunities for achievement in a discriminatory manner and that resentment can be fuelled by the exacerbating inequalities of wealth and lifestyle.

For most of the last fifty years, France has employed territorial definitions of citizenship, rather than basing entitlements to citizenship on ethnicity. In general, the children of migrants born in France are French citizens. However, the legal entitlement to French citizenship has not automatically translated into social acceptance. The general status of migrants and whether they are adequately integrated into French society have been continually questioned. These tensions are particularly focused on the significant populations from former colonies like Algeria. Despite its limited electoral success over the past two decades, the racist reaction represented by the French National

Front has been one overt indicator of these tensions. The French model of social integration is based on the application of universal principles and equal treatment, but this model can be experienced as intolerant and even licensing double standards in relation to certain migrant practices. French citizens of non-European migrant backgrounds are more likely to be subjected to surveillance and identity checks as a result of the intensive policing in recent years of illegal migrants and possible terrorist networks. The view that the French state authorities are indifferent to the circumstances of migrants received sustenance from the three Paris apartment fires earlier in 2005 that resulted in nearly fifty deaths. French discussions of cultural pluralism have often concerned its potential to weaken the Republican ideals that are central to French society. The secularist policy of *laïcité*, based on the separation of state and religion, has in recent years been invoked to justify bans on headscarfs and veils worn by some Muslim school pupils. In this context, the supposed integrative function of public institutions is partly inverted and rights to self-determination and equal participation are diminished on the grounds of cultural practices.

Given the French republican model of national identity, half-positions limit the options of citizens to construct (or reconstruct) a distinct cultural identity. According to Dominique Schnapper, compared to the immigrant descendents of England and Germany, 'the children of French migrants are more ignorant and more detached from the culture of origin of their parents, more totally acculturated to the local language and culture', but 'they are also the ones for whom access to the world of work is the more difficult' (Schnapper 2006, 766). In France, there is a greater discordance between cultural integration and structural integration (Schnapper 2006, 766). This analysis suggests that integration is more problematic in France, in spite of the French welfare state's achievements such as greater access to social housing, comparatively higher school retention and access to university education in France.

These problematic dimensions of half-positions have been opposed by other forms of political contestation and movements, such as *SOS Racism* (Lentin 2004), but these modes of resistance involve forms of practices that are somewhat distant from the concealed and underlying experiences of subordination and marginality. These structural dimensions of half-positions intersect with the diffuse background of symbolic violence that is associated with the 'hidden injuries' of race and class. In a sense, the hidden injuries are connected to the 'in-between' situation of social integration that is conditional on consent or acquiescence to a position that is relatively subordinated and largely precludes the public expression of aspects of identity (Sennett and Cobb 1972, 118). For these reasons, the hidden injuries are the *debilitating self-relations* that can develop from occupying a half-position and the constant denial of reciprocity in social interaction. Balibar's description of 'internal exclusion' of the 2005 rioters captures the subjective binds of these contradictory processes of exclusionary forms of social inclusion.

> The object of destruction is in large part a 'thing' from which the young rioters are contradictorily *excluded* as 'non-citizens', to which they only have limited, illegitimate access, but of which they are *themselves a part*, that in a way is part of themselves and their identity. This is why they can be characterised neither absolutely outside nor as really within the social system, but only in the paradoxical terms of an *internal exclusion*, which must produce its effects at the deepest levels of subjectivity. (Balibar 2007, 51; Balibar 2001)

The type of social exclusion that is then typical of half-positions generates a kind of accumulation of damages and a corresponding experience of the violation of rights and legitimate expectations of equal treatment. As the fractured channels of the welfare state and the capitalist economy mean that those in half-positions are incompletely integrated, an everyday moral order evolves that is adapted to the shared experiences of hidden injuries as well as related to the overarching value system of the social order as a whole. As we will see, this kind of disrespect may engender destructive forms of collective behaviour when the conflict that is normally veiled by everyday moral orders, and 'unarticulated condemnations' of social subordination are brought out into the open by events that undermine the legitimacy of the coercive powers of the state (see Honneth 2007, 93). In this context, the damages of acquiescence can reach a point of precipitating some form of action. In our opinion, the actions of the rioters in 2005 were driven by an impulse for retribution and involved practices that could be defined as those of creative disrespect.

The creativity of disrespect

Although there are persistent tensions and sources of discontent, there is no inevitable connection between half-positions and violent conflicts: half-positions more often generate feelings of demoralisation and resignation. However, diminished citizenship and insecure employment expose individuals to the tension between, on the one hand, the normative expectation of the respect for the rights of members and contributors to French society and, on the other hand, the experience of the forms of symbolic violence and material inequalities that are associated with half-positions. The somewhat paradoxical supposition that the half-positions actually contribute to integration can then unravel when confronted with situations that reveal the discrepancies involved, such as the seemingly gratuitous deaths of the youths hiding from police and the incivility of racial taunts. For this very reason, measuring the 2005 riots against some defined political objective is to misconstrue the nature of the conflict. Instead, it is necessary to focus on the internal dynamics of this violent action and to explicate the processes that 'turn a single incident into a wave' (Joas 2003, 189). In a similar vein, it is important to relate the riots to the comparatively limited opportunities that the dominant institutions of the public sphere provide for expressing the tensions of half-positions and the distance, in any event, of this model of political-will formation from the context and experience of the rioters. The riots may then involve a quite different manner of contestation, one that is conveyed in actions that respond to experiences of disrespect.

At the risk of imputing a shared motivation to different agents and the destructive consequences of the violence, we could describe the distinctive action orientation of the riots as one of 'creative disrespect'. The Australian anthropologist Gillian Cowlishaw adapted the term creative disrespect in an analysis of violent outbreaks among Aboriginal communities in Australian towns (Cowlishaw 2004). Cowlishaw importantly drew attention to 'actions other than speech' that express the frustrations of those with the least access to a public voice and the salience of such practices to the Indigenous populations that are marginalised as a consequence of race. For all the many differences between the situation of Indigenous Australians and young *banlieue* dwellers in France, there is some commonality in the response to powerful racialising objectifications that act to deny groups of people an 'equal' citizenship, or the status of being fully moral subjects (see Cowlishaw 2004). This commonality can be located in the bypassing of 'legitimate' channels of complaint about injustice and hurt in favour of more performative or 'creative' acts that attempt to take the initiative in a losing situation by moving outside of the conventional framework of representation. Creative disrespect would seem to point to actions that (however momentarily) bypass the discursive domination and symbolic violence that is a necessary accompaniment to groups who have highly limited means to argue or even to formulate a normative consensus.

Yet, what Cowlishaw described as creative disrespect would be more accurately conceptualised as performative disrespect or performative disobedience. In our opinion, performativity can be an important dimension of creative action, but to focus exclusively upon this aspect is to obscure some of its other dimensions and potentially misrepresent the characteristics of creativity. In Cowlishaw's account, confronted with situations where the game of public speech seems heavily loaded against them, Indigenous people will often enact and exaggerate the negative stereotypes that are projected onto them. These performative actions temporarily refuse integration through creatively playing with a highly stigmatised and interpellated identity. 'Because they cannot be approached, answered or treated as legitimate social events,' in Cowlishaw's opinion, 'such performances interrupt and temporarily silence white voices. That is, they do not institute a dialogue, but rather seem to confirm the grotesque images of a damaged Aboriginality' (Cowlishaw 2004, 74).

The ethnography of performative disrespect provides significant insights into the specific embodiments of the agency of those marginal and racially stigmatised groups that lack effective access to public voice. In this sense, it describes a thwarted dialogue that is carried on by other means and it draws attention to the production of subjectivity in the acts of violence. Nonetheless, it is necessary to distinguish our analytical position on creative disrespect from those focusing on 'transgressive' performance. In our opinion, such an interpretation of creative disrespect is in danger of a too romantic celebration of transgressive performativity. As a consequence, it is liable to misconstrue patterns of contestation that do not conform to its image of revolt. For example, William Beik (1997, 254) distinguishes the more earnest episodes of urban violence and revolt in 17th-century France which sought to 'punish wrong-doing and see that it never happened again' from the more playful and theatrically stylised chastisement and mockery of *charivari* rituals. In order to understand the differences between these modalities of contestation, Beik recommends that one attend to 'the anger, the existential risk, and the uncertainty' in the moments of genuine revolt.

The performative conception is then insufficient to carry the full weight of an explanation of the internal dynamics of violent action, and to some extent it simply inverts the emphases of the strategic-rational explanations. For instance, a more complex self-relation is involved in the enactment of violence than that of a shift from rage and frustration to the thrill and pleasure of transgression. These elements were certainly present in the 2005 French riots, but other considerations are relevant to the enactment of creative disrespect, including the rituals of the familiar repertoires of contention and the phasing of the escalation of the conflict. Hans Joas has argued that the creativity of action is occluded in the two dominant explanations of violent resistance. The first explanation is based on the model of translating socio-structural disadvantage into rational claims and demands, while the second is anchored in assessment of the significance of values and norms. The latter type of explanation tends to assert that a decline or change in values initiates a type of spiral that culminates in violence, but sometimes takes the opposite form of highlighting the normative content of a culture of violence, such as those of masculinity or street gangs. While Joas admits that these two explanatory frames are legitimate and potentially insightful, he believes that each shares a common tendency to treat the enactment of violence as a secondary consideration. In other words, they neglect the dynamics of violent action and turn away from its genesis in the practical engagement with a particular interpersonal situation in favour of the general traits of implementing strategic-instrumental objectives or following value-commitments.

In Joas' opinion, the analysis of the immediacy of violent situations discloses the significance of the 'creative nature of human action'. Specifically, close analyses of violent situations demonstrate that neither the implementing of strategic-instrumental objectives nor the following of value-commitments is simply a straightforward process of enactment; rather these depend on a creative response to alternatives that only reveal themselves in the action process itself. For Joas, this pragmatically situated creativity is not only relevant to the application of norms and values, but also to understanding their emergence in the first place, as well as the genesis of types of collective solidarity (Joas 2003, 190). He claims that it 'is collective action itself that defines the problems it relates to; it generates motives and identities, shapes new social relations and communities, gives rise to profound changes in identity (conversion and regeneration), produces affectively cathected symbols and leaves behind symbolic attachments capable of structuring biographies' (Joas 2003, 192). Now, while it would be difficult to substantiate each of these contentions in relation to the 2005 French riots, the notion of the creativity of action opens the way to a more complex sociological consideration of experience. Specifically, it draws attention to the flows of affect that can propel acts of violence and the awakening of a sense of injustice. No less significant to action processes are corporeal dynamics; the more visible aspects of these bodily practices are highlighted in the description of performative disrespect, but they have a broader importance in establishing the integrity of experience and its inverse, such as translating into a form of self-relation the fractures of half-positions. Further, the violent reactions to insults and injuries points to the intersubjectivity of action and its incorporation into forms of sociality. Sociality makes action a symbolically meaningful exchange and opens up creative possibilities that are not available to the individual in isolation. For example, participation in collective practices can induce some experience of the transcendence of the self and it is the forms of sociality that are especially involved in confrontations between institutionalised norms and informal moral economies.

In some respects, the transgressive feature of performative disrespect is a mode of dramatising the contradictions of the social structure. At the same time, the fact that the performance of this disrespect typically draws heavily on the self-representation of the status hierarchy and reassigns it for a limited period points to its limited interpretative frame. The most influential recent discussions of disrespect have emphasised the extent to which it involves the experience of a sense of the potential loss of personality and of self-control (Honneth 2007; Margalit 1996). In the context of the 2005 French riots, the performance could be understood as a kind of traumatic enactment of the binds of half-positions, while the creative disrespect is located more precisely in those collective actions that attempt to reassert some form of self-control and self-identity in relation to institutional subordination. The creative component of disrespect originates initially then in the immediate situation and the insight action provides into the contest of values. This is propelled less by performativity than by the experience of a radical transformation of the grounds of legitimate authority and the unintended clarification of the contradiction of the social order. As the riots exemplify, the sustaining of acts of creative disrespect hinges on the temporal unfolding of a dialectic of control and the degree to which the context of action is shaped by norms of reciprocity or the lack of mutuality.

Riots as retribution

We understand the riots of November 2005 as a retaliatory marking of the limits of tolerable attack—both on physical bodies and on social honour in general—in a manner that bypassed engagement in dialogue in a public arena, in favour of actions that did not aim to generate public speech. We interpret the actions of the rioters as a new kind of popular 'retributive justice', as distinct from governmentally implemented systems that operate on some principle of proportionality or 'the punishment to fit the crime'. In this instance, retributive justice aimed not to enforce claims to compensation or establish statutory rights, but to demonstrate and maintain a sense of collective pride against incursions seen to threaten the acceptable boundaries of interaction with the state. In utilising the notion of 'retribution' we are in part suggesting another line of analysis to those of the politics of recognition and of distribution.[4]

In introducing the concept of the half-position, we have pointed to how certain citizens may be integrated into national membership in such a way that causes a blockage to their participation beyond a certain point in both the political sphere and the market. This half-membership precludes subjects' full access to the means of redress of traditional politics and social movements, such as the use of citizenship rights to make claims in the public sphere. In this respect the half-membership differs from both proletarian membership of parties and labour unions and the 'not-yet' political membership of the first generation of immigrants. Half-positions are constituted where the recognition of legal and citizenship rights of a specific group are effectively *eclipsed* by an inability to command publicly recognised honour or social esteem.

We can broadly sketch the problematic dimensions of half-positions of relevance to young *banlieue* dwellers. In the domain of citizenship, rather than the formal inability to present an alternative cultural model of identity, the experience of half-membership is one of a silencing and spoiling of identity particularly through racialisation (see Goffman 1968). On the level of social allocation, half-membership can be experienced as the bind of being implicated in forms of inclusion that

---

4 We draw on historian William Beik's account of a 'culture of retribution' in seventeenth-century France in which violent attacks on agents of the state attempted to mark boundaries and limits of a particular (inevitably unequal) social equilibrium 'built upon ritual interaction between the symbolic authority of magistrates and the collective pride of popular groups' (Beik 1997, 1). Direct physical attacks on individual tax collectors, magistrates, lawyers, councillors, police etc. sought reprisal for particular attacks, attempts at insult or humiliation, or a threatened shift in balance affecting reciprocal dealings with the state such as a new or increased tax.

simultaneously function to exclude. For example, there is the contradiction of a schooling system which strongly demarcates and legitimates inequality while promising to provide opportunities to redress disadvantage; the widespread provision of public housing that the state has allowed to deteriorate; and the increase of concentrations within a spatial economy that negatively marks out difference and hierarchy. In these cases, allocative processes clash with the political orthodoxy of *laïcité* with its assertion of universal rights. These are further undermined by experiences of casualised employment and a diminishing prospect of life-chances.

However, these aspects of half-positions can only be understood as a general context for indignation, although this is hardly determining in relation to outbreaks of violence. The 2005 riots emerged from the everyday experience of specific subjects in concrete locations—young people in *cité* and *banlieue* environments. The riots instantiated a kind of retribution on the particular frontier most sharply exemplifying the constraints of the half-positions and invoked creative disrespect in encounters with the mechanisms of law and order. In this zone a number of conflictual convergences are brought together: the escalated policing of the *banlieue* as an imagined zone of racialised criminality; the liminality of youth caught between the jaws of school failure and labour market disadvantage; and the recourse to struggles over spaces where young males can assert a kind of autonomy in an ongoing riposte with police surveillance. In these social spaces, a residual sense of honour (and this is no doubt highly gendered, in general a masculine honour) tends to be located in a 'code of the street' (see Sennett 2003, 222)

That the actions were a kind of retribution can be demonstrated with reference, we believe, to the orientation that generated the rioting, the determination of its targets, and the typical format of this contestation. This is not to deny that one could discern some order of claims for redistribution and recognition in the riots, but the action of retribution accentuates a lack of mutuality. Retribution belongs more properly to a moral economy that differs markedly from 'individual rights' and procedural claims to justice: it is a form of popular will and it reflects very limited means of redress. The primary aspect of retribution is to affirm the collective pride of the aggrieved group by challenging the expectations of the state concerning compliance to its authority. In the case of the French riots in 2005, retribution was enacted on the most direct 'messengers' of state violence and regulation (police), as well as on parts of the physical environment, especially mobile forms of property like cars, and certain public facilities like school buildings and public transport.

In our opinion, that perceived police contraventions of the informal 'rules of engagement' provided a trigger for the rioting serves to locate the fractured moral economy of this form of violence. Retribution does not have the normative underpinnings that characterise, for instance, civil disobedience. The illegality of acts of civil disobedience is often justified in terms of normative principles that are accepted, though currently unfulfilled, by institutions. Cohen and Arato (1992) even contend that civil disobedience and acts of violence are mutually exclusive. By contrast, the understanding giving rise to acts of retribution is one in which the boundary between legality and illegality is in question and the power of the affective experience of indignation takes precedence. As Cowlishaw says of creative disrespect:

> There are actions other than speech which take place on the border, not of the unsayable, but of the undoable. In these cases the boundaries of legitimacy are also boundaries of legality. (Cowlishaw 2004, 74)

In other words, the state, especially through the coercive agency of the police, is understood to have itself undermined the 'negotiated equilibrium' and the legitimate boundary that separates its authority from the stigmatised community. Retribution challenged the excesses of policing of the *banlieue*, the gratuitous acts of humiliation and racialisation that served to take the exercise of authority beyond the purely regulatory power of law. This rupture of a 'negotiated equilibrium' altered the ongoing contestation and momentarily suspended some of the informal rules that had organised it.

Retribution responds to indignation. In premodern contexts, the popular justice of retribution was related to the contravention by authorities of boundaries that were closely connected to the spatial organisation of social relations and the hierarchical nature of the social order (Beik 1997). The contemporary form of retribution that we have analysed is grounded in the paradoxical occupation of the half-position, where subjects are blocked from the experience of 'full' or untainted membership in French society, while being too 'French' to claim alterity. Retribution in this modern context is a form of action and moral assertion that is situated in relation to the forms of justice that are implicit in the positions of citizens and employees, welfare clients and consumers. In modern societies, the complexity of integration generally involves some delegation of the justice related claim of these social positions and roles. However, those in half-positions are unable to take for granted the actualisation of their legal claims and social rights. Retribution is enacted at those junctures where consent to authority requires the denial of subjectivity without recompense.

Conclusion

In conclusion, the riots of late 2005 in France were unusual in their extensiveness and our analysis has drawn attention to the various factors that contributed to their distinctive unplanned coordination. Although the riots did not conform to the dominant models of social movement contestation and political mobilisation, we have shown that there was a particular dynamic of structuration to the riots and that this can be traced to the half-positions that the (largely, though not exclusively, immigrant) populations of the *banlieues* and *cités* tend to occupy in France. Due their social-structural marginalisation and the forms of deprecation to which these French citizens are subjected, the half-positions give rise to a significant commonality of experience and a sense of indignation. However, it is only under certain conditions that this context is translated into violent actions and our analysis has high-lighted the importance of focusing upon the actual actions of the rioters in order to understand the nature of the conflict and its implications. In our opinion, the specific action orientation of the riots was one of creative disrespect; although our use of this category draws on related usages it also differs from them. Namely, creative disrespect contains elements of the performative disobedience of dramatising a stigmatised identity, but it equally involves more complex layers of modifying the relationship to the self, transforming norms and values, and practically engaging as a collective in a dialectic of control with state authorities. The perceived transgression by the police of legitimate legal authority created a context for the enactment of aspects of an everyday moral order that had been shaped by the experiences of half-positions and disrespect from the dominant institutions of French society. On the basis of this analysis, it is possible to perceive how the riots comprised practices of retribution for the injuries that had been sustained and sought to assert some order of collective pride, whilst seeking to demarcate boundaries against state incursions.

References

Balibar E (2001). Outlines of a topography of cruelty: citizenship and civility in the era of global violence. *Constellations* 8(1): 15–29.

Balibar E (2007). Uprising in the *banlieues*. *Constellations* 14(1): 47–71.

Beaud S & Masclet O (2006). Des 'marcheurs' de 1983 aux 'émertiers' de 2005. Deux generations socials d'enfants d'immigrés. *Annales, Histoire, Sciences Sociales* 4: 809–43.

Beik W (1997). *Urban protest in seventeenth-century France. The culture of retribution.* Cambridge: Cambridge University Press.

Benjamin W (1979). *One way street, and other writings,* London & New York: Verso.

Bourdieu P, Accardo A, Balazo G, Beaud S, Bonvin F, Bourdieu E et al. (1999). *The weight of the world: social suffering in contemporary society* (trans. P Ferguson, S Emanuel, J Johnson & ST Waryn). Cambridge: Polity.

Castel R (2006). La discrimination negative. Le deficit de citoyenneté des jeunes de banlieue. *Annales* 4: 777–808.

Cohen J & Arato A (1992) *Civil society and political theory.* Cambridge, Mass: MIT Press.

Cowlishaw G (2004). *Blackfellas, whitefellas and the hidden injuries of race.* Malden MA: Blackwell.

Donzelot J, Estèbe P, Jaillet MC & Lagrange H (2006). November nights 2005: the geography of violence, a round table discussion [Online]. Available:

www.eurozine.com/articles/2006-02-01-donzelot-en.html. [Accessed 30 March 2010].

Economist (2006). 28 October–3 November.

Esping-Andersen G (1990). *The three worlds of welfare capitalism.* Cambridge: Polity Press.

Goffman E (1968). *Stigma.* Harmondsworth: Penguin.

Habermas J (1987). *The theory of communicative action Vol. 2: Lifeworld and system.* Cambridge: Polity Press.

Honneth, Axel (2007). *Disrespect: the normative foundations of critical theory.* Cambridge, Malden MA: Polity.

Joas H (2003). *War and modernity* (trans. Rodney Livingstone). Cambridge: Polity Press.

Lagrange H & Oberti M (Eds) (2006). *Émeutes urbaines et protestations.* Paris: Presses de Sciences Politiques.

Lentin, A (2004). *Racism and anti-racism in Europe.* London: Pluto Press.

Levy JD (1999). *Tocqueville's revenge: state, society, and economy in contemporary France.* Cambridge Mass.: Harvard University Press.

Margalit A (1996). *The decent society.* Cambridge Mass.: Harvard University Press.

Marx, G (1970). Issueless Riots. *Annals of the American Academy of Political and Social Science,* 391, 1: 21–33.

Mitchell K (2007). Marseille's not for burning: immigrant cities and the production of peace. Seminar, Centre for Cultural Research, University of Western Sydney, August 30.

Moore Jr B (1979). *Injustice: the social bases of obedience and revolt.* London & Basingstoke: Macmillan.

Offe C (1996). *Modernity and the state.* Cambridge: Polity Press

Roy O (2005). The nature of the French riots. Social Science Research Council [Online]. Available: riotsfrance.ssrc.org/Roy/. [Accessed 30 March 2010].

Schnapper D (2006). L'échec du 'modèle républicain'? Réflexion d'une sociologue, *Annales, Histoire, Sciences Sociales,* 4: 759–76.

Sennett R & Cobb J (1972). *The hidden injuries of class.* New York: Alfred A. Knopf.

Sennett R (2003). *Respect in a world of inequality.* New York and London: W.W. Norton.

Silverstein PA & Tetreault C (2006). Postcolonial urban apartheid. Social Science Research Council [Online]. Available: riotsfrance.ssrc.org/Silverstein_Tetreault/ [Accessed 30 March 2010].

Smith TB (2004). *France in crisis*. Cambridge: Cambridge University Press.

Thompson EP (1991). *Customs in common*. New York: New Press.

Tilly C (2003). *The politics of collective violence*. Cambridge: Cambridge University Press.

Turner RH (1994). Race riots past and present: a cultural-collective behavior approach. *Symbolic Interaction* 17(3): 309–24.

Wieviorka M (2005). Violence in France. Social Science Research Council [Online]. Available: riotsfrance.ssrc.org/Wieviorka/ [Accessed 30 March 2010].

Notes on contributors

Robert Aldrich is Professor of European History at the University of Sydney. Among his works are *Greater France: a history of French overseas expansion*, *Vestiges of the colonial empire in France: monuments, museums and colonial memories* and an edited collection, *The age of empires*.

Craig Browne is a senior lecturer in the Department of Sociology and Social Policy at the University of Sydney. His current research interests include critical social theory, praxis philosophy, social imaginaries, democracy, social conflicts and modernity. He recently published in *Thesis Eleven*, *Critical Horizons* and *European Journal of Social Theory*.

Gillian Cowlishaw studied anthropology at Sydney University in the 1970s, taught at Charles Sturt University and the ANU in the 1980s and at the University of Sydney in the 1990s. Her first research in Southern Arnhem Land led to *Rednecks, eggheads and blackfellas* (1999). Other works, *Black, white or brindle* (1988) and *Blackfellas, whitefellas and the hidden injuries of race* (2004) explore existential questions and living dramas arising from the racial binary in rural Australia. Now working in Sydney's western suburbs, her latest work, *The city's outback* (2009), analyses the nature of social research, contrasting conceptions of the suburbs, as well as local Indigenous self-perception. Gillian currently holds an Australian Professorial Fellowship at UTS.

Didier Fassin is James D. Wolfensohn Professor of Social Science at the Institute for Advanced Study in Princeton and Director of Studies at the École des Hautes Études en Sciences Sociales in Paris. He directs the Interdisciplinary Research Institute for Social Sciences (CNRS–Inserm–EHESS–University Paris North). His recent publications include *When bodies remember: experience and politics of AIDS in South Africa*, (2007), *The empire of trauma: an inquiry into the condition of victimhood* (with Richard Rechtman, 2009), *Contemporary states of emergency: the politics of military and humanitarian intervention* (with Mariella Pandolfi, 2010), *La raison humanitaire: une histoire morale du temps présent* (2010).

Deirdre Howard-Wagner has worked for 15 years as a senior policy officer and academic focusing on key Indigenous law and policy issues, including working within the Office of Indigenous affairs in the Department of the Prime Minister and Cabinet in the 1990s. She has conducted fieldwork in Maningrida in the Northern Territory and Newcastle in New South Wales. While working as a Senior Policy Officer, she spent periods of time in Indigenous communities in areas around North Queensland working with, for example, the Kuku Yalanji peoples in the Mosman Gorge and Wajul Wajul settlements. Her socio-legal work explores the state governmentality of Indigenous rights and justice in the context of land rights, Indigenous heritage protection, criminal justice, Indigenous customary law, self-determination, and more recently child protection. She is currently a lecturer in socio-legal studies at the University of Sydney.

Phillip Mar is presently a researcher with the Centre of Cultural Research, University of Western Sydney. He completed a doctorate in social anthropology in 2002, and has lectured in cultural sociology and anthropology at the University of Sydney, the University of New South Wales and Macquarie University. His research interests include transnational migration and culture, political affect, contemporary Hong Kong and Chinese society and culture, urban spaces, and the sociology of art.

Justine McGill is a lecturer in the Department of Philosophy at the University of Sydney. Her current work brings together her teaching speciality in political philosophy with her earlier love of Nietzsche, in the form of a study of responsibility and irresponsibility in modern life.

Emmanuel Renault teaches philosophy at the École Normale Supérieure de Lettres et Sciences Humaines (Lyon). Editor of the journal *Actuel Marx* (PUF) and co-editor of the journal *Critical Horizons* (Acumen), he has written books and articles on Hegel, Marx, and critical theory. His publications include *Marx et l'idée de critique* (1995), *Mépris social. Ethique et politique de la reconnaisance* (2000), *Hegel. La naturalisation de la dialectique* (2001), *Philosophie chimique. Hegel et la science dynamiste de son temps* (2002), *Où en est la théorie critique?* (edited with Yves Sintomer, 2003), *L'expérience de l'injustice. Reconnaissance et clinique de l'injustice* (2004), *Souffrances socials: sociologie, psychologie et politique* (2008), *Lire les manuscrit de 1844* (Editor, 2008), *Lire Marx* (with G. Duménil and M. Löwy, 2009).

Elizabeth Rechniewski is a senior lecturer in the Department of French Studies at the University of Sydney. Her current research interests lie in the area of Memory Studies and commemoration, and she is a member of a project coordinated by Professor Olivier Wieviorka undertaking a comparative study of the significance of commemoration in contemporary national life. She has researched and published widely on French intellectuals and engagement, including *Suarès, Malraux, Sartre: antécédents littéraires de l'existentialisme* (1996) and *Sartre's nausea: text, context and intertext,* (with Alistair Rolls, 2005). Reflecting a continuing research interest in discourse analysis of the media, she undertakes comparative analysis of the news media within a systemic-functional and appraisal framework.

Irene Watson is an Aboriginal legal scholar and critical legal theorist who belongs to the Taganekald and Meintangk peoples, also known as the Ngarrindjeri. She is currently Leader of the Research and Research Education portfolio of the David Unaipon College of Indigenous Education and Research at the University of South Australia. Prior to this, she was a research fellow with the Sydney Law School. In addition to her career in academia, Watson has worked as a legal practitioner and was a member of the Aboriginal Legal Rights Movement SA from 1973 to 2005. She has taken part in the UN Working Group on Indigenous Populations and has extensive experience working on questions of international law and Aboriginal peoples.

Index

www.ingramcontent.com/pod-product-compliance
Lightning Source LLC
Chambersburg PA
CBHW071212240726
48654CB00009B/744